Maps of Heaven,
Maps of Hell

D0209692

Maps of Heaven, Maps of Hell

Religious Terror as Memory
from the Puritans to Stephen King

— ▦ —

Edward J. Ingebretsen, S.J.

M.E. Sharpe
Armonk, New York
London, England

Library of Congress Cataloging-in-Publication Data

Ingebretsen, Edward.
Maps of heaven, maps of hell : religious terror as memory from
the Puritans to Stephen King / Edward J. Ingebretsen.—1st ed.
p.   cm.
Includes bibliographical references and index.
ISBN 1-56324-871-9 (alk. paper).—ISBN 1-56324-872-7 (pbk. : alk. paper)
1. Horror tales, American—History and criticism.
2. Gothic revival (Literature)—United States.
3. Fiction—Religious aspects—Christianity.
4. American fiction—English influences.
5. Puritan movements in literature.
6. Christianity and literature.
7. Heaven in literature.
8. Hell in literature.
I. Title.
PS374.H67I54   1995
813'.0873809—dc20
94-39041
CIP

Printed in the United States of America

The paper used in this publication meets the minimum requirements of
American National Standard for Information Sciences—
Permanence of Paper for Printed Library Materials,
ANSI Z 39.48-1984.

EB (c)   10   9   8   7   6   5   4   3   2   1
EB (p)   10   9   8   7   6   5   4   3   2   1

*Dedicated to my sisters Yvonne and Carol
and my brother, Charles:*

Love to them they love.

*and to my brothers in the Society of Jesus
who take away the terror*

I owe a debt of gratitude to many people who have discussed, read, advised, argued with me, and who in small and large ways helped to make this a better book. In particular I wish to acknowledge John Glavin for his initial guidance in this project and John Hirsh for his encouragement and advice throughout.

I thank all those who read this manuscript in its various incarnations and whose suggestions improved it immensely: Mary Lee Settle, Randy Bass, Sam Sara, S.J., Jewel Spears Brooker, Dennis Todd, Joe Sitterson, Jo Glorie at Paragon House, Anne Weston, George Lensing, Jerry Cobb, S.J., John Rudnick, Dan Coran at the Northern Illinois University Press, Gary Fisher, Roland Pool, Michael Reed, Thomas Brady Murphy, Jeff Resetarits.

To Jim Slevin, Lucy Maddox, Paul Betz, John Pfordresher and John Witek, S.J., for their general guidance and critical acumen.

To my students, especially in "The Fantastic" and "American Gothic" courses, whose eagerness to teach me what I need to know is reflected in this book.

For Michael Hardt and Adam Rue for technical support.

For Ken Pribanic, for too many debts either to mention or to forget.

I gratefully acknowledge and thank the Graduate School at Georgetown as well as Georgetown's English Department for making time-release possible to finish this book.

Finally, my parents, Edgar and Annabelle; Leo Rock, Don Merrifield, Tom Rausch, for the kindness and unfailing courtesy of my long-time friends: Brian Copple, Joe Dever, Scott Martin, Bill Williams, Curtis Bryant, John Breslin, Kevin Wildes, Tim Gilman, Jason Juffras, Javier Romanach. To echo Faulkner, they endured.

Contents

———— ■■ ————

Ours is indeed an age of extremity. For we live under continual threat of two equally fearful, but seemingly opposed, destinies: unremitting banality and inconceivable terror. It is fantasy, served out in large rations by the popular arts, which allows most people to cope with these twin specters."

(*Sontag, "The Imagination of Disaster," p. 224*)

"The American romancer's concern with the deeper art is synonymous with his search for the buried life; and he is of necessity an evoker of ghosts and a resurrector of dead bodies."

(*Joel Porte,* The Romance in America, *p. 97*)

"Our fiction is not merely a flight from the physical data of the actual world . . . It is, bewilderingly and embarrassingly, a gothic fiction, non-realistic and negative, sadist, and melodramatic—a literature of darkness and the grotesque. . . .

(*Fiedler,* Love and Death, *p. 29*)

Last Things First:
A Dante-esque Digression

And now for love you vengeance prove,
  it is an equal thing.
Your waxing worse, hath stopped the course
  of wonted clemency:
Mercy refused, and grace misused,
  call for severity.
—"THE DAY OF DOOM," MILLER, P. 138

■■

I propose to show how a map of Heaven could only be constructed, as it were, by inversion, beginning with Hell. But first a diversion to another time and to another country, since to explore heavenly maps I must talk about endings, the final things. However, diversions, as the word implies, can be entertaining, and entertaining diversions— especially about Final Things—are, after all, my subject.

The perennial, always-returning subject of American fantasy is the Divine—hidden and disguised, it is true, but, that's why its search is called a *diversion*, since we are deflected from it at every turn. The Divine is that which must be revealed, the secret hidden away till the end of time. Indeed, the Divine's uncovering *will be* the end of time. After all, what are the diverting and entertaining qualities of the Apocalypse, if not the grammar by which the Sacred shall be discovered, (recovered, uncovered) and written in time?

Yet it needs to be remembered that the Apocalypse does not come at the *end* of time, as is conventionally thought. Its terror lies behind, not ahead. Even our foundational narratives tell us this. The Book of Genesis, that first map of western culture, makes it clear that the terror we anticipate has already been experienced, at that moment in the garden when immortality and mortality first intersected, before they went their separate/separating ways. Human drama begins at the East Gate, where the messenger (*angelos*) with the flaming sword compelled the fictive couple out of *U-topos* (no place) and into time: "The world was all before them, where to choose/Their place of rest, and Providence their guide." In that first diversion into topography was the promise of narrative. And in that beginning, then, was the word, the terror. And while the telling of origins in Genesis provides the metaphor of apocalypse, Milton made it myth, a necessary part of the popular iconography of the terrible. For Milton, of course, the apocalyptic *figura* was an actual fact. He had seen the angel's admonitory sword in the death of King Charles and in the Interregnum's subsequent collapse of social hierarchies. He had lived through the terrible revelation and witnessed the passing of the "old heav'ns and earth." So how better than as social chaos to figure the war in heaven? In *Paradise Lost*, Milton captured the anxieties of cultural displacement, describing first the revelation of transgression; then the cost of seeing god's awe-ful face; and, finally, the long search for haven. After such knowledge, what forgiveness?

In the beginning, then, all the themes and motives of a Gothic novel were there: scrutiny, expulsion, dispossession; grace and fate; transgression and expiation: the first shock of recognition at the perils of being chosen. There would be others. Like Milton's Adam and Eve, we've been wondering ever since, wandering in the terrors and terrains of history. Eternally seeking return, we try to divine the Divine, the Absent(ing) Father, our trial and expiation. Commemoration is in our blood; ritual, the fate of those lost in time.[1] And yes, the Divine is *still* diverting. The secret "sits in the center and knows" (see Frost, "The Secret Sits") while we stand around and suppose. The secret enchains us; enchants. In His absence you will know Him.

---

1. In "In Horror Movies, Some Things Are Sacred," Leonard Wolf observes "The great frenzies of chaos, creation, disobedience, disaster, solitude and evil which have been rendered vague or bland in the well-bred church and synagogue services . . . are restored to their terrifying proportions in the half-light of the movie theaters. . . . These are the ways in which the most representative myths of the horror film genre are able to strike chords of religious feeling." (p. 19) *The New York Times Arts and Leisure*, Sunday, Apr. 4, 1976, pp. 1, 19.

The Semiotics of Terror

. . . fantasy structures are given by a society as maps . . . by which a lost audience can find its way.
—JAMES TWITCHELL, *DREADFUL PLEASURES*, P. 87.

You must *look through the surface of American art, and see the inner diabolism of the symbolic meaning.*
—D. H. LAWRENCE[1]

. . . all ghost stories presupposed a life after death . . . no matter how scary the ghosts are, isn't that optimistic?
—STEPHEN KING[2]

———————— ▦ ————————

Introduction

There are apparently two books in every American household—one of them is the Bible and the other one is probably by Stephen King.
—CLIVE BARKER[3]

At the core of American cultic memory is a rhetoric shared by colonial theological text, civic ritual, and contemporary pulp horror formula. This rhetoric is partly habit, partly pragmatic social strategy: the duty of remembering the Holy, writing it into society as transcendent origin and authority. Traditionally, however, to speak of the Holy is to enter a realm of experience that could not be enunciated within earthly grammars; speaking the Holy, therefore, is to invoke the limits of human comprehension.

In addition, the history of religion shows that to speak the Divine is to invoke a metaphysics of uncertainty: God's (or the gods') eye; scrutiny and judgment from on high; human transgression and expiation. In short, to remember the Holy is to acknowledge its horror as well.

This study attempts to dis-cover the connections that exist between the rhetorics of religious terror and the consumerist technologies of horror. I explore, that is, how a theological map of Heaven—a metaphysics—almost by necessity produced its inverse companion, a politically useful map of Hell. I argue that the religious imperatives woven into the fabric of American culture keep its citizenry dutiful during the day and frightened at night. These narratives take many forms, and are active still as polemics, sermons, admonishings. The communal rites of the religious imagination, ill-at-ease with itself, are replayed through misanthropic populist fantasies such as the Ku Klux Klan and the Moral Majority; more indirectly and diffusely, their politics inform the ostensibly nonpolitical genre of fantasy.[4]

I argue that the habit of religious uncertainty (the threat of mystical self-loss, otherwise understood as the promise of conversion and change) articulates and focuses aspects of the American imagination that otherwise remain opaque and unreadable; and further, that the pieties of a traditional American religious discourse, inverted and debased, drive a fertile tradition of dark fantasy.[5] This then is the paradox situating this study: as mystics from Moses to Calvin understood, God's awe-ful face is complex and ambiguous, awful to behold, at once a dreadful promise as well as terrible threat—as the confusing amalgam of rapture and apocalypse in popular rhetoric suggests. Further, as Calvin the social theorist knew, God's awfulness is politically useful in forming a social order. Terror, then, in the name of religion, whether invoked as positive action or negative threat, functions as an epistemology as well as a semiotics—it is a way of knowing as well as a rite of communal identity.

Nor were the uses of terror lost upon those who organized the Puritan Migration in 1630. One of my themes is that this renegade theological movement begot a separatist political fantasy off a presumptively "new" land, and then, deeply suspicious of its unauthorized and possibly illegal action, distanced itself from this first transgressive ambiguity by justifying it in a rhetoric of Manifest Destiny and chosenness. The social order established by this movement was predicated upon a holy turn of heart, a return to God involving a basic and radical self-revision. And while the language of conversion was private, nonetheless conversion was public in its effects, as over time the language of the *polis* gradually subsumed the language of God. Consequently, conversion came to embody complex political, even eschatological meanings, as a people hungry for righteousness found themselves adrift between continents, adrift between civic and theological orders. Wavering between the promise of conversion and the implicit threat of apocalypse, they found themselves lost between hope of the Promised Land and threat of dispossession and spiritual landlessness.

History, however, is rarely kind to rhetorics of the ideal, and as declension and perceived failure beset the New England social order, a similar metamorphosis occurred in its institutional rhetorics. As conversion—*metanoia*—was the religious motivation in the first place, change and metamorphosis of various kinds became the great fear, a shadowy threat articulated in sermon and text as a fear of declension, slippage, or falling away. Original visions of inheritance—theo-national dreams of a new Heaven and Earth, for instance—slipped, slid, coalesced, and mixed with less-clear fears of apocalyptic Hell and civil dispossession. Conversion, it was seen, had another face, an unholy metamorphosis covering a range of social distresses.[6] From this original theological metaphor, I argue, derive the texts of horrific conversion, declension and unwanted metamorphosis commonly gathered under the rubric of American Gothic: dark tales of psychic humiliations, collapsing identities, enslavements, enticements, spontaneous self-annihilations; tales of seduction, scrutiny, and moral bondage—all eroticized, because a culture enthralled by the spirit nonetheless found that while it could repudiate carnal bodies, it could not escape the gravity of their desires.[7]

Linking religious discourse to the transgressive complexities and ideological erasures of fantasy texts may seem, at first sight, surprising. Nonetheless, the alignment of the rhetorics of theology and entertainment is not a recent marketing development, nor merely an exchange of God for gore. The errand into the wilderness and the errand into the movie theaters are, and have been, long-time associates. To anticipate my argument a bit, I cite Daniel B. Shea who makes the point that "Puritan spiritual narratives" compare in strategy with current "entertainment media" (*Spiritual Autobiography in Early America*, p. 92); both are moralistic, spectacular, and confessional. Indeed, our word for the ephemera of social diversion—entertainment—has a complex and possibly lethal theological past. In Salem, for example, witches were brought to trial charged with "entertaining Satan." Even Cotton Mather, that great architect of Puritan interiority, understood the almost necessary association of the Holy and the Horrible, the Deity and the Demonic.

From the very beginning, then, religious habits of imagining the New World spilled messily into other discourses, shadowing everything from its theology to politics. The chapters of this study seek to show how a geo-national metaphysics of uncertainty, deriving ultimately from a tradition of religious eschatology, bred fantasies of nostalgic moralism on the one hand and moralistic, horrid fantasies on the other. The deflective energies of a largely forgotten metaphysical history live on, not only in churches, but in a myriad other centers of displaced worship. Endlessly reappropriated and refigured, commodified for imaginative export, as it were, a habit of religious nationalism provides a compendium of useful policies and civic strategies—producing, on the one hand, technologies of social control (methodologies of witch detection, for one) and, on the other, systems for social diversion and distraction (movies *about* witches, for instance). "Distraction" and "diversion"—the words are significant for what they portend. What are we being distracted or diverted from? Further, a rhetoric of the godly (moralism) would be invoked to manage human societies (Winthrop through Falwell, for instance), while a "theology" of the demonic would be arrayed to display, explain, and perhaps argue the Almighty (Edwards, in particular). Lastly, as Max Weber has famously argued, the language of the Holy has been used to encourage personal discipline in the interests of civic zeal— although as Foucault observes, that same rhetoric effaced the line between public and private altogether, rendering private and interior public and spectacular by means of a rhetoric of confession and communal revelation.[8]

At least two important consequences followed from such a confusion of political and theological grammars. First, in this society of Revelation and imminent Apocalypse, God would inevitably become linked to the *monstrum*—the divine warning and remonstrance. Second, in this order one's soul was, in a manner of speaking, potentially monstrous and always on display; the prospects of its conversion and mystical effacement in God would always be a spectacle. Thus, two early rites of the religious imagination, scrutiny and confession, would become, in time, performance and voyeurism. A need to tell and expose begot a need to watch.[9] In the secularization of the religious imagination, an epistemology of uncertainty would remain, functioning as popular constraint and as boundary and limit of the civil (and in some cases uncivil) imagination. In the gradual evacuation of theological content, only the forms of religious authority survived, leaving a frisson of terror as emotional trace to mark where the Sublime once had been. Out of the Holy would be born the Horrible.

In *Horror Fiction in the Protestant Tradition*, Victor Sage argues that the horror genre "is not a literary genre, in the narrow sense, at all. It is a cultural response, which implies a broad series of relationships with the whole of the culture in which it is produced" (p. xiii).[10] In *Dreadful Pleasures*, James Twitchell concurs: "Essentially, horror has little to do with fright; it has more to do with laying down the rules of socialization . . ." (p. 66).[11] Traditionally much the same could be said for theologies, as well, which, in their pursuit of God always have at least one eye turned earthward. Thus, to remember the Holy as divine principle is in effect to remember, and in some cases to set, boundaries or limits beyond which the human does not or can not go. In American theological practice, for instance, the rhetoric of religious hierarchy and conformity found in John Winthrop's "A Model of Christian Charity" complements Cotton Mather's language of religious grotesquery in *The Wonders of the Invisible World.* Jointly they invoke a metaphysics of transcendent scrutiny (Judgment) that operates in mundane and earthly ways as communal admonishment and fraternal correction. These religious rhetorics establish civic rituals which in turn are useful for policing the body politic. Already one can observe how private religious metaphors had public civil consequences. Nonetheless, given a cultural confusion around the appropriateness of the private, lines between the private and the public existed, often enough, only in rhetoric and rarely in practice. Thus, in such a civil order as we are discussing, acts of fraternal- or self-correction would be perceived as a communal gesture; toning the private soul would be tantamount to exercising the body politic. But for this reason, then, the threat or fear of transgression becomes an ambiguous metaphor, since transgression is both evidence of sin as well as the possibility of amazing grace. Publicly, too, transgressions were complex events. For instance, Mather was concerned with demonstrating the presence of witches in Salem; he knew well that "dis-covering" evil was a righteous religious duty, but that, in addition, its spectacular display in the courts and other public places gave it value as "entertainment."

Generally speaking, then, I am arguing that once-religious imperatives can be traced across a variety of American genres, modes, and texts. This prescriptive grammar—routinely unseen for the significant presence it is—accounts for the intimate speech of confessional autobiography; it accompanies the mystification of the universe (Christian allegorizing) in apocalyptic texts; it can be heard in the diabolization of God and the rhetorizing of the self—either downward in ritualistic self-abasement or upward in the rhetoric of civic exaltation. The language of the Holy buttresses civic normalcy, and its various mythifications in civic texts show how extensively a founding politics of the Enlightenment rests, often uneasily, upon other premises as well. Beneath or perhaps to one side of the Jeffersonian abstractions and committee compromises of a patchwork Constitution can be discerned other memories—in particular, of vernacular American Christianities (for there were more than one). For example, the secularized City of God familiar to nineteenth-century utopic thinkers barely disguises its origins in seventeenth-century apocalyptic discourse. If Locke and Jefferson emphasized the reasonability of Social Contract, the protesting religious communities formed throughout the colonies emphasized something rather different. They focused upon God's unknowability and upon the futility of social covenant (works) without grace. Thus, the metaphysics of uncertainty that had given them origin by providing a hierarchy of divine terrors, still continues to shape a civil order in its image. Over time these terrors, disavowed and repudiated as theology, took refuge in discredited, weird texts of all kinds—perhaps by way of ironic reminder that dispossessed religionists themselves had once taken refuge in a geographic fantasy called the New World.

New Worlds Westward

Religion is the soul of culture and culture is the form of religion.
—PAUL TILLICH

The genre of "American Gothic" consists, in the main, of what one critic calls a tradition of "terroristic literature" (Coad, p. 73).[12] This literature has roots in the theological distress of an Old World order; I argue, in fact, that the history of Reformation theology continues to have political and social consequences. Indeed, the New World and its foundational old-world eschatologies cannot be separated.[13] For example, the Puritans fled to New England in fulfillment, as it were, of the fantastic end to which their zealotry committed them. Seeking a kind of communal dark night, they first embraced dispossession, then exile, and finally, death by final fire—that last rapturous and apocalyptic intimacy with God. The New World was to be for them a type of Paradise Found, the Imagined Land Eastward. These immigrants thought of themselves as spiritual vigilantes, a homeless people blown outward through history beyond the angel's flaming sword. In the extreme of their narcissism they likened their New England settlement to a city on a hill, a light lit for all the world, rising phoenix–like from the ash of old theological hopes. It was to be a Promised Land where they could take their rest, as they left the lost (or perhaps abandoned?) garden behind them. This habit of ecstatic fantasy continued beyond their time, refined and shaped by new generations to new needs and ends. The habit of religion found new avenues, created for itself new, sometimes surprising, homes. So it was that political and theological dream-weavers (from Shakespeare to Stephen King, from John Winthrop to Ronald Reagan) would find in this blustery wilderness what they needed: New World, Utopia, Prooftext, Escape, Paradise, Providence, *exemplum*.[14] All these geographies of the imagination, these conditionals and night visions would be cobbled together as *religio,* the binding sacred myth—the way a culture lies to itself in public.[15]

Thus it was that the rhetorical place called "America," sentimentalized in political speech and populist myth, began as an act of repudiation—a rejection of the failed spiritual order that the Reformation was to have been.[16] Indeed, the rhetoric of apocalyptic fantasy was already a cliché, old and worn long before the land was discovered whose terms it was thought to fulfill. For example, the phrase "New World" itself indicates its provenance in Renaissance geo-mythology, a memorial preserved in the dreambanks of a culture. Even the language used to describe the New World is language-at-its-end (metaphor, *figura*), and thus, a grammar of eschatology:

> *Westward the Course of Empire takes its Way;*
> *The four first acts already past,*
> *A fifth shall close the Drama with the Day;*
> *Time's noblest Offspring is the last.*[17]

Bishop George Berkeley's sentiment expressed an understanding common to the time, that the "westernmost country . . . was destined to become the seat of the most highly advanced civilization and of mankind's greatest achievements" (Freese, p. 81). Thus, the place now called "America" is an *arriviste,* the *Novus Ordo* a come-lately ideological dream, whose "individualistic, pietistic, perfectionist, millenarian" (McLoughlin, p. xiv) politics were ideals heavily hammered into place by equally violent rhetoric, hope, and law.[18]

Reading this theologically dense but diverse culture is like reading a palimpsest; one uncovers literal pretexts hidden beneath later accretions and additions, and sometimes one finds texts willfully erased and silenced. Religion is one such silence; displaced and hidden from public view, it shows itself as a kind of shadow or trace, which is perhaps what D. H. Lawrence meant by the "inner diabolism" he finds characteristic of American culture. But to start at the beginning, we must acknowledge that the term "American" itself contains more than its share of ambiguities. As numerous commentators have pointed out, it functions poorly either as a geographical or political description, although its metaphysical duplicity is evident in that the expression is routinely used for both purposes. Nonetheless, "America" ought to be considered a rhetorical strategy rather than descriptive term. That is, while neither descriptive of any demographic or empirical data, "American" represents a utopic, imaginative topography—a template of often unconscious responses operating more or less rigidly as emotional habits. Perhaps "instincts" might not be too strong a word, since for all practical purposes these visceral, personal investments lie, as the word implies, in the comforts of flesh, hallowed by habit beyond the reach of conscious reflection. Now widely dispersed through all levels of American culture, these habitual patterns function as ideological buttresses to a rhetoric of the Sacred. This transcendent, ideal order is presented as authority and justification of a civic order by means of a network of interlocking rhetoric and civilly authorized restraints.

In this study, I shall use the word "American" in a limited sense to represent a broad set of attitudes toward self and society traceable to the scrutiny and transgression-based theo-social order of colonial Massachusetts. Bits and rhetorical pieces of this New England Way, as this order came to be called, would later be recommodified, shaped into a homogenizing rhetoric of identity, functioning as national ideology (as, for example, in the phrase "popular American culture").[19] Here fantasy and politics function in inverse ways, showing how a putatively geographic or nationalistic discourse can nonetheless disguise a coercive and moralistic subtext. Indeed, the utopic origins of the word "American," as well as its continued deployment in a grammar of nationalist fantasy, reflects the hegemonic tension of "the melting pot" that belies it.[20]

My point in these initial reflections is simply that the geographic mapping of the New World followed, and depended upon, a prior metaphysical mapping of the imagination, with all the proscriptions, imperatives, and repudiations that such a governance reflects. A culture authorized by Revelation in effect organized itself according to a semiotics of terror and uncertainty. Such a culture moved toward self-identity and self-possession by way of a "negative dialectic" (Jameson, p. 51). Broadly speaking, an allegorical privileging of the spiritual resulted in a denial of the carnal—in Puritan phraseology. This denial would be located in the body itself, since the health of the communal body politic could—

indeed, would—demand the effacement of the individual. Other repudiations followed; the quest for interior perfection (the spiritualized self) eventually registered a fear of exterior difference, as religious perfection came to signal civic conformity. Finally, interiority itself was sacrificed to the demands of religious correctness and social compliance. A discourse of surfaces and style would be the result—a denial, in effect, not only of history but of community, evident most especially in the American apocalyptic mode. Finally, the Sacred itself would be sentimentalized, emptied of any significance except as political icon. Though everywhere present in civic language and public emotion, it would thereby be safely and routinely denied any power. Its once transcendental authority would be used to buttress a rhetoric of coercion in the service of a politics of comfort.

In this discussion of the origins and meanings of American theological rhetoric, it must be kept in mind, finally, that the Puritans did not so much find a new world as recreate the transgressive and hierarchical (and, paradoxically, antinomian and lawless) one they thought to repudiate. They did not so much *pursue* the Holy as *construct* one in their own dispossessed and land-hungry image. Thus did writing the Holy become for them and subsequent generations an exercise in detailing the Unholy, as a society-wide effort at righteousness compelled the language of terror and fantasy in order to do so. If the lands of New England were thought to be utopic and gracious, its wildernesses, conversely, were demonized—darkened, populated with demons (and later, by their agents, the Indians, or "heretical" persons like Anne Hutchinson and Roger Williams). Both mappings—utopic and "infernal"—reflect the early colonial strategy of allegorizing the cosmos. Reading its powers into the particulars of daily life is a tactic still covertly employed in varying ways to define—and police—the "American." Victor Sage explains, "Protestant theology contains, at the subjective level, a complete preemptive description of the most obscure processes of the mind; it also consists, at the outward or objective level, of a sophisticated set of models for the recognition and control of social behaviour" (*Horror Fiction*, p. xvii). A most uncivil religion, the New England Way; under pressure of time, habit, and market, it would become increasingly more so.

Religious Culture and Gothic Religion: Mapping Interiors

"It's a poor sort of memory that only works backwards," the Queen remarked.

—LEWIS CARROLL, *THROUGH THE LOOKING-GLASS AND WHAT ALICE FOUND THERE*

I wish now to consider the problem of "reading" culture—and, implicitly, the difficulties of reading a so-called "pop" culture that inevitably connives with, while parodying, some other, "higher" culture. There is always a public dimension to the seemingly private contours of the imagination, despite often rigid, sometimes defensive attempts to render the private as "personal," and therefore, by implication, "not public."[21] Yet private and public cannot be kept separate. Indeed, Victor Sage makes a "direct connection" between the "essentially random activity of the individual subconscious and the determining pressure of the political culture" (*Horror Fiction*, pp. xi–xii). Similarly, Fredric Jameson points out:

> To imagine that . . . there already exists a realm of freedom—whether it be that of the microscopic experience of words in a text or the ecstasies and intensities of the various private religions—is only to strengthen the grip of Necessity over all such blind zones in which the individual subject seeks refuge. . . . (*Political Unconscious*, p. 20).

The political, the *social*, as Jameson suggests, must be the "absolute horizon of all reading and all interpretation" (p. 17). It is this space between private and public—the place of tension between nightmare and the conventionalities of social mores—that must be negotiated and which is always being transgressed. This is the site of contention I wish to consider in this study: where intimate encounters of an imaginative kind are, in every sense of the word, socially produced; and where they are theologically constructed to provoke a range of useful affects. Two in particular interest me: the civic emotions of sentimentalized love and eroticized terror, especially as each is framed in a rhetoric of paradoxical self-aggrandizement and self-loss.

A culture's main task is to survive its own imaginative demise—
when, that is, its long memory ceases to wield any effective power.
That is why custodians of culture, those who monitor core values
and imperatives, must act as moral topographers. Their job (generally self-appointed) is to map the lands of the imagination, to
draw its permissible terrain, and, in particular, to define the
realm of the emotionally acceptable: What are the limits of love?
Whom may one love, and how? Who and what ought to be
feared?[22] For example, a popular version of contemporary American self-speak insists loudly that its citizens are politically free. We
are, as the rhetoric suggests, in effect free to love and fear whom
we wish. However, upon reflection one can see that this is hardly
the case. Self-narrative—personal or cultural—is rarely descriptive of *praxis*; one must not be seduced by point of view. For
example, the posturing of the Religious Right around so-called
"family values" is a case in point. The call for a return to "traditional" forms of domesticity—subsumed within, and authorized
by a debased and therapized biblical rhetoric—means precisely
that one *may not* love just *anyone*, nor in any way one pleases.
Love, unlike terror in this respect, has its limits. The target of
such rhetoric, of course, is the perceived threat of homosexuality
(among other irregular sexual modalities) to the social order,
here understood as an economic construct that maintains an
abiding interest in controlling all sexual technologies. Indeed,
social deviations are moralized by religious rhetoric in order to
permit their criminalization. Yet this is not a new political strategy, nor is it even particularly religious. Quite to the contrary.
The rhetoric is political in intent and its current vogue reflects
the argument's proven success in organizing social emotions."[23]
For example, in *Growing Up Straight: What Every Thoughtful Parent
Should Know About Homosexuality* (1968) Peter and Barbara Wyden
cut to the chase: "No parent sets out deliberately to produce a
delinquent—or a homosexual. Yet it is recognized today that
delinquency and homosexuality are both rooted in the home."[24]
Part of the energy behind this book is to show that the identifica-
tion of the deviant is often a case where a political order creates
ex nihilo the monsters it needs to delineate and protect its boundaries. In the struggle to claim the imagination, it is never good to
leave such strategic choices to chance. Where cannons are few,

fear must suffice. Terror must be authoritative in order to be effective.

In point of fact, then, love and hate are both socially construed; both are purposefully shaped by practical politics. Love presumes focus, permission. It suggests a passion for possession, particularity, and thus, implicitly, it easily can be inserted into a capitalistic social economy, because the institution that grants permission to love also can withhold it. Love, then, or at least its permissions, are conservative in their effects. "Deviants"—"criminal or homosexual" (p. 48) (Wyden's explicit linkage of the two should be noted) are in surprising ways supportive of the status quo. In the same way, terror likewise presumes a prior discrimination and its use suggests implicit authority. Those who create the monster (or the monstrous) must either continue reminding us of the fact or convince us to do that work ourselves. Consequently, neither love nor terror can be considered "merely" natural or, in a democratic regime, "freely chosen." If a society is to survive its own inevitable tensions and contradictions, the power it gives away to love or hate—in liberal discourse, its putative "rights"—must be carefully monitored. For beyond these limits lies the Unspeakable, the unimaginable, even the Ineffable: the nightmare of limitless possibilities, metaphorized as Holy and Horrible, against whose death-filled yearnings culture shields itself.

Theologies—stories of God—are, of course, also poignant reminders of the human condition. In effect they are stories we tell on ourselves, reflecting our conditions and possibilities. Entangled and complex webs of speaking and silence, spelling and dispelling, theologies weave political needs together with seemingly transcendent valuations. I find particularly interesting the way religious discourse in its many hybrid forms serves as a flexible American paradigm of personal *and* civic identity. To switch again to a metaphor I employ throughout, religious discourse *maps* the individual onto a civic terrain; permits her or him to be located in respect to questions of Self and Other, and to the *civitas*, whose permissible boundaries are established and maintained by community sanction.

In this way American theologies and its traditions of horror support each other as discourses of the outer limits; each demarcates in different ways the domain of the Divine and the monstrous. Theological discourse can be said to police the vertical dimension of the human, since it establishes the necessary boundary between the community and the Divine. Gothic discourse on the other hand polices a horizontal boundary; its texts expose tensions and struggles, areas of silence and the unspoken that constitute the self in relation to its society (DeLamotte, p. 8). Theology and Gothic, then, are in effect narratives of the Unspeakable; together they fence off that which cannot be spoken—either because it exists *beyond* boundaries of grammar (and thus beyond human knowing) or because it cannot *permissibly* be spoken within human boundaries.

However, it must not be thought that this blending of metaphysics, politics, and entertainment is merely a "New England" phenomenon. From time immemorial witches have been burned and saints canonized; the pragmatic functions they serve are clear. What is feared, of course, from the witch or monster is contagion—the collapse of boundaries and human definitions. The witch, then, conjures up curse and imprecation, while the saint invokes prayer and blessing. In either rhetorical direction—Hell or Heaven—human society is protected, bounded, and fenced. The rhetoric (and bodies) of the Holy and Unholy proclaim social boundaries secure at each end, while offering, at the same time, models, *exempla*, spectacles—rhetorics of moral suasion. Fear, then, keeps a community vigilant, and in that word we should hear yet one more theological echo: vigil.[25] Rhetoric and fantasy—the Holy and the Horrible—keep vigil over the imagination, and for this reason, on the metaphysical map holiness and hellishness are contiguous.

Further, I argue that America's metaphysics of the Sacred and its traditions of Gothic fantasy are intimately linked as "mode of history" and, therefore, as "mode of memory" (Punter, *The Literature of Terror*, p. 409).[26] One could, however, argue that American theological history is, in its more recent forms, merely a nostalgic tale and not history at all—a deliberate forgetting rather than remembering.[27] These insights are not necessarily new. I differ from previous scholars (Joel Porte, Louis Gross, Victor Sage, for instance) only by making a more radical, or perhaps more basic, claim—arguing that the American tradition of the forgotten and unadmitted (its Gothic tradition) *is* its tradition of idealizing theologies, covered (hidden) and recovered as something else.[28] To name two places in particular where metaphysics and politics (maps of Heaven and earth) intersect: first, in the very place we say they do *not*, in our social policies, where we erase and expunge the Sacred—literally "unsay" it—through means called, rather unpoetically, Disestablishment.[29] However, traces of religious habits of reflection nonetheless remain visible around the edges of public civic economies, as, indeed, the scrutinizing eye is literally visible on our money.[30]

A second connection will prove more central to this study, and this is where metaphysics and poetics cross, and sometimes collide, in texts of dark fantasy and so-called Gothic pulp. Jonathan Edwards inadvertently provides a name for the connection I seek: the "Images or Shadows of Divine Things." His phrase is felicitous, as will become apparent. Where does religion hide when by law it can no longer be spoken as (civic) discourse? It is locked in the literary basement with the "nasties" (Barron, p. 207), hidden in the wickedary of a culture. A society authorized by divine revelation is, also and therefore, a society of secrets and scrutiny, its social order one of undressing and exposure. Such a theology, then, offers in effect an erotic grammar of transgression and expiation, of covering and uncovering, and *this* secret—the Divine's twin faces of fear and ecstasy—*is* the secret hidden away in repudiated pulp horror. The Sublime—erased by law and denied by commodity economics— nonetheless continues to speak. By its terror you shall know it, whatever forms its denial takes.

I propose, then, to uncover the American Holy by reading its traces in the Horrible; I will read the Divine by tracing its shadows in the contrived, constructed, and generally formulaic terrors by which the Holy is, traditionally, deflected into and through public discourse—and in which the Sacred is misspoken, as it were, in the Scary. In *The Idea of the Holy*, Rudolf Otto builds on Edmund Burke's theories of the Sublime, arguing that terror and the Holy are closely, even intimately, associated. Otto writes that "the sense of the numinous, cut loose from a context of rational religious belief, could return in the most primitive form, that of demonic dread" (cited in Geary, p. 19).[31] Unlike Otto, however, I do not posit a numinous, post-Kantian category in which terror inheres.[32] For my purposes, the word "terror" itself hints at its provenance and its mundane purpose. Though often associated with the conventional structures of religion, simply stated, terror is less of

Heaven than of *terra*, earth. It survives, even thrives, from age to age because it is good for commerce. The use of God to damn this or that "monstrous" person or "infernal" cause may be politically expedient and socially effective even when not doctrinally clear. In *Powers of Horror*, Kristeva argues that "Abjection accompanies all religious structurings and reappears, to be worked out in a new guise, at the time of their collapse" (p. 17), and I argue, ultimately in agreement with her, that the fertile field of American horror is the "socialized appearance of the abject" (p. 16). In short, and again, where can theologies of scrutiny and abasement be found? These religious structurings reappear, discarded and devalued, in works of horrorists like Lovecraft, or Stephen King, whose tales unintentionally remember Jonathan Edwards's divine pyro-technics or Mather's demonic energy. Thus it is that the traditional focus of theological narrative—the deity, the unnameable creator—becomes, by slight of hand, the darkly unspeakable—admissible, as Fiedler puts it, only at "the backdoor of culture" (Underwood, *Kingdom of Fear*, p. 52).

Textual Mappings: Maps of Heaven and the Road to Hell

> . . . *so we understand how the highest angel can turn into the most*
> *base devil by a simple act of renouncement.*
> —FRANCIS FORD COPPOLA'S
> PRODUCTION JOURNAL, *DRACULA*

Why *is* it easier to imagine Hell than Heaven? Why does Milton's Satan have all the best lines? Even Dante knew that Hell was always the more familiar site on the metaphysical map; preachments and policements from time immemorial made sure of that. Perhaps in some deep chamber of the soul Hell was a comforting thought because for most people—or at least for many—Hell was, pre-sumptively, their imagined lot, cold and claustrophobic, gray and cheerless—a domestic sort of end, after all. Hadn't Calvin and his interpreters made it perfectly clear that the road to Hell was well paved? And that only a chosen elect would survive the revelation of God's awe-ful grace? In terms of the great masses of humanity, as a matter of fact, only a mere handful would. It is no wonder, then, that the expressions "Holy Terror" or "Holy Hell" survive, or that terms of piety such as "awe-ful" and "dreadful" twist like a snake upon the teller. Nor is it a surprise that the Puritans' efforts to map the City of God onto the *civitas* of man reads like a Gothic novel: weak mortals straining against unknown fates and destinies—or, in the fittingly apocalyptic language of Henry James, ". . . the spirit engaged with the forces of violence."[33] In retrospect it can be seen that the Puritans' spiritually civilizing project was doomed to fail; that the Holy strained at its own limits, since righteous orthodoxy and woeful declension alike led to apocalypse and annihilation. No surprise, then, to twentieth-century H. P. Lovecraft, as he read seventeenth-century Cotton Mather, that reasoned explications and theologies of God's mercy quickly gave birth to monstrous tales of cosmic terror. Hell might be hellish; but so was Heaven— or at least so it seemed to the architects of Puritan interiority.

This book is, partly, the story of *that* story. Chapter One, "Nostalgia and Terror: Holy Ghosts," argues the construction of a theonational myth of the Holy, a federal eschatology both transcendent *and* transgressive, broad enough to serve church as well as meeting house. I will consider John Winthrop's "A Model of Christian Charity" to see how he derives a taxonomy of corporate identity and self-reflection from primarily religious categories, images of which—possession, dispossession, conversion, to name a few— were then dispersed through a variety of cultural discourses and socializing gestures. Chapter Two, " 'Entertaining Satan': The American Rite of Deviancy," examines how the allegory of transgression organizes a grammar by which to write/right the social self. Evil is rarely allowed to remain abstract in any society. God might be faceless; the demonic, never. For Salem authorities in 1692, the stability of the body politic necessitated, and was used to justify, the rhetorical (and *actual*) effacement of individuals. This ritual of necessary deviancy lives on still; in time the authorized violence of civic dismemberment would become a routine civic strategy, occasioning communal self-reflection for the body politic. The pleasures of perversity would always succeed as spectacle. Finally, Salem is an important national event because, as the Red Queen insists to Alice, memory works forward as well as reverse. As narrative, history is less concerned with *what happened then* than with *how it is remembered now*. Nor can the past ever be safely forgotten; it must always be made over, written over, drawn over, to provide fictions needed to live by.[34]

Chapter Three, "Writing the Unholy: Chanting the God Demonic," moves from political fantasies of *civitas* to the problematic of language. It locates the dilemma of writing the Holy in the complexities of discourse itself. My discussion will center on Jonathan Edwards and his fantastic theologies. Edwards attempts to write the Holy as converting grace only to find the language itself slipping away from him, as the discourse of theology gives way to the "horrors of the mind." Yet Edwards's progress, or perhaps descent, into theological fantasy, as exemplified by "Sinners in the Hands of an Angry God," sets a precedent from which others will profit. The moral authority once possessed by theology will be displaced into a poetry of high, moralistic civility. From this latter position, I argue, it is only a small step for the complete inversion of theological imperative in the equally moralistic incivility of contemporary horror. Chapter Four, "The Shape of the Dark: Robert Frost and H. P. Lovecraft," considers another link between theology and fantasy—cosmology and its dreadful Outer Spaces. Not for nothing does Lovecraft sound like John Calvin of *The Institutes* gone mad. Whether you choose Lovecraft's so-called Elder Gods or his dancing, blind, and tyrannous Cthulhu, or the One God of Calvin—each is inscrutable, and thus incomprehensible and quite literally unspeakable. Theology takes its fantastic metaphors seriously, even literally, and so the family resemblance among them is obvious.

In Chapter Five, " 'It Came from Beyond': The Sacred and the Scary," I consider the metaphors of ingression and intrusion—outer spaces as they impinge, intrude, break through into human spaces, violating the very patterns of normality their existence establishes. Bloch writes that "the majority of writers who deal with the supernatural have repudiated the tenets of organized religion" (*Kingdom of Fear*, p. 27). Perhaps. But what is important about King, Lovecraft, and other such horror writers, is not their pseudo-religious referentiality, nor the crypto-religious excitations their fantasies provide for the unchurched. More significant than these is the way the stirring and prompting of a deeper religious crisis—the fear of the intrusive transcendent—informs their work. Lovecraft's "The Dunwich Horror," for example, offers a horrific take on a canonical New Testament image—indeed, so does William Blatty's *The Exorcist*. King's *'Salem's Lot* continues the theme of metaphysical violation, showing how a system of conflict and transgression; scrutiny and voyeurism; exclusion and expiation *are* the meaning of socialized religious practice.

Throughout these discussions it is important to observe how a theological model provides a template for civic self-definition, which functions, when all is said and done, as a form of metaphysical determinism—ironic, of course, in a culture whose rhetoric privileges the prerogatives of the single, separate self (although more often than not, this rhetoric only buttresses the economics of consumer desire). The final chapter, the Postscript, "End Runs: Toward the American Gothic," argues that the excitation of beyond-the-edge horror in contemporary dark fantasy reflects this Christian metaphysics of uncertainty in operation. Through an economy of symbolic displacement, the horror industry assumes some of the functions once largely managed by the discourse of religion. Indeed, I argue that horror serves as a misappropriated religious response to mystery. It is part ritual of memory, part dismissal. Old theologies become movies, commemoration becomes repetition, repetition becomes formula; the cinematic staking of the witch or other socially derived deviant, for example, organizes the new ritual of communal identity.[35] Gothic literatures and low-market pulp fictions, then, are not merely diversions *from* a Howellsian, high-canonical perspective of realism. They *are* the real thing, the contentious deflections of a culture profoundly diseased with and by its metaphysical abstractions and denials. Indulged in as entertainment, the Freddy-style dismemberings and violent fantasies in the *Nightmare on Elm Street* genre can hardly be considered innocuous. Nonetheless, they need to be read *beyond* their trite moralisms and simplistic cosmology of good and evil. However perversely as it might seem, these texts of horror are politically invested, civic gestures of identity. Contemporary horror texts rewrite originally *religious* allegiances into other terms, situating formerly metaphysical or supernatural horrors—such as fragmentation, bondage, captivity, possession, loss of self—in the political or social fabric of the society itself. (For examples I think, immediately and easily, of King's *Gerald's Game*, or *Carrie*, or any number of his texts. In *Misery*, for example, King asks, not always indirectly, what better place for hate to hide than in the horrible intimacies of altruistic, coercive love—where of course it is not expected and therefore not seen?)

The texts that remark themselves as appropriate to this study will be ones in which religious memory and political strategy conjoin at the level of metaphor and symbolic expression. In these texts, the master theological narrative will reflect itself in moments of confession, conversion, expiation, or possession—these gestures to be read as Revelation, sometimes of grace, sometimes of dis-grace.[36] So while a high-canonical writer like Flannery O'Connor would seem to be perfectly suited for a study of this sort (especially her dark tale of religious possession, *Wise Blood*), I focus instead on the genres of paracanonical, populist productions of fantasy and horror. Meaning, after all, is to be found in those places we are told not to look—which is why we are directed not to look there in the first place. But even limiting myself to these discredited genres I needed to be selective. Many contemporary texts came to mind, including Shirley Jackson's classics, "The Lottery" and *The Haunting of Hill House*. Anne Rice's early vampire novels most directly invoke the metaphysical inscrutabilities involved here, though Rice's Harlequin horror is considerably less moralistic—and considerably more Catholic—than Stephen King's, and that comparison would make an interesting study in itself.

There are many, many other texts which similarly derive their terms, if not their overall intent, from an originating religious discourse. Reflect, for example, on American political fantasies, ranging from John Winthrop's spiritual imperialism to the pulp racist fictions of *Weird Tales*; or perhaps, on a higher literary level— a doubtful assertion—think about Dixon's *The Clansman*. Dixon's novel seems superficially more realistic than the pulps; thus, by the casual alliance made between the *real* and the *worthy*, Dixon's frightening novel of racial revenge is often granted a canonical status denied other texts. Beyond the scope of this study, but nonetheless important, is L. Frank Baum's *The Wonderful Wizard of Oz*. Its later metamorphosis as screen spectacle during the Great Depression is a wonderful demonstration of how wilfully American nostalgia masks a fundamental despair. (A similar point could be made about Margaret Mitchell's *Gone With the Wind*.) From another perspective, consider the waves of porno-Gothic horror that flood the markets—either the domestic fixes designed for a love-addicted society, or the treacly, sentimentalized transcendent of *ET, Close Encounters of the Third Kind,* and similar products. These examples, picked pretty much at random, show how an institutionalized metaphysics of Christian love, discredited and trivialized, in turn generates its converse face: a nightmare order of intrusion and violation.

American dark fantasies range wide. By definition, they are transgressive, subversive, upsetting to the status quo. Crossing genre lines, sometimes they are written by custodians of culture like Wigglesworth and Edwards and Melville and Hawthorne, although they are mostly written by those who, in one way or another, culture would silence—presumably because they speak it too plainly. These "pulp" writers—for instance, Lovecraft, Burroughs, King—occupy the aesthetic margins. Their texts are consigned to the great unwashed and (in theory at least) the great unread. Social custodians presume their "lowbrow" texts to be meaningless, even dangerous to public morals—or, shifting away from moral evaluation toward a presumably "neutral" ground, these texts are considered to be inferior aesthetic products.[37] As we shall see, however, the converse is true. These texts are precisely meaningful to the extent that they speak what the culture would silence.

Finally, some of the links I will make have already been made for me, as Lovecraft reads Mather and Hawthorne; as Twain reads Edwards; as Edwards reads Calvin—indeed, as Calvin reads the Bible; and finally, as King reads his amnesiac culture. Especially in the early part of my study I have purposely chosen well-known texts—sermons and poems that from one point of view might be considered conventionally "American." I selected so-called "canonical" texts (with all the ideological burden the word carries) rather than more arcane examples in order to underscore the repetitive, indeed formulaic constraints—the genre and ideological expectations, in short—that even from early on shaped theological discourse, unwittingly diverting it toward other, more diverting ends. What Lovecraft learned of ghosts and haunts, he learned from Hawthorne. What Hawthorne needed to know of ghosts, spiritual vigilantes such as Mather, Edwards, and their theological masters taught him. The poetics of the troubled spirit characteristic of Frost (and others), are, indeed, not new to him, and are one of the reasons Frost is considered so accessible and "American" (and why certain of his poems, rather than others, are anthologized). These texts of variously horrific intimacies are, then, to be found in all generations and at all levels of culture—each intending, with varying degrees of self-awareness and craft, to scare the living Hell out of listeners, readers, and today, viewers.

This study reflects, I think, the concerns of a socio-religious culture that in the first place distrusted symbol and fiction, turning instead to the universalizing congruences of type and allegory. Suspicious of fiction's seductive, enchanting lies, these early religionists nourished their imaginations upon a theoretically safer genre—the sermon, whose minatory and didactic fancies were acceptable because they were, after all, "lessons." Thus would be born the spectacle, blood spilled that we might live and be saved. How pious it all sounds! Yet piety, too, plays a fundamental role in the development of American values. It must be remembered that these are the writings of a powerful interest group, whose purpose it was in 1630 to enter the land and to subdue it, armed only with theology and a rhetoric of great desires. Subsequent generations proposed to maintain the hegemony of God, and their writings defined, often by omission, society as life lived by the godly. Yet the texts that they would repudiate have much to teach, since in its own way the disallowed is revelatory of what is permitted. So to return to my original point, it is no surprise that the rhetoric common to theological text and horror fantasy focuses on terror. In the first place, terror was read as a sign of the encounter with God. And then, almost inevitably, terror came to signify a primary revelation of God's order (and thus, by extension, of *their* social order). There is no little irony here; the experience of the Divine would signify both authority and apocalypse, revelation and disaster.

Fantasy writes its story in the margins—in the blank, white spaces around the normative, hegemonic story that culture insists on telling, and telling loudly. Works of fantasy thus give voice to what a culture chooses to silence. That is, in the lives of individuals and cultures, the unspoken becomes unspeakable. This study argues that by knowing someone's fantasy you will also know, indirectly, the prison that holds them bound. In addition, this study presumes that although prisons can be constructed of metal and steel, for entrapment words are nice, and will suffice. Prisons can be merely symbolic, or perhaps, more covertly, just metaphysical. In the New World, a theology of the *Word*, born again, is the *Weird*.[38] Born again *and* again, it is both good politics and good business.[39]

NOTES

1. D. H. Lawrence, *Studies in Classic American Literature* (New York: The Viking Press, 1964), p. 83.
2. Cited in "Riding the Crest of the Horror Craze," William Wilson, *The New York Times Magazine*, May 11, 1980, p. 42.
3. "On Censorship," in Stephen Jones, ed., *Clive Barker's Shadows in Eden* (Lancaster, PA: Underwood-Miller, 1991), p. 402.
4. In *Revivals*, McLoughlin writes, "The Puritan Awakening in effect gave America its own culture core, its sense of being a differently constituted people, covenanted with God on a special errand into the wilderness. The millennial hopes of the colonists, their pietistic perfectionism, their belief in further light and a higher law, their commitment to freedom of conscience and separation of church and state, and, above all, their profound sense of individual piety made the Americans different. . . . It was a land committed to the reformation of God's world and the freedom of the individual in his calling, though its settlers also possessed a large share of self-interest, aggression, and acquisitiveness" (p. 25).
5. For convenience sake, I will generally use "terror" and "horror" as synonymous terms. While theorists from Edmund Burke and Ann Radcliffe onward have argued their differences, for my purposes "horror" (as in the "horror" market) functions descriptively to signify a "contrivance" or "construction" that maintains, even obliquely, traces of an early ritual of religious self-effacing—in short, metaphysical terror. For discussions of these terms and their various differences, see Will H. Rockett, *Devouring Whirlwind: Terror and Transcendence in the Cinema of Cruelty* (Westport, CT: Greenwood Press, 1988), who argues that horror "couples fear with disgust or loathing" while terror "couples fear with awe" (p. 31), and pp. 43–51; in *The Delights of Horror: An Aesthetics of the Tale of Terror* (Urbana: University of Illinois Press, 1987), Terry Heller argues simply that "terror is the fear that harm will come to oneself" and that horror "is the emotion one feels in anticipating and witnessing harm coming to others for whom one cares" (p. 19). But see his concluding chapter, "Terror and the Sublime," pp. 191–206. Barton Levi St. Armand, in *The Roots of Horror in the Fiction of H. P. Lovecraft* (Elizabethtown,

NY: Dragon Press, 1977), argues, more or less in agreement with Ann Radcliffe ("On the Supernatural in Poetry") that "terror expands the soul outward" toward the ineffable while horror is a "species of devolution toward . . . 'the unspeakable' " (pp. 2–3). Noel Carroll argues against this distinction in *The Philosophy of Horror: or Paradoxes of the Heart* (New York: Routledge, 1990), pp. 161–68 *passim*. Even Stephen King, in *Danse Macabre* (New York: Berkley Books, 1982), distinguishes terror and horror: "terror on top, horror below it, and lowest of all, the gag reflex of revulsion." (p. 37). The classic text, of course, is Edmund Burke, *A Philosophical Enquiry into the Origin of Our Ideas of the Sublime and Beautiful* (Notre Dame: University of Notre Dame Press, 1968).

6. The connections between secular and religious uses of terror have been made before, notably by Machiavelli, Hume, and Hobbes. Hobbes, in *Leviathan*, examines at length the place of religion in the social contract. Most contemporary theorizing on the subject owes a debt to René Gerard, *Violence and the Sacred*, trans. Patrick Gregory (Baltimore: Johns Hopkins University Press, 1977). See Michael Walzer's "Puritanism as a Revolutionary Ideology," *History and Theory*, III (1963), p. 88; "The Study of Religion and Violence," by Richard C. Martin, in *The Morality of Terrorism*, David C. Rapoport and Yonah Alexander, eds., second edition (New York: Columbia University Press, 1989), pp. 349–73.

7. See Walter Evans, "Monster Movies: A Sexual Theory," in *Planks of Reason: Essays on the Horror Film*, Barry Keith Grant, ed. (Metuchen, NJ: Scarecrow Press, 1984): "The key to monster movies and the adolescents who understandably dote upon them is the theme of horrible and mysterious psychological and physical change; the most important of these is the monstrous transformation which is directly associated with secondary sexual characteristics and with the onset of aggressive erotic behavior." (p. 54) In *Dreadful Pleasures: An Anatomy of Modern Horror, op. cit.*; James Twitchell makes similar points.

8. See Robert Bruce Mullin, *Episcopal Vision/American Reality: High Church Theology and Social Thought in Evangelical America* (New Haven: Yale University Press, 1986), esp. 135 ff.

9. In *Policing Desire: Pornography, AIDS and the Media* (Minneapolis: University of Minnesota Press, 1987), Simon Watney writes about pornography, arguing that notions of indecency as legally defined "involves display." (p. 65). One wants to "see," of course, but not too much. Too much display is "scandalous"—and welcome to the extent that it provides a daily dose of social reassurance. See Watney's chapter, "AIDS and the Press" (pp. 77–97).

10. *Horror Fiction in the Protestant Tradition* (New York: St. Martin's Press, 1988), p. xiii.

11. *Dreadful Pleasures: An Anatomy of Modern Horror* (New York: Oxford University Press, 1985).

12. Oral Sumner Coad, "The Gothic Element in American Literature Before 1835," *Journal of English and Germanic Philology*, vol. 24, 1925: 72–93.

13. For example, in what seems an example remote from my topic, Dennis Altman argues that the moralistic/monstrous rhetoric that saturates discussions of AIDS is more typical of "Anglo-Saxon societies, where puritanism

and a fear of contamination from outside seems particularly developed."
(pp. 184–85) See *AIDS in the Mind of America* (Garden City, NY: Anchor Books,
Doubleday, 1986).

14. Before "America" the land had other names, of course. Plato's Atlantis had
been considered; El Dorado, the Edenic island, the land Columbus called
"the earthly paradise." See *the Voyages of Christopher Columbus. Being the
Journals of His First and Third, and the Letters Concerning His First and Last
Voyages, to Which Is Added the Account of His Second Voyage Written by Andreas
Bernaldez*, p. 252. Cited in Peter Freese, *America, Dream or Nightmare?: Reflections on a Composite Image* (Essen: Ver Die Blaue Eule, 1990), p. 78. See also
First Images of America: The Impact of the New World on the Old, Fredi Chiappelli,
ed. (Berkeley: University of California Press, 1976).

For a "summary view" of old-world national mythologies that helped
shape that of the New World, see Slotkin, *Regeneration Through Violence*,
pp. 14–24; for its Arcadian, "dream kingdom," background, pp. 29–35 and
passim. See also "The Puritan Vision of the New World," Sacvan Bercovitch,
Columbia Literary History of the United States (Emory Elliott, general ed., New
York: Columbia University Press, 1988), pp. 33–44.

15. One could argue that the myth was sacred *because* it was socially binding,
because the process of constructing it was, as Richard Slotkin writes, "simultaneously a psychological and a social activity." (p. 8) See *Regeneration
Through Violence: The Mythology of the American Frontier, 1600–1860* (Middletown, CT: Wesleyan University Press, 1973).

16. Joseph Campbell defines myth as "traditional metaphor addressed to ultimate questions" (cited in Richard Slotkin, *Regeneration through Violence*, p. 20).

17. "On the Prospect of Planting Arts and Learning in America," *The Works of
George Berkeley, Bishop of Cloyne*, A. A. Luce, ed. (London: Nelson, [1948–57]),
vol. 7: 373.

18. William G. McLoughlin, *Revivals*. Peter Freese, *America, Dream or Nightmare?:
Reflections on a Composite Image*, (Essen: *op. cit.*, argues that three general
traditions come together in the iconography of America: 1) the mythic
tradition which "envisaged America as the pastoral country in which a new
golden age would flourish"; 2) the religious tradition of millennial Protestantism which considered America to be "the New Canaan where God's
chosen people were to create a new earthly paradise"; and 3) the political
tradition, dating "as far back as Sir Thomas More's *Utopia* (1516)" and
which "found its lasting expression in the Declaration of Independence."
(pp. 89–90)

19. In *The New England Soul: Preaching and Religious Culture in Colonial New England*
(New York: Oxford University Press, 1986), Harry S. Stout argues that the
"recent surge of scholarship on the Middle Colonies and Chesapeake confirms how atypical and nonrepresentative New England was in certain key
social, cultural, economic, political, and demographic respects" and that
qualifications are necessary "lest we fall into the trap of reading America as
New England writ large" (p. 9). Nonetheless he admits it would "be a mistake
to under[score] the importance of New England's religious culture . . . and

more particularly, the influence of Puritan rhetoric on the American identity" (p. 9).

20. See, for example, *A Mirror for Americanists: Reflections on the Idea of American
    Literature*, William C. Spengemann (Hanover: University Press of New En-
    gland, 1989); also, see "New Literary History: Past and Present," Emory
    Elliott, *American Literature*, vol. 57, no. 4, December 1985: 611–21.

21. For a discussion of the difference between private and public, see Patricia
    Spacks, *Gossip* (New York: Knopf, 1985). Spacks writes, "the sharp differentia-
    tion of public and private belongs to a relatively recent moment in history."
    She cites Richard Sennett, "The line drawn was essentially one on which the
    claims of civility—epitomized by cosmopolitan, public behavior—were bal-
    anced against the claims of nature—epitomized by the family." (p. 6) Ameri-
    can culture has, as a rule, in practice if not in rhetoric, privileged the self (i.e.,
    privatization) over the body politic. Indeed, this is one of its major fantasies,
    and the reason why overtly fantastic texts are categorically denied the privi-
    lege of "realism"—in an effort to keep the suspect genre precisely "private,"
    their implications limited, at best, to a few.

22. "For when the novel is conceived of as a successful act of truancy, no other
    role for the police is possible than that of a patrol which ineptly stands guard
    over a border fated to be transgressed. . . . I shall be considering what such
    views necessarily dismiss: the possibility of a radical *entanglement* between the
    nature of the novel and the practice of the police. . . . And how does the
    novel—as a set of representational techniques—systematically participate in
    a general economy of policing power?" D. A. Miller, *The Novel and the Police*
    (Berkeley: University of California Press, 1988), p. 2.

23. See R. Laurence Moore, *Selling God: American Religion in the Marketplace of
    Culture* (New York: Oxford University Press, 1994).

24. (New York: Stein and Day, 1968), p. 48.

25. See Keith Thomas in *Religion and the Decline of Magic* (New York: Scribner's,
    1976). He writes, "The search for a scapegoat sprang from the conviction that
    every natural disaster must necessarily have a moral cause." (p. 92) For a
    contemporary example of this argument, in *Policing Desire: Pornography, AIDS,
    and the Media, op. cit.*, Simon Watney argues that a "model of contagion"
    structures not only the "entire dimension of AIDS commentary" (p. 43),
    homosexuality itself is structured as a "contagious condition, invisible and
    always threatening to reveal itself where least expected" (p. 23). See also
    Dennis Altman, *AIDS in the Mind of America*, cited previously.

26. David Punter, *The Literature of Terror: A History of Gothic Fictions from 1765 to the
    Present Day* (New York: Longmans, 1980).

27. See Julia Kristeva, *Powers of Horror: An Essay on Abjection*, trans. Leon S.
    Roudiez (New York: Columbia University Press, 1982), p. 34.

28. See especially Mason I. Lowance, Jr., *The Language of Canaan: Metaphor and
    Symbol in New England from the Puritans to the Transcendentalists* (Cambridge:
    Harvard University Press, 1980); Ann-Janine Morey-Gaines, *Apples and Ashes:
    Culture, Metaphor and Morality in the American Dream* (Chico, CA: Scholars
    Press, 1982); *The Haunted Dusk: American Supernatural Fiction, 1820–1920,*

Howard Kerr, John W. Crowley, and Charles L. Crow, eds. (Athens: University of Georgia Press, 1983); "Calvinism and Literary Culture," Horton Davies, *John Donne Journal*, vol. 3, no. 1, 1984: 106–12; "Aesthetic Strategies in Western Religious Thought," David Chidester, *Journal of the American Academy of Religion*, vol. 51, no. 1, 1983: 55–66; *Puritan Influences in American Literature*, Emory Elliott, ed., *op. cit.*; Richard Ruland and Malcom Bradbury, *From Puritanism to Postmodernism: A History of American Literature* (New York: Penguin, 1991), esp. pp. 3–60.

29. See Garry Wills, *Under God: Religion and American Politics* (New York, Simon and Schuster, 1990), esp. part 8, "Church and State."

30. Although Will Herberg provides the background in *Protestant, Catholic, Jew* (1957), Robert Bellah coined the expression "Civil Religion" in "Civil Religion in America," originally printed in *Daedelus* (Winter 1967), and since reprinted in Richey and Jones (see below). See also Bellah's later *The Broken Covenant: American Civil Religion in a Time of Trial* (New York: Seabury Press, 1975). For responses to Bellah see especially *American Civil Religion*, Russell E. Richey and Donald G. Jones, eds. (New York: Harper & Row, 1974).

31. See Rudolph Otto, *The Idea of the Holy*, trans. J. W. Harvey (New York: Oxford Galaxy Books, 1958). See also Robert F. Geary, *The Supernatural in Gothic Fiction: Horror, Belief, and Literary Change* (Lewiston, NY: Edwin Mellen Press, 1992).

32. In "Otto and Freud on the Uncanny and Beyond" Lorne Dawson argues that while "Otto's theory depends on a suspect neo-Kantian metaphysics" nonetheless his theory usefully can be compared to Freud's "Uncanny"—especially with regard to the relationship of "numinous, aesthetic, and erotic experiences," *Journal of the American Academy of Religion*, vol. 57, no. 2, 1989: 284.

33. Preface to "The Jolly Corner," *Novels and Tales*, the New York edition (1907–09), vol. 17: xvi.

34. Robert J. Stoller defines societies as "individuals soaked in history." *Observing the Erotic Imagination* (New Haven: Yale University Press, 1985).

35. Roger Dadoun specifically addresses the role of the cinema in this process of confirming repudiations. He observes that "in the cinema the spectator's potential for perversion is managed by the institution." See "Fetishism in the Horror Film," in *Fantasy Cinema*, James Donald, ed. (London: British Film Institute, 1989), p. 59. For a discussion of what Terry Heller calls the "reenactment of Repression, see *The Delights of Horror: An Aesthetics of the Tale of Terror*, *op. cit.*, pp. 72–73, 83–86; Rosemary Jackson, *Fantasy: the Literature of Subversion* (New York: Methuen, 1981).

36. Under this rubric, as well, although in a different genre, many presidential campaign speeches will situate themselves, as political variants of the dark fantasy tradition, and as Gothic texts. As for American Gothic, see most of George Bush's campaign for the presidency (thanks to Lee Atwater, political Gothicist extraordinaire); indeed, Reagan, from whom Bush learned the more-or-less polite arts of terror, is an able practitioner. Reagan is instructive

as an example of the trivialization of post-Christian rhetoric. He demonstrates the tendency of American religious discourse to displace itself into either sentimental moralism or foundationalism.

37. The work of Charlotte Perkins Gilman, one of the earliest to articulate a specifically "feminist" position, was likewise published as fantasy—and thus, her feminism easily dismissed. See the publication histories of "The Yellow Wallpaper" and *Herland*. See Ann J. Lane, *To Herland and Beyond: The Life and Work of Charlotte Perkins Gilman* (New York: Pantheon Books, 1990); *Critical Essays on Charlotte Perkins Gilman*, Joanne B. Karpinski, ed. (New York: G. K. Hall, 1992); *The Captive Imagination: A Casebook on "The Yellow Wallpaper,"* Catherine Golden, ed. (New York: Feminist Press at the City University of New York, 1992).

38. See *American Horror Fiction: From Brockden Brown to Stephen King*, ed. by Brian Docherty, ed. (London: Macmillan, 1990).

39. My argument is partly indebted to Joseph Grixti, *Terrors of Uncertainty: The Cultural Contexts of Horror Fiction* (London: Routledge, 1989). Grixti argues that "works of horror fiction and the texts which explain them have a similar ideological base; by cultivating fear within well-determined codes, with the help of an increasingly lucrative horror industry, they propagate a sense of personal helplessness and political impotence which is central to the maintenance of consumer culture" (p. 1).

CHAPTER ONE

Nostalgia and Terror: Holy Ghosts

There are terrible spirits, ghosts, in the air of America.
—D. H. LAWRENCE, "EDGAR ALLAN POE"

We shall be made a story and a by-word through the world.
—JOHN WINTHROP, "A MODEL OF CHRISTIAN CHARITY"

To know God is to be struck with horror and amazement, for then and only then does one realize his own character."
—CITED IN SAGE, P. 74

———— ■■ ————

A Troubled House

How like an iron cage was that which they called Liberty.
—HAWTHORNE, "MAIN STREET," P. 1031

Old habits die hard, although none die so hard that they can't be resurrected in new guises, as people in addictive processes discover. So it is not surprising that after three hundred years, a cultural habit of religion, legally silenced, still speaks loudly enough to be heard. Like the vampire, that ironic cultural icon (also a religious image, once removed), the discourse and rhythms of religion seem unkillable, endlessly adaptable. On the one hand, a habit of religious reading encouraged budding young naturalists like Jonathan Edwards (and *his* errant student of the spiritual,

Thoreau) to read into the world of nature "some kind of moral order" (Coale, *In Hawthorne's Shadow*, p. 37).[1] Indeed, discerning the "Shadows of Divine Things" in the woods and hills of western Massachusetts, Concord, and other places has produced a genre of writing distinctively American in style and content. However, the "inexpressible weight of things Eternal" (Richard Baxter; cited in Caldwell, p. 136) also helps shape and fence other landscapes, too—notably the darker geography of the imagination.[2] For instance, it was the habit of looking for God in all the wrong places, as it were, that prompted Cotton Mather to scan the streets and skies of Salem for God's will. Then, endlessly confident that he had found it, to decry the "wonders of the invisible world" breaking through into witch-plagued Salem. His action would dramatically shape the subsequent American political imagination.

Chapter One considers the politics and consequences of this theologized imagination. It examines the way metaphors of spirit and body entangled, and the practical confusions that resulted, when the earliest religious immigrants to this country established the *civitas* in spiritual terms. To Perry Miller, "Puritanism" was "not only a religious creed," it was, additionally, a "philosophy and a metaphysic . . . an organization of man's whole life, emotional and intellectual" (cited in McLoughlin, p. 24). And so, however discreetly, religious discourse continues to be an all-purpose, civic narrative of self-description, populist motivation, and terrible self-haunting. As we shall see, the rhetorical pattern of the Puritans' zeal is still written in civic self-address; their moralistic energy still fills movie theaters and sways public emotion.

Although economics and religious motives were deeply mixed even in 1630, the actual *land* settled as a religious sanctuary and called New England was somewhat less important than the various new worlds of rhetoric and cult derived from it. Even before the Puritan migration, of course, the crucial attraction of the New World was, really, that it was a never-never land in the classic sense: a utopic geography perfectly situated in the mind's eye to be unrestrained by problematic conditions of land and weather, while at the same time being free from the messy *gravitas* of earthly politics. In short, the Puritans sought a spiritual landscape, perhaps even a fantasy one. However, they were not the first to yearn for Utopia; nor were they alone in blending desire for a new world with nostalgia for the old: " 'America' entitled a carnival of European fantasies" (Bercovitch, "The Puritan Vision of the New World," *CLHUS* p. 35).[3] It was just that the unworldly hopes of the Puritans differed from other European visions, so they thought, because theirs had biblical warrant.

The Puritans read history in reverse, beginning with Revelation—the end. Biblical typology explained to these strict religionists the complexity of their lives, and even lent a measure of authority to their history that it otherwise lacked. To a culture long on reading and short on books, allegory was a necessary habit and the Bible, life's primary text: "All demarcations of the Sacred, all ways of linking nature, man, and God, rested on moral allegory" (Hall, *Worlds of Wonder*, p. 212). For the dispossessed Puritans the newly vernacular Bible offered a template from Genesis to Revelation, from origin to apocalypse. It made possible an easy-to-follow map through a geographic wilderness that metaphorically embodied a range of issues—psychological and emotional, nationalistic, civic, even religious: Who am I? Where am I from? Where am I going? Manifest Destiny would later become a nationalistic rallying cry, even a cliché. But it could be applied to exterior geography because for decades it had already expressed popular sentiment about being able to read the soul's destiny rightly.

The Puritans struggled to build a society conceived as worship and the difficulties of the task soon became apparent. For one thing, a hidden assumption behind governance and theology became clear. So entwined were the two impulses of church and *polis* (state would be anachronistic in this context)—evangelical federalism, as it were—that in the new republic, laws would eventually have to be enacted *precisely* to keep church and *polis* separate.[4] As if this were not complication enough, the social order rising on the Massachusetts strand implicitly presumed that God's love— whatever else might be said of it—was so overwhelming that few individuals survived its revelation unchanged. And what could be said about individuals would be said about social orders, as well. The society rested, often uneasily, upon a politics of apocalypse. That is, as Puritan rhetoric put it rather more ingenuously, their world was to be radically converted *by* love *to* love. In practice, things did not always turn out that simply, of course. Grace was, in a word, devastating, even awful. Indeed, Salem would provide practical confirmation that metaphysics had civil consequences, and that the intrusion of the transcendent, whether demonic or divine, portended ill to individuals and to societies alike. Caution and restraint would prove theological necessities as well as civic strategies.

Nonetheless, to the conversion of love by love were organized the exclusions, denials, and prohibitions of their dissenting social polities. Further, the very *idea* behind Puritanism—an "emotion of dissent" (Heimert, p. 15)—casts light upon the Puritans' greatest contradiction. As Larzer Ziff suggests, "antinomian belief [is] at the core of Puritanism" (Heimert, p. 13). Dissenters themselves, the Puritans showed zealous devotion to the law, relentlessly pursuing the lawless, whether freethinker, Quaker, or other "perversely creative minds" (Starkey, p. 234). So by a curious reversal, the same antinomian impulse engendered both John Cotton, radical dissenter, originator and guardian of New England's law, *and* Anne Hutchinson, herself a sharp-witted and formidable dissenter against the constraints of external law. The urge to dissent and to speak the soul freely produced the most law-*conscious* culture in the world, while making inevitable its necessary subversion. In time, even the Divine—inscrutable, unmanageable, and above the law, clearly an antinomian of sorts—would draw their fire.

The separatists and come-outers who fled war-torn England were not by any means, then, persons given to works of airy accommodation. John Demos notes the "ubiquity of conflict in early New England life" (*Entertaining Satan*, p. 297). Demos observes, for instance, that conflict was viewed "not simply as an invitation to God's wrath but also as an *expression* of it" (p. 371). (Indeed, as one commentator suggests, Salem, which we will consider in the next chapter, was considered to be "one of the most contentious little communities in the Massachusetts Bay Colony" (Starkey, p. 26). This general attribute of the colonies was due in part to the naturally fierce challenges the people faced merely to survive, for the Puritans' strenuous practice of Christianity seemed a fitting response to the rough weather in New England and rougher conditions at home. Nor did the vast spaces of the not-yet colonies appease or even much temper their contrariness. Further, it is crucial to understand that the first New Englanders neither sought nor hoped to find religious toleration; they "were in no sense pioneers of religious liberty" (Miller, *American Puritans*, p. 94), and freedom of expression, at least as we understand the term, was not what they sought. Quite to the contrary; it was precisely to demonstrate their bondage to the Covenant and their submission to God's spiritual law that the Puritans undertook the Great Migration, choosing in literal fashion to follow the biblical injunction, "be not conformed to the world. . . ." And so they were not, and would not be, ever; to be dispossessed *and* captive would always be their emblematic spiritual condition.

Still, while resisting the (new) world, these early immigrants rigorously imposed upon it a characteristic religious sense and shadow. It was, in Wallace Stevens's phrase, as if they had left "with [their] bones . . . what still is / The look of things. . . ." ("A Postcard from the Volcano," p. 159). Fleeing popery in the Old World, they reinstated in the new a system of religious scrutiny as baroque as any old-world Catholicism. A zeal for hierarchy the Puritans lived out as submission. Although they escaped the burdens of priestcraft, they reinstated the weight of priestly subjugation in the meetinghouse, whose very pews wrote out a pattern of conformity and hierarchy at the same time. And although they spoke long and eloquently of God's love, it was God's unescapable terror that compelled their allegiance; and, as resistant to other people's laws as they were, they considered submission to God's inscrutable law— and, paradoxically, to his confounding mercies—their greatest virtue. The English expatriates who fled Queen Mary's zealous persecutions, removing first to the lowlands, and then to New England, were indeed a ragtag lot of dissidents and separatists—fanatics, their own peers would call them. As Alan Heimert observes, "their name and even their sense of who they were" the Puritans received "from those who reviled them. Theirs was a movement invented . . . by its enemies" (*The Puritans*, p. 1). Indeed, their very name— "Puritan"—was meant as a derisive insult.

The Puritans were convicted—one must hear the word's theological echo—by the need to write the Holy into the temporal order as civic principle, and their efforts to rewrite theological disputations as nationalist policies and governmental systems had precedent.[5] As incentive, source, and model, they could draw upon various theological and social polities of the Reformation, beginning with Calvin's social theories—or, closer in place and time, with Oliver Cromwell's model for the Commonwealth of England. In effect, both governmental models were attempts to spiritualize the *polis*, or perhaps in reverse, to police the spiritual. While the religious settlers in New England may thus be distinguished for being the earliest practitioners of a modified democracy, nonetheless, this liberal political position was derived not so much from any putative *value* of the Self, but by the exact reverse. The Puritans emphasized the Self's precise *valuelessness* in light of the Holy, upon whose authority their society depended and in whose transcendent image they proudly abased themselves.

It can be seen, then, that the New England mind "was seldom, if ever . . . a single or simple one" (Heimert, *The Puritans*, p. xii). Alan Heimert argues that the consequent irony of its social history, through which it undergoes a transformation from "dissenters to lawgivers" is "manifold and deep" (p. 15). Indeed, the Congregationalists enterprisingly learned from Saint Paul that devotion to the law in effect *compels* transgression and that, more oddly still, transgression authorizes, even confirms, the law it violates. This perverse fact would constantly surprise and dismay their leaders: "It was not long before they were rooting out their own deviants from their midst" (p. 15). Nor did the Puritans lose that initial habit—a distrust, even paranoia of the Sublime—that would first surface in the antinomian crisis. Indeed, they had a right to distrust the Divine; for one thing, the constant search for revelation naturally, if unwittingly, implied God's hiddenness. The anticipated Second Coming of Jesus underscored His First Loss; future hopes, then, confirmed in the present a sense of God's *absence*. As a consequence, longing and exaltation; abasement and submission; freedom and captivity would be the polarities of the religious mind upon whose rhetoric would be organized a social order. Their governance of the soul was predicated upon the necessity of revelation; upon a distrust of the actual in favor of the allegorical. Central to its spirituality was the imperative of conversion, with its attendant public consequences.

The Protestant movement since its founding in the Reformation had always been preoccupied with literacy, and in New England the politics of reading engendered crucial civic metaphors.

David Hall argues that complex ecclesiastical (and civil) politics were mobilized around the notion of a vernacular Bible, and that questions of literacy and theological justification could hardly be separated: "Learning how to read and becoming 'religious' were perceived as one and the same thing" (Hall, *Worlds of Wonder*, p. 18). To know one's letters was to experience firsthand God's saving power as revealed in the Testaments. Reading was tantamount to private revelation: a duty and right that in its willful vanity the popish church had withheld from the people. Indeed, to a people who felt they had very little worldly clout, being able to read the Scriptures was a worldly significant, yet spiritually visionary, act—even a radical gesture of religious (and thus political) defiance.[6] Consequently, in this rigorously democratic society even the poorest were kingly, since the ability to read presumed a direct access to God unbeholden to priestcraft or other forms of magic.

In sum, the colonists who fled Old England were a complex people, zealots lured by expanding markets in two worlds, spiritual and geographical. They were practical in business, wordy and contentious in religion. Nor did they separate the two. As John Higginson warns, " . . . this is never to be forgotten, that *New England is originally a plantation of Religion, not a plantation of Trade.*"[7] Their many sermons and diaries reveal, sometimes compulsively, the anxieties they carried with them to the New World.[8] Writing the soul, the "spiritual account book" (Shea, p. 88) had been a Protestant genre since the time of Elizabeth (although the form derived from the *Confessions* of Saint Augustine). The spiritual autobiography, sometimes known as the Puritan's genre, was a detailing of interiority, and the early New Englanders were relentless diarists.[9] They rendered the soul in words, tried it as text.[10] By their writings we know them, and indirectly, ourselves, since our culture still mirrors theirs in so many ways. The colonists' preoccupation with issues of identity and authority, even destiny—their awareness, too, of the transgressive nature of the enterprise—made for "a highly self-conscious literature with a tendency toward polemic and apology" (Slotkin, *Regeneration through Violence*, p. 15). Defensiveness, as Heimert comments, "was a part of New England's initiation" (p. 7).[11] Subsequent generations would inherit these ambiguities; even yet a restive mixture of conformism and individualism; a confusion of bodies and spirits in public rhetorics registers the intensity and conflict of this early enterprise.

In summary, in the political theorizing that had derived from Calvin's *Institutes*, eschatology (the study of the last things) governed first things. Consequently, for most Puritans the notion of private identity was subsumed in a larger, communal sense of mission. The Puritans conceived this mission to be divinely mandated by God, and they themselves chosen, in effect, to help God in His work of bringing closure to time—when God would reveal (be revealed?) as the end of history. Yet the new Heav'ns and Earth the Puritans sought would be found only after they had, practically speaking, imagined and constructed them in the first place. So, Godlike, they created and mapped a world in their own image: zealous, imperfect, fallen, transgressed. Their model had scriptural warrant: "Be ye therefore perfect, even as your Heavenly Father is perfect" (Matt. 5:48). For this reason conversion—of the soul, of the state—lay at the core of their hopes, while the terrors of inappropriate or unauthorized conversions, personal and civic instabilities, lurked on the fringe. On the one hand the successful establishment of Winthrop's "city upon a hill" would betoken a radical transformation of the world—a conversion already in process, as more than one Divine (Mather, Edwards) confirmed. On the other, the failure of the "errand into the wilderness" (in the title of Samuel Danforth's 1670 sermon) would signify an equal, if downward, transformation of society.[12] Conversion and metamorphosis: those who could read the signs of instability in either direction would never want for work, for the Puritans read their fallen world through a semiotics of revelation, just as they read themselves by means of the metaphors of captivity (outward) and scrutiny (inward) that increasingly governed public and private life. Ironically, while the quest for the perfect society—one "converted" in terms of the Holy—was in theory a place to begin, it became in practice an often appalling apocalypse, because, as time went on, "perfect" and "conventional" became exchangeable terms. Conforming the exterior replaced exploring the interior. In the Congregational Way of New England, the reformation of the body politic began with the individual, while the monitoring of the soul began with the exteriors of the body.[13] As duty claimed the interior warrant of love, uncertainty and terror enforced a moralistic, sentimentalized conformity. Gradually the spirituality of the visible saints presumed, and finally came to mean, the study of civility.

Origins and Beginnings: Looking Homeward

[The great achievement of the Fifth Monarchy forces] is what is known in the sociology of revolution as the terror, *the effort to create a holy commonwealth and to force man to be godly.*[14]

Cambridge-educated John Winthrop, justice of the peace and squire of Groton Manor, first governor of the Massachusetts Bay Colony, could have died happily, and rich, in England. His family had profited from Henry VIII's 1535 break with Rome; they had received lands from the monarch's dissolution of the monasteries, and with these as a firm base Winthrop could have been secure. However, like other restless young people of the time, he began reading the Bible at an early age and soon fell under its spell. The rest, as the expression has it, is history. So in 1630, when Winthrop reflected upon his tenuous position as commander–in–chief of the Great Migration, he may have wondered at the ironies of fate. Here he was—lawyer, layman, governor of the not-yet colony—spelling out in dry detail for the assembled charter colonists the spiritual how and whyfores of their mission: why they were rocking at sea rather than still in exile in Leyden or home in Old England. Winthrop had been given command over the *Arbella* and its fleet of ships because he was a practical leader as well as soberly religious. A short address he delivered on board ship before landfall shows Winthrop's economy: it was justification, description, exhortation, and threat, all at once.[15]

Winthrop's "A Model of Christian Charity" contains a taxonomy of a social order. He describes his boat-bound people as a "community of peril" (p. 85). He exhorts them to "walk by" one another, appealing to religious idealism—love, "the bond of perfection" (p. 86). Nonetheless, good lawyer that he is, Winthrop appeals as well to more practical bonds—the "law of nature and the law of grace" (p. 83). These twin principles, he suggests, will govern the community in its efforts to build a new society. However, in its concluding three paragraphs Winthrop's address changes tone; careful explication and exhortation gives way to minatory charge, threat, and lively admonition:

> But if we shall neglect the observation of these articles which are the ends we have propounded and, dissembling with our God, shall fall to embrace this present world and prosecute our carnal intentions, seeking great things for ourselves and our posterity, the Lord will surely break out in wrath against us, be revenged of such a perjured people and make us know the price of the breach of such a covenant. (pp. 90–91)

It is almost as if what preceded these lines was a warmup. Winthrop rises to his subject, and with some vigor here emphasizes the subjunctives and conditionals, the dicey quality of the immigrants' "extraordinary" task: the community's health depends on "if" the Lord "shall please to hear" them. But Winthrop's declarative intent is clear: communal disaster *will* follow "if we shall neglect" the Covenant and, "dissembling with our God, shall fall to embrace this present world" (p. 90). The colonists were still cooped up aboard ship following a long, tiring sea voyage. Already at sea in a real sense, Winthrop made it clear to the colonists that they risked being at sea in other ways, too. Not only were they between diverse countries and diverse laws; in addition they were between kingdoms as well—earthly on the one hand, heavenly on the other.

In effect, Winthrop outlines to his homeless people the hazards of being metaphysically homeless, also. Thus the injunctions Winthrop raises—the fears of "shipwreck" and the "curses" he invokes—double and slip from one referent to another, from one kingdom to the other. And lest his people doze and mistake the point, Winthrop repeats the threat twice more in his short sermon; to "avoid this shipwreck" they must be "knit together" (p. 90) lest "prayers . . . be turned into Curses . . . till we be consumed out of the good land whither we are agoing" (p. 91). Again a few lines later he admonishes these spiritually dispossessed colonists to stay true or else, as Winthrop concludes, "we shall surely perish out of the good land whither we pass over this vast sea to possess it" (p. 92).

Possession, shipwreck; home, dispossession: behind Winthrop's articulated fears, then, lay others, their importance signaled by the fact that they remained unspoken—although, in the nature of such things, not unheard. No one of his auditors would miss the point; none needed to be told that Winthrop's penultimate threat—"till we be consumed out of the good land whither we are agoing"—referred not *only* to the land visible off the rocking bow of the *Arbella* (a land described by Cromwell as "poor, cold, and useless" [Heimert, p. 7]). The colonists knew that Winthrop had his final eye on another land, as theirs should be, as well. After all, the city they would have in that rocky new land, such as it was and would become, would not after all be a lasting one. Although they had not yet even set foot on the fantasy land they sought, even at this early date they were already looking ahead—or beyond—to another fantasy world elsewhere.

The title of Winthrop's "A Model of Christian Charity" (1630) is surely ironic, since it is long on distress as well as charity. Yet in addition, it also reflects a curious notion of time. With the fleet anchored in Boston Harbor, one forgets that the frontier, the imagination's limit of exploration, was the rocky beach a few hundred yards away. There would be time yet to discover how far that frontier extended, and what creative use could be made of the idea. But for the moment Winthrop turned away from the frontier, perhaps underestimating its aesthetic possibilities in the way future generations of mythologists would not. Winthrop faced the worries of an unknown future by calculatingly inventing a past— to which he could then turn in vindication of the Utopia he imagined for the present. He looked first backward to England, and then, more remotely in time *and* in fictionalized memory, he traveled back even further to the Jerusalem of the primitive church. Still, this was not far enough for the authority he sought, and Winthrop pushed his inventive memory back further, reaching into the Old Testament to the "return out of captivity" as recorded in Nehemiah (p. 85). And there he hit pay dirt. Winthrop shaped his community's future by appealing to a largely fictitious—that is to say, a textual—memory, the once and future captivity that would always be so spiritually resonant. Winthrop's "memory" becomes in effect the first "American" captivity narrative, a form that would again and again fit—or be made to fit—the spiritualized conflicts of life on these new shores.

And so it probably didn't strike his listeners as odd that the memory Winthrop stitched together had to accommodate Old and New Testaments *and* England in one very short text. After all, invention, *figura* was a hallmark of the tradition. Nonetheless, Winthrop's imaginative exercise presents a telling moment in cultural politics, since a community invokes the authority of the past only when it considers itself to be in "peril." Practically speaking, this occurs when social authority is either lacking or its enforcements fail. A community under the pressure of such a moral panic thereby acknowledges that it has reached the limits of physical persuasion and must resort to less tangible weapons. Of these, rhetoric and polemic are two favorites. Given his double responsibility, then, Winthrop must have realized that memory is especially critical—or dangerous—to a people who suspect that they have nothing to remember or, contrariwise, that they have a great deal to forget. (He anticipates Lincoln's "Second Inaugural" speech in this respect). And this suspicion the immigrant separatists in Plymouth (and their nonseparating brethren in Boston) must have felt. Having repudiated their history (or, in their estimation, been repudiated *by* it, as evidenced by England's blasphemous turn away from the true church under James I) these protocitizens had little justification either for their political actions or for their strenuous theological beliefs. As a result they needed a new set of memorial traditions by which to explain and justify themselves.

Looking backward, but meaning forward, part dreamy nostalgia, part nightmarish threat: the Puritans remembered what never happened and anticipated what never would—herein lies the singular complexity of Puritan historiography. Their self-descriptions often took the form of fantasies in two directions, utopic nostalgia and dystopic collapse. J. Gerald Janzen, in "The Terror of History and the Fear of the Lord," explains the dilemma of the Christian imagination:

> For to live in the venture of faith is to face the *terror of history*, the terror of the unknown future, an unknown future which in the

form of present potential both threatens and invites, which yawns
. . . as an abyss of uncertainty and yet, somehow, beckons with
promise.[16]

Doubleness would always complicate the religious project, a need
to look—and listen—in two directions at once, which partly explains the sometimes histrionic tones of lament found in colonial
texts. The habit of divine irony—a kind of double-hearing, or even
double-dealing—was, and would be, an enduring fate of religious
language in this culture. And, as is always the case, the memories
conjured up by these early immigrants' speeches and prayers, their
sermons and histories, would be more significant the way they were
told than the way they actually happened. Listen, for instance, to
Thomas Tillam, "Upon the First Sight of New England" (1638):

> *Methinks I heare the Lambe of God thus speake*
> *Come my dear little flocke, who for my sake*
> *Have lefte your Country, dearest friends, and goods*
> *And hazarded your lives o'th raging floods*
> *Posses this Country; free from all anoye*
> *Heare I'le bee with you, heare you shall Injoye*
> *My sabbaths, sacraments, my minestrye*
> *And ordinances in their puritye*
> *But yet beware of Sathans wylye baites (p. 127).*

Tillam's poem begins in the mists of nostalgia and ends with the
suggestion of a lurking threat. Perhaps one should not call it a
poem at all, or perhaps it is a poem as Emerson defined the genre,
a meter-making argument. For Tillam *is* conducting an argument
with himself, while pitching it loudly into text to be overheard by
the entire community. Indeed, much of Puritan polemic has this
quality of talking out loud for all to hear. In this case, Tillam, new
to New England, uses verse to confirm his chancy decision to
migrate; in addition, he anticipates—arguing in advance as it
were—the terrors he and other immigrants would face. There's
also Tillam's dramatic sense; by adding a note of heroism to what
must have been already an exquisite human drama, he casts the
adventure into the struggle of a cosmic melodrama, in which are
pitted the most unlikely adversaries.[17] For left to its own devices
how could the "dear little flocke" survive "Sathans wylye baites"?

Forewarned is forearmed. And besides, heavily costumed in cosmic fury as it was, the drama makes a terrific story.

So if Winthrop's backwards look took his mind off present complexities, early colonists like Tillam found that a similar strategy worked for them as well. One *could* remember the future, if one tried—a point Lewis Carroll's Red Queen was yet to make. The continual iteration of expected (perhaps half-*wished* for?) ruin and devastation took one's mind, even briefly, off thoughts of the daily failures accompanying so elaborate a mission as the settling of New England.[18] Even fairly mundane tasks in the new land were characterized by overwhelming difficulty and defeat; no wonder, then, that physical, geographic metaphors carried over to Puritan discourses of interiority. Symbols of struggle lay beneath their feet. Declension, slipping, backsliding, possession, and dispossession—all were daily, common, and harrowing experiences in the wild country of Massachusetts, especially in winter, but even in muddy spring. It was with just such an eye for slippery geography, remember, that a century or so later Jonathan Edwards would make a name for himself as a preacher of slippery theological places.[19]

Fear, socially applied, was not Winthrop's invention, of course. He learned from the masters in the Inquisition, who had good learning of *their* elders in religion. Yet how well Winthrop understood the divided heart, intuiting that terror is not only good church policy; occasionally it is a serviceable political tool as well, useful for convincing moral sluggards of the need "to walk one towards another" (p. 83). His insight was fairly common, really. In fact the fleet of the Great Migration had barely sailed for Boston when Thomas Hooker anticipated Winthrop's efforts. Less restrained than Winthrop, Hooker provided a dramatic and breathless apocalyptic context for the mission: "May God unchurch or discharge a people, and cast a nation off? Oh, then let this teach us to cast off all security; for miseries are nigh at hand in all probability!" ("The Danger of Desertion," Heimert, p. 65) Hooker, like Winthrop, wanted to warn his people away from the edge of communal failure, where, it seemed, like schoolboys they were so often wont to go. He probably intended no irony as he continued in a similar vein: "When we observe what God hath done for us, all things are ripe to destruction" (p. 65). In the tradition of God-speak, terror was the other end of love—its last resort, as it were, especially when phrased in the eternal verities and serviceable images of submissive Christian expiation and gratitude. Nonetheless, Hooker and Winthrop understood that spiritual language was *always* partly directed at this world, even when it pretended not to be—a denial made most frequently by those who had most to profit from the deception.

Thomas Hooker looked for disaster to "teach." Unlike his interest in the pedagogical aspects of disaster, Winthrop was more interested in its aesthetic potential, arguing that the failure of the Great Migration would make his people a "story and a by-word" for all the nations. He thereby acknowledged what literary critics and theoreticians had yet formally to recognize (Edmund Burke's theorizing about the Sublime was still one hundred twenty-five years in the future): terror in some odd way could be a source of pleasure, the pain (and pleasures) of perversity at least aesthetically interesting. However, neither Winthrop nor Hooker would have guessed that in addition to being good church and good politics, recounting the "miseries . . . nigh at hand" would prove to be an enormously profitable business venture as well. A few years later, Michael Wigglesworth would make just such a connection between prophecy and profit. But even for that historical period, however, Winthrop's minatory efforts were fairly tame; moral hysteria and incendiary language were not part of his lawyerly training. Other polemicists would follow, more practiced in the arts, whose images of dark portents and consequences left little to the imagination. So numerous became the cries of catastrophe, and after awhile so similar, the one to the next, that Sacvan Bercovitch cites with approval Perry Miller's point that the New England jeremiad is America's "first distinctive literary genre" (*The American Jeremiad*, p. 6)—a genre in which terror, turned upside down, betokens an odd form of "unshakable optimism" (p. 7).

Terrible Narrations: Confessing the Body Politic

Let us not be like a Troubled House, *altho' we are so much haunted by the* devils.
—COTTON MATHER[20]

Despite the self-absorption evident in the early colonial narratives (or, perhaps, as evidenced by that narcissism), the story of New England's "Religious Way" is a chronicle of the colony's failure, in Winthrop's phrase, to "walk together."[21] One can read signs of the slippage of communal myth as early as John Winthrop's journal (1642) and Bradford's *Of Plymouth Foundation* (1630–50). After the first generation of immigrants had died, and as the pace of personal disorder and civic decline accelerated (to those in authority these seemed to be related events), religious leaders responded by increasing the energy of their rhetoric, as if to stem the tide of immorality by sheer volume of sound. They also increased the scope of their scrutiny; the result was a "staggering compendium of iniquity" (Miller, p. 7) that became in time an "unending monotonous wail" (Miller, cited in Bercovitch, *The American Jeremiad*, p. 5).

For example, in 1662, Michael Wigglesworth, Malden's versifying pastor, took up his pen to protest the Half-Way Covenant, an arrangement by which children of "non-professing" members could be baptized. Wigglesworth believed this covenant to be an outrage, a shameful concession to human frailty and, thus, a visible sign of spiritual entropy. In "The Day of Doom," Wigglesworth energetically took the side of what today might be called the family values school, detailing at length what Hooker earlier had more circumspectly termed the "miseries . . . at hand." Wigglesworth's ode to woe echoed and built on themes Hooker and Winthrop (and others) had especially prized, which all came down to one recurrent theme. The collapse of the body politic, as evidenced by "sloth and frailty," signified a wider declension:

> *Wallowing in all kind of sin,*
> *vile wretches lay secure;*
> *The best of men had scarcely then*
> *their lamps kept in good ure;*

*Virgins unwise, who through disguise
amongst the best were numbered,
Had closed their eyes; yea, and the wise
through sloth and frailty slumbered.*

(MILLER, *AMERICAN PURITANS*, P. 283)

Probably for reasons of propriety Wigglesworth never actually details the "erroneous notions and lustful motion" (p. 289) that exorcise him at such length. However, he does something strategically better. He manages to keep his reader rapt through two hundred and twenty-four eight-line stanzas, as he hints and guesses, glancing obliquely but demurely at "all filthy facts and secret acts, / however closely done" that will be "revealed / before the mid-day sun" (p. 289).

Not for nothing does Perry Miller call Wigglesworth's eschatological diatribe "the first American best-seller" (p. 282).[22] The first printing consisted of 1,800 copies, read to pieces; until the publication of Franklin's "The Way to Wealth," a century later, "The Day of Doom" was the "best-selling of all colonial writings" (Heimert, p. 229). Nonetheless, even as enlightened an observer as Perry Miller reflects a persistent bias. Miller associates the popular with the inept; Wigglesworth, he says, was "a man of much greater culture, and in this work was deliberately stepping down to the popular level" (p. 282). No matter; literary critics notwithstanding, people knew what they liked, and they liked Wigglesworth. No doubt about it, he had the formula: "grosser facts" detailed at length for spiritual edification; the private and "concealed" uncovered and revealed, and all, alas, available for public delectation. Secret, secret: who has the secret? Apparently the average believer resembled the inscrutable Divine in this respect—they relished their secrets and their revelations. Finally, throughout this discussion it must be remembered that in the Protestant dispensation, the soul was considered to be public property, even *the* public property. Its evangelization and scrutiny would be the primary interest of a people given to fits of reformation, just as its confessing (and, dare I say, its exposure) would become an endless business from which much profit would one day be made. In this manner, confessionalism, like the Apocalypse, became a well-worn habit. Indeed, in nineteenth-century politics of reformation, an energy to confess would be one face of civic admonishment—and as such considered an act of righteousness. This trend helps explain Twain's acerbic comment that the great virtue of the Protestant sensibility was that nothing so needed correcting as other people's faults.

Some thirty years after Wigglesworth, Cotton Mather, a third-generation New Englander, would take up the cause begun by his elders. Mather was the grandson of the famous John Cotton, and descendant of two generations of ministers. Like them, he considered himself a spiritual marshal, charged with a mission of righteousness in whose pursuit he was endlessly vigilant, and one in which he inveighed roundly against perceived civic backsliding. Mather was aware that events in Old England had not exactly turned out the way New England had hoped (the Civil War; the Cromwellian Interlude; and the Restoration). And something far worse, potentially even disastrous, loomed ahead on the horizon: as a result of the near-revocation of the Royal Charter in 1684, the small communities in New England had been left, essentially, to founder in a kind of religious backwash. Cotton Mather was perplexed. If theirs was to be a "city upon a hill," as Winthrop had expressed it, why was no one in Old England—or elsewhere, for that matter—watching? For it was apparent that across the seas no one was paying attention to the New England experiment—a "confession," if you will, that depended on being "watched." The spiritual program of New England had, all along, depended implicitly upon this sense of an audience, and from that need *to be watched* (and *to exhibit*) its literature would never be completely free.[23]

Of course, Mather was really more interested in New England's present complexities than in its past, and he would make a name for himself by bringing his lively imagination to its study. In his narrative of the Salem witch trials, penned hastily in order to take advantage of local interest, Mather grafts a Winthropesque version of inventive nostalgia onto a sense of lurid voyeurism he may have found in Wigglesworth. Mather's narrative was an immediate hit—in some ways, an early form of the longed-for Great American Novel; it presented a labyrinthine world of secret dangers, hidden mysteries, surreptitious delights, hapless heroines—in short a Gothic world.[24] *The Wonders of the Invisible World* outdid any of Mather's predecessors in uncovering "long concealed . . . erroneous notions and lustful motion" (p. 289, v. 58, 59). But in important ways Mather's telling of the witch trials, which we shall examine in a subsequent chapter, didn't differ much from earlier texts in the "wonders and providences" mode. The model of transgression and spectacular expiation remained the same; only the names were changed to suit the circumstances.

Across the decades, then, terror and a memory of anxiety, real or imaginary, would usefully serve the society. Bercovitch argues that while the European jeremiad "fused fear and trembling to teach acceptance of fixed social norms" (*The American Jeremiad*, p. 23), the American Puritan jeremiad "went much further. It made anxiety its end as well as its means. Crisis was the social norm it sought to inculcate" (p. 23).[25] From the very beginning, civic aims, especially social stability and personal conformity, helped organize and map Puritan interiority. The memory of Hell would be invoked as figure and polemic to serve as a secure anchor, especially when the community threatened to blow away in windy and contested metaphysics—as it did, for instance, in the Hutchinson affair, and later, during the time of the Half-Way Covenant. Indeed, Hell was a necessary place of *terror firma*. While the early divines were fairly workaday in imagining it, others intent on terrorizing (both religious and lay) would take to their subject with vigor and creativity. In *The Language of Nightmare: A Theory of American Gothic Fiction*, Gary Green argues that negativity was a characteristic aspect of Puritan discourse, a rhythm of affirming by denying, distinguishing and clarifying by negating. This same habit, pressed into civil service, would see double duty as nationalistic myth. Spiritual dissembling, as it were, came to be written into personal and social narratives. For a people bent on Heaven, Hell, too, was a very popular place.

The presence of threats, dispossessions, and the language of eschatological terror (along with its nostalgic subtext), made itself at home in a variety of discourses and situations. It can be found in a colonial poem bewailing human frailty (and acknowledging God's never-flagging energy to correct same); in Election Day sermons exhorting fidelity by describing infidelity rampant. More recently, eschatological terrorizing can be found in civic rhetoric and presidential speech (Lincoln and Reagan are two notable examples); as well as in the terroristic politics of religious sentimentality (the Moral Majority, most recently, for instance). Last but not least, the shadow of divine admonishment can be observed in the subterranean religious energies of the horror market, whose adaptation of eschatological theorizing in contemporary film and text is certainly neither random nor accidental. On the contrary, the various expressions of terror-of-endings show how persistently religiously derived formulas of destruction shape a social and communal memory of crisis, confirming Bercovitch's point cited earlier. Finally, this public iconography of the terrible shows how ostensibly private fears nonetheless resound in corporate speech. Private terror, publicly formulated, resembles Hooker's "magistracy and ministry." Religious terror keeps the city civil, its people vigilant; its walls guard the body politic.

Confessing the Uncivil Self: Captivity and Conversion

> 'Twas Grace that taught my heart to fear,
> And Grace my fear relieved
> How precious did that Grace appear,
> The hour I first believed.

Complicated sets of tensions intersect here. Contrast Winthrop and Wigglesworth in their roles as civic police, on the one hand, and, on the other, in their roles as ritualists. In both respects they serve as tellers of the "story and by-word," the story of malediction and curse that bonds a society together. Let me explain. The construction of a nationalized religious imagination—by turns stark and baroque; violent and sentimental—as an initial, master allegory, was all but inevitable in the early years of the colonies. *Civitas* and Self served quite naturally as analogues for each other, although this so-called "natural" fit was more a result of rhetoric than actual fact, of course, for the fit was hardly natural. Still, religious categories defined the social imagination and even shaped its calendar (to this day the celebrations of a repudiated religious past are called "red letter days"). In such a tightly interwoven form of political expression, "ritual practice" served as the "heart" of religious duty as well (Hall, *Worlds of Wonder*, p. 167). Ritual in effect brought the Divine out of the air, embodying it in time and space and in civic bones and flesh.

So closely aligned were the discourses of the Self, the Holy, and the *polis* that over time once-private acts of devotion (diaries and journals, for instance) encouraged, abetted—perhaps even in the public mind *authorized*—public rituals by which the private soul was symbolically tried, rendered, read, and made over. Diaries and spiritual journals, of course, had always been traditional forms of self-scrutiny, although in latter New England they assumed a wider dimension of interest; perhaps the *public* appetite for ritualized forms of worship—scrutiny, transgression, and expiation—encouraged their private equivalents in the devotional lives of the citizenry. The invention of print surely helped this process, as did the underlying sense of audience, noted earlier. In the city upon a hill, all was confession and spiritual display, and over time display took on a life of its own. In *Dark Eros: The Imagination of Sadism,* Thomas Moore notes the close resemblance between the genres of confession and pornography. To confess, says Moore, "is to let some of one's own perversion into the light" (p. 110)—and into the community, as well.[26] So it is understandable, then, that perversity, like transgression noted earlier, had a certain limited usefulness—in the right places, of course, where its pleasures could be displayed under appropriate religious constraints.

Daniel Shea notes that accounts of Puritan narratives of grace— a qualification for church membership—"indicate how limited the Puritan's freedom of movement could be as he prosecuted his inward exploration" (p. 91).[27] One understands, then, the extreme anxiety evidenced by the colonists with regard to their spiritual lives. Individual citizen as well as state—the body and the body politic—lived in constant vigilance against failure, declension, slippage. If the society itself seemed prey to endless threats of downward conversions and declensions, so, too, did the individual—who likewise faced a variety of conversions, possessions, dispossessions, and unwanted metamorphoses. As Stout observes, "By 1662 everyone's attention had turned inward" (*The New England Soul,* p. 59). The agents of imagined decline were many—and the Indians, those "swarthy demons," were always on hand as potential scapegoats to channel this negative energy. Yet the dangers were neither exterior nor all demonic. Even conversion to God had its negative consequences, rendering individuals beyond the reach of civil authority as they became caught up in divinely inspired ecstacies. Thus, the dangers were double; an individual could be lost in selfless raptures of love, as religious rhetoric encouraged, or, more darkly (and, according to sermon, more likely), one could be negatively converted, possessed by "Sathans wylye baites" (p. 127). This generalized anxiety would find expression in the ritual cry of the apocalypses—those great and small moments of revelation by which a society declared itself godly. By courting annihilation, a social order living on the edge remembered its sense of itself. Thus, while personal diaries, filled as they were with a rhetoric of conversion, wonders, and revelation, were meant to be comforts for family and friends, in practice they were just the opposite, replaying privately the doom featured publicly in sermon after sermon. The diaries and private journals revealed how people *lived*, held captive as they were by a theological frame of fierce, Divine Love in which fear rather than bliss was the face of the Holy most often perceived. Or maybe fear *was* the bliss; and maybe God's awe-ful face, with a slight change of perspective, could be truly awful. As we will note, Edwards would make much spiritual profit from the divine duplicity.

Conversion, then, was considered a great—possibly even the greatest—personal moment. Nonetheless, it was also thought to be profoundly public, even *cosmic* in its effects. Indeed, conversion to God in an open, public forum of the visible saints was both socially formative and politically expedient, since being chosen for the Lord's Supper was, in effect, also conversion to the state. Indeed, along with incorporation into the church came social power.[28] Turning from darkness, the converted individual found true identity in public confession, true communion with the visible saints. Thus, in one stroke the separatists in New England organized the body politic by reforming the individual soul. To confess the soul (especially its incivility: its sin) meant to own the covenant. In this public order "Obedience and self-denial, the acceptance of prohibition, were demanded" (Slotkin, *Regeneration through Violence*, p. 53). For this reason, one's conversion to grace was not an event to be wasted in solitude; as diaries and records attest, few persons ever lost a moment to tell about it.[29]

If the jeremiad, then, served as the indictment of a community, the diary served as the discourse of self-indictment and customary self-display. Nonetheless, it must be understood that while early Puritan diaries were intimate and personal documents of piety, they were inevitably allegorical documents, translating the visible world into messages and meanings of the invisible. This double focus—reading the world as moral sign, reading the heart as spiritual text—helped shape another genre entirely. Herein lay the first inkling of the way cultural politics would reassert familiar theology. And, not incidentally, herein could be found the first traces of an emerging and curious ritual, compounded partly of a need to efface the Self, and, at the same time, a need to watch this process in someone else. Voyeurism would became acceptable as a civic ritual, a form of participatory piety. The example of Samuel Sewall underscores this point. In 1697 he stood before his church in Salem while his pastor read an apology from Sewall's diary in which Sewall in effect publicly acknowledged and repudiated his role in Salem's recent bloodbath of witch killings.

Sewall's example registers a crucial change in sensibility, indicating the gradual shift by which publicized acts of transgression/expiation replaced their private equivalents. In odd ways an older oral tradition here overcame newer, written forms. Confession became the usual, corporate expression of religious piety. From that point it was only a short distance as gossip replaced confessionalism; as voyeuristic looking *in* replaced an individual's "speaking *out*" as the communal religious rhythm and normative rite of social interaction.[30] In this way, by slow absorption, the soul became the property of the state—or at least increasingly inhabited by state functions and surely inhibited by its imperatives. This gradual elision of the private into the discourse of the public would profoundly affect generations far removed in space and time from New England. Those who inherited the Puritan's imaginative world never lost the habit of terror, and the ritual titillation of *spectacle* would always find an audience for gossip—the "thrill of secret knowledge" (Spacks, p. 10). Although subsequent generations probably couldn't tell you where the energy came from, and though they found fewer and fewer pious motivations to induce the spectacle, nonetheless latter-day religionists were to become legendary for the enterprise and creativity they brought to the re-creation of moralistic terror for piety's sake. The irony, of course, is clear; the telling of perversity's pleasures for communal uplift was built into the confessional act. Indeed, spectacular sin was a prerequisite for converting grace.

The close association of awe and fear; spiritual conversion and terrible change; piety and voyeurism becomes clearer when the diary-goes-commercial in the form of the captivity narrative.[31] To the dispossessed immigrants in New England, who sensed themselves victimized by history and maybe even by fate, the captivity metaphor would prove to be as fertile and varied as the geographic topography of the New World. Nonetheless, victimization is a fairly common trope in Christian rhetoric, part of a religious grammar that predates Christianity itself. However, with its central focus on the icon of the bloody Jesus, victim and political martyr, the apotheosization of the victim is symbolically crucial to popular Christian practice, even if not always articulated that way as doctrine. And in the fertile and vast New World, possibilities for captivity and for telling about its terrors seemed as endless as the wilderness. Nor, in the aforementioned zeal for baring it all, were any opportunities overlooked for witnessing the glories of God's inscrutable Providence. Captivity would become the "first American mythology," a drama in which the "hero was the captive or victim of devilish American savages and in which his (or her) heroic quest was for religious conversion and salvation" (Slotkin, *Regeneration through Violence*, p. 21).

The captivity narratives were simple enough in theme, if not always so simple in motivation. Their theme was "deliverance . . . framed in images of constraint and release" (Caldwell, p. 8). Mary Rowlandson's captivity narrative is both an early example and perhaps *the* foundational document of the genre, setting the tone and form for later emulation, in which entertainment was at least as important as spiritual edification. In 1676 when the town of Lancaster was sacked by Indians, Rowlandson was abducted and carried away, perhaps for the purpose of ransom. Rowlandson, a minister's wife, was released some three months later, and her detailed account of her many "removes" is heavily anecdotal and quite graphic. Take, for instance, her description of the moment of capture in which the Indians swiftly come upon "the Father, and the Mother and a sucking Child" whom "they knockt on the head." Similarly, she recalls another hapless victim: the Indians "knockt him in head, and strip him naked, and split open his Bowels" (p. 118). First published in 1682, Rowlandson's "witness" of her "dolefull" (p. 120) suffering went through four editions that same year. Indeed, as Derounian suggests, although there had been little reason "to anticipate its immediate popularity" (p. 244), the book was to be a "steady seller" (p. 248) in New

England from its earliest printing.[32] Yet it doesn't take Nielsen ratings to understand why the narrative was so popular. Rowlandson's lament may have served a complex set of purposes, but as a narrative it was demonstrably full of action: "But out we must go, the fire increasing, and coming along behind us, roaring, and the Indians gaping before us with their Guns, Spears and Hatchets to devour us" (p. 119). In addition, her text was immediately linked to an already extant tradition of pilgrimage and travail; an advertisement for Rowlandson's "Captivity, & Redemption"— "Being pathetically written with her own Hand"—appeared on the last leaf of the first American edition of *The Pilgrim's Progress* (1681) (Derounian, "Publication," p. 244).

Rowlandson's narrative was primarily marketed as spiritual autobiography. Written "especially to her dear children and relations" (as the original title says), it thereby supported ideological purposes by establishing Rowlandson's "willingness to convert personal experience to public belief" (Derounian, "Publication," p. 252). Finally, Rowlandson's soul-baring, including her moving account of the "wounded babe" she carried till his death ten days later, was exhortation, admonishment, entertainment, and news all at once. Rowlandson herself suggests the combination of viewpoints when she makes the allegorical dimension—and minatory function—evident:

> There was one who was chopt into the head with a Hatchet, and stript naked, and yet was crawling up and down. It is a solemn sight to see so many Christians lying in their blood, some here, and some there, like a company of Sheep torn by Wolves . . . (p. 120).

So inevitably the narrative of the Christians versus the "Barbarous Creatures" (p. 121) found its market in other than religious houses. As David Hall remarks, in New England "printers intervened to publish tales of terror and despair for reasons of the marketplace" (p. 137). No surprise here, at any rate. Rowlandson easily put to her own uses the traditions of sentiment/benevolence in which such moral dichotomies as rapacious wolf and hapless victim were commonplace.

In *The Colonial Roots of American Fiction*, Marilla Battilana argues that the captivity formula is "a uniquely American genre" (p. 8):

"Pamphlets and booklets in this line, mostly written in a popular vein, kept being eagerly read by people of every season and station in life" (p. 9). John Demos, in *Remarkable Providences 1600–1760*, concurs. Captivity narratives are, he argues, a "unique literary genre. . . . As adventure stories (with blood, gore, and at least a hint of sex), as morality plays, as theological statements, the captivity narratives are among the most compelling indigenous products of the New World culture" (p. 344).[33] Indeed, the metaphor of captivity remained a vibrant, fertile source of inspiration long after colonial history, since it served needs for individual and community mythology long after the last actual Indian captivity.[34] Over time spiritual narratives of bondage and captivity, retold for spiritual profit, seemed insensibly to slip into darker tales in which captivity for the sake of captivity, rather than the uplift of spirituality, seemed more the focus. These encomiums of woe were sermons of suffering for a discriminating reader, one who might be too squeamish for fictions of other sorts. Typically they featured hapless women (captive men, there were, of course; yet unaccountably their tales seemed not so compelling). Held captive, these women found providential release, only, it seemed, that they might then tell of their suffering in as breathless detail as possible—and all, certainly, in the interests of spiritual uplift.

Richard Slotkin argues that the captivity is a "primary vehicle for the American Puritan's mythology" (*Regeneration through Violence*, p. 101); moving forward some centuries this literary "formula" is still so thoroughly a part of American literary tradition that its familiarity blinds us to its considerable and varied presence. Evidences of these narratives often go unremarked. In Rowlandson's narrative, of course, release meant quite specifically escaping from the hands of Indians (demonized, incidentally, for added symbolic punch). But consider the variations possible as the formulaic "release" came to be interpreted, even interpolated, into a variety of new contexts. The most typical variant was probably the narrative of the escaped or freed slave. A 1760 text, for example, is entitled, "A Narrative of the Uncommon Sufferings and Surprizing [sic] Deliverance of Briton Hammon, A Negro Man" (Sekour, p. 102). In numerous nineteenth-century texts release is refigured as a providential escape from brute husband or brutalizing conditions (examples would include Chopin's *The Awakening*, or most particularly, Gilman's Gothic masterpiece,

"The Yellow Wallpaper"); or escape from the tyrannies of Demon Rum (in temperance tracts). As time and distance intervene, one sees the formula change to reflect a new emphasis—release from the complex captivities of Self (in the confessional poetry form, for instance, from Bradstreet through Dickinson and contemporary poets).[35] In *Uncle Tom's Cabin*, as her title indicates, Harriet Beecher Stowe blurs the lines between race and gender, rewriting the captivity formula as a domestic drama. In Stowe's gothicized tale of slavery and decadence, the epiphanic moment of release will be doubly figured: Tom, the slave, cast in a feminized role, finds his death is a release from two captors—the death-in-life of slavery, and death as release from the brutal hands of Legree, the northern white slave owner. As observed earlier, in general the captivities are written by women; it may be, as Carol Clover observes in her study of slasher films, that gender considerations are always important in horror films; certainly they also carry traces of a theological history in which absent patriarchy *defines* a Christian metaphysic.

Will Rockett reads the formula of "threat and deliverance" as the "primary story for most horror films" (*Devouring Whirlwind*, p. 30). Here we begin to see more clearly a connection between the economies of the soul and its entertainments. Reading Rowlandson's famous captivity, for instance, one senses that its value as entertainment perhaps eclipsed its spiritual worth. The captivity narratives were "official, sanctioned, establishment literature" (Zanger, p. 130) and thus, these often stylized and dramatic renderings had the effect of authorizing, and channeling, a wider range of public anxieties. Jules Zanger, citing Richard Slotkin, explains, the "Rowlandson model provided a narrative myth for colonial New England which dramatized the frontier community's perception of itself and of its precarious situation in both the material and spiritual worlds" (p. 125). This would be the case a few years later when Mather linked the "sooty Devils" and the "hellish Indians": "New Englanders are not *Swarthy Indians*, but they are *Sooty Devils*; that are let loose upon us" (emphasis Mather's, p. 85). This may be a theological statement; it certainly verges on entertainment, as spirituality and triviality entwined; as the need to show and tell connived with a growing need to sell.

In *Worlds of Wonder*, Hall argues that literacy and the life of the spirit could not be separated. For all their spiritual significance, books "were also artifacts in a commercial marketplace and counters in a complex politics that sometimes set the people at odds with the clergy" (pp. 18–19). The technologies associated with printing and marketing would therefore further complicate matters by adding another dimension to the struggle for spirituality/literacy: "It was crucial to the success of the ministers that . . . they mated terror and the evangelical inquiry with genres that had proven sales appeal" (p. 56). The formulaic nature and number of texts typical of the captivity genre indicate that like the slave narrative, it, too, had at least one eye on the market: "In effect, the marketplace made room for two quite different understandings of the book, the one that moralists preferred and another that printers and hack writers made their own, a frank embracing of inventiveness and competition" (p. 55). Thus an originally "spiritualized" text—Rowlandson's, for instance—derived its essential form from variations of a then-familiar benevolent tradition; yet what was familiar, increasingly, was spectacle, especially the spectacle of the Self, exposed, opened, viewed from outside. And, as we will see, Mather's hastily written account of the Salem witch trials reveals *his* sharp eye for market timeliness, while his details show him responsive to reader interest. Perhaps it *is* true that Jesus saves; it was demonstrably true that the devil—along with a hint of sex—*sells*.

Conclusion: Something New, Something Old

> The completest religions would . . . seem to be those in which the pessimistic elements are best developed. . . . They are essentially religions of deliverance.
> —WILLIAM JAMES[36]

It may be that form dictates content; that art shapes life. Let me here consider briefly a recent example of the captive woman. In *Out of Bondage* and *Ordeal*, its sequel, Linda Lovelace tells of her forced life as a porn star. While not quite the mixture of devil and sex suggested by another porn title—*The Devil in Miss Jones*—the titles themselves make clear the text's complex heritage, part theological formula and part commercial prurience. These "witness texts" are, I presume, unintentionally parodic, since these narratives about sexual captivity have literally forgotten the original intentions of the "possession" genre, which I will take up in a later chapter. In *Ordeal*, Lovelace continues the narrative of the forced carnal knowledge she suffered at the hands of a man named Chuck. Its opening chapter tells how Linda, then a naïve twenty-one-year-old girl recovering from an automobile accident, is introduced to a handsome photographer who drives a Jaguar XKE. Linda admits herself to be starstruck, or at least dazzled by the car, and confesses that she readily accepted a marijuana cigarette from the photographer. From this first slippage followed the long downward cycle of her captivity by a man whose every action "was designed to degrade" her (p. 156). Narratively, then, one can read the religious context: it was Lovelace's initial moral failure—accepting the cigarette—that entails, or at least permits, her resulting slavery to "carnal intentions." Nonetheless, while detailing the days and kinky sexual alliances to which "that demon" Chuck subjects her, Lovelace is at pains to exclaim her essential purity: "I was known as Miss Holy-Holy and for a time even wanted to be a nun" (p. 7). Perhaps secretly suspecting that her readers might not be totally convinced, she equivocates a bit, and declares that after all, she was not "always Miss Holy-Holy." So the text would indicate. Nonetheless, Linda insists that she is basically a "real prude" (p. 140) who "didn't like doing any of that stuff." In fact, she says, so naïve was she that when she "got [her] period for the first time, [she] was sure it was God's punishment for one sin or another" (p. 6). To anticipate a bit; in his fantasy novel, *Carrie*, Stephen King will employ a similar narrative ploy to establish Carrie White's innocence.

Lovelace asserts sexual experience on the one hand, while in effect denying it on the other: "I want to state this as clearly as I can. There was no pleasure. There was no love, no affection, no normal sex with anyone. . . . I did not have a single orgasm for six or seven years, I never had any enjoyment from any of it at all" (p. 57). This deflection is only part of the curious disjunction a reader experiences in this narrative; explicit details of manipulative, tawdry sexual activities are punctuated by pious homilies: "I have always believed in God and I knew that God would get me out of my troubles. I know today that God will take care of Chuck without any help from me or anyone else." Yet the aggression underlying this noble sentiment becomes evident in the very next sentence, as Linda moralizes, "If people do bad all the time, they're going to suffer" (p. 169).

Presumably the people who will suffer most are those like Chuck who are "sick," those who do not have "a normal, healthy, and happy love life" (p. 261). Presumably sickness here is characterized by "swapping mates and having affairs with each others' wives and going to sex clubs" (p. 261). Linda's ideal, as she states, is simple: "Marriage has always been important to me, perhaps too important. From when I was a small girl I had imagined what marriage would be like. That was all I ever expected from life—to get married to a good man, to have children, and to someday have a home of my own" (72). In the closing pages of *Ordeal,* Lovelace shares with the reader her current financial difficulties (suggesting perhaps a motive for her writing?). In addition, she again foregrounds some of the same gender concerns we have seen earlier. She makes a point to underscore to the presumptively female (although perhaps male?) reader her essential domesticity: "I'd like someday to live in peace and quiet, with my husband able to go out and work for a living. I would like one more baby, a girl, and I would like a garden of my own" (p. 261); and "My vices aren't much to talk about these days. When we can afford it, I like nothing better than a beer while I'm watching a football game on television. Sometimes I think I'll drive my husband nuts, the way I like sports" (p. 263).[37] Middle America, no doubt about it: domestic Gothic with a vengeance.

In conclusion, the entangling theological and social discourses of New England resulted in some curious alignments and misalignments, as "religion came to permeate a national identity at its deepest cultural and intellectual levels" (Stout, p. 10). First, as noted earlier, the entangling discourses shaped literary politics and made inevitable the repudiation of a whole range of fantasy texts. This already complex process, which is largely beyond the scope of this study, is further complicated by the fact that spiritual autobiography *is* a primary cultural gesture, partly political, although essentially and derivatively religious. Less charitably, and in political practice, one could call it a habit of telling fictions, if not outright lies, in public. These diaries and conversion narratives gradually evolved into the complex captivity narratives, and thence into a conventional, even emblematic, American genre of victimization and release. A second consequence followed, a form of participatory theater, as it were, in which individuals are laid bare for communal profit. This ritualized form of civic dismemberment we will examine in the next chapter, specifically in the context of the New England witch hysteria that resulted in the arrest of more than two hundred persons and the execution of more than fifty women and men. Here the tyranny of a religious imagination reflects itself not as literary genre and as discredited fantasy, but as social and political strategy in which religious imperatives are reappropriated as political rites of constraint.

The fears of personal annihilation, dispossession, and civic decline—and, conversely, hopes for deliverance—evident in Winthrop and Wigglesworth become standard images in American iconography. Motifs of self-effacement, self-denial, victimization, and expiation would be endlessly replayed in daily sermon. Evident, as we shall see, in theological texts—Cotton Mather, for instance—they find their way into contemporary texts of fantasy, Stephen King, for example. In private speech and in public exhortation, the fragile body politic was constantly shored up and buttressed against its enemies, within, without. Fantasy and polemic played against each other. And while individual sermon or Election Day speech may have been insignificant, when taken together, like a chord their images and terms, rhetorics and assumptions, heavily influenced the music line. The language of the ever submissive, ever interiorly vigilant soul—self-effacing yet spiritually proud—became standard public address, as well.

Immigrant anxieties, disowned and dispossessed, returned under new rhetorics. To this day public self-address of the *civitas* features a language of nostalgic authoritarianism, largely defensive and elegiac, whose anticipated threats of destruction are couched in images of slippage and declension, anxieties of having, holding—or being held. Repudiated bodies return, sexualized and demonized, as the tradition of witchery and captivity reflects, and as Linda Lovelace demonstrates in her adaption of that moralistic tradition. No wonder, even today, such originally religious expressions as "possession" and "inheritance" are so loaded with emotion. Traces of these anxieties can be observed in historically problematic moments, when the language of annihilation signaled a corporate gesture of penance. Witness, for example, during the traumatic Civil War, the particularly thundering rhetoric of terror of "The Battle Hymn of the Republic." Consider how Lincoln first articulates the possibilities of a civil religion by reworking Christian apocalyptic as civic expiation. His "Second Inaugural" speech (1865) is replete with a customary and familiar language of transgression and expiation:

> If we shall suppose that American Slavery is one of those offenses which, in the providence of God, must needs come, but which, having continued through His appointed time, He now wills to remove, and that He gives to both North and South, this terrible war, as the woe due to those by whom the offence came, shall we discern therein any departure from those divine attributes which the believers in a Living God always ascribe to Him?[38]

Similar religious assumptions, spun off into rhetoric, still provide an element of emotional dissonance to a social order based upon an abstracting, transcendent image of the Holy. This is the point of this study: self-loss is, indeed, a moment to which American narratives of self-description continuously return, probably because self-loss—the encounter with the Holy—is where these early religious narratives obsessively began.

NOTES

1. See William L. Howarth, "Travelling in Concord: The World of Thoreau's Journal," in Elliott, *Puritan Influences in American Literature* (pp. 143–66). Samuel Coale, *In Hawthorne's Shadow: American Romance from Melville to Mailer* (Lexington: University of Kentucky Press, 1985).
2. Patricia Caldwell, *The Puritan Conversion Narrative: The Beginnings of American Expression* (Cambridge: Cambridge University Press, 1983).
3. Indeed, considered as an expression of geography, the term "New World" renders the ambiguities transparent. It expresses a wish, not *precisely* for a new world, but merely for one that is *not old.* Even as iconography, the "New World" imagines not so much a positive geographic site as a negative condition, an imaginative lack.
4. George M. Marsden observes that John Winthrop, the first governor of the

Massachusetts Bay Colony, citing Deuteronomy almost verbatim, "assumed that he could transfer the principles of nationhood found in ancient Israel to the Massachusetts Bay Company with no need for explanation" (p. 246). Marsden concludes that the "practical confusion of church and state" logically followed this "overriding presumption." Other presumptions followed, and other confusions and accommodations as well, some of which this study seeks to explore. See "America's 'Christian' Origins: Puritan New England as a Case Study" in *John Calvin: His Influence in the Western World*, W. Stanford Reid, ed. (Grand Rapids: Zondervan, 1982). In a point that will be relevant to my next chapter, Marsden also argues that the Salem witch hysteria, the "major miscarriage of justice of New England," was based legally "on the assumption that New England law should duplicate that of ancient Israel" (p. 247).

5. For background on the American religious heritage see, of course, Sacvan Bercovitch and his magisterial studies, *The American Jeremiad* and *The Puritan Origins of the American Self* (New Haven: Yale University Press, 1975); also William A. Clebsch, *American Religious Thought: a History* (Chicago: University of Chicago Press, 1973); Robert Booth Fowler, *Unconventional Partners: Religion and Liberal Culture in the United States* (Grand Rapids: William B. Eerdmans Publishing Co., 1989); "Sidney E. Mead's Understanding of America," LeRoy Moore, *Journal of the American Academy of Religion*, vol. 44, no. 1, 1976: 133–53; "On American Religious Thought," Denise Lardner Carmody and John Tully Carmody, *Religion and Intellectual Life*, vol. 5, no. 1, Fall 1987: 43–58; "The Enlightenment and Calvinism: Mutual Support Systems for the Eighteenth-Century American Wilderness," Elizabeth I. Nybakken, in *Transactions of the Fifth International Congress on the Enlightenment* (Oxford: The Voltaire Foundation, 1980): 1126–35; "Ideology and the Protestant Principle," Terence M. O'Keeffe, *Journal of the American Academy of Religion*, vol. 51, no. 2, 1983: 283–305. For Puritanism, see *Puritanism in America: New Culture in a New World*, Larzer Ziff (New York: Viking Press, 1973); *Puritan Influences in American Literature*, Emory Elliott, ed. (Urbana: University of Illinois Press, 1979); *Saints and Revolutionaries: Essays on Early American History*, David D. Hall, John M. Murrin, and Thad W. White, eds. (New York: W. W. Norton & Co., 1984); Harold J. Berman, "Religious Foundations of Law in the West: An Historical Perspective," *Journal of Law and Religion*, vol. 1, no. 1, Summer 1983: 3–43; Ralph C. Hancock, *Calvin and the Foundation of Modern Politics* (Ithaca: Cornell University Press, 1989); Nathan O. Hatch, *The Democratization of American Christianity* (New Haven: Yale University Press, 1989).

6. Consequently, in the fragile collection of pre-Colonial beachheads, villages, and encampments that would one day be known as New England, reading represented a communal theological imperative rather than the secular, largely privatized, experience it is today. In its repudiation of an established religious order (the Roman church), literacy prophetically announced a new world order of spiritual equality. No more would religious tyrannies have the city upon a hill to itself. Not for nothing did the early churches gathered in the wilderness dispense altogether with the iconography (and architecture)

of churches, binding themselves instead in the covenant of the meeting-house.

7. *The Cause of God and His People,* cited in Harry S. Stout, *The New England Soul: Preaching and Religious Culture in Colonial New England, op. cit.,* p. 72.

8. This is one reason why New England zealously persecuted witches long after Europe had ceased doing so. Reading God's will—even, unhappily, in the all-too-fleshy tablets of the heart—had become a ritual in itself. If the people could read their own spiritual states by closely monitoring their immediate worlds (and, implicitly, the worlds of those around them), they could better read the larger typological, apocalyptic significance of New England: "Within this context the physical and psychological torment to which they subjected their neighbors, friends, and sometimes members of their own families was nothing other than a desperate hermeneutic practiced at the edge of time." See Michael Clark, "Witches and Wall Street: Possession is Nine-Tenths of the Law," in *Herman Melville's Billy Budd, "Benito Cereno," "Bartleby the Scrivener," and Other Tales,* Harold Bloom, ed. (New York: Chelsea House Pub., 1987), p. 130.

9. Although, as Daniel B. Shea, Jr. observes in *Spiritual Autobiography in Early America* (Princeton: Princeton University Press, 1968), "As long as the Puritan magistracy held sway, enthusiastic autobiography was for the closet only" (p. 90).

10. If in their public description they spoke of the errand into the wilderness in metaphors of exploration and revelation, just as zealously they set about describing the topography of the inner Self, using similar images of travel *and* travail: "Whatever we doe, and wherever we goe we should always be travailing towards Canaan . . . " (cited in Hall, *Worlds of Wonder,* p. 226).

11. Listen, for example, to the note of hesitation in John Winthrop's 1629 defense of the Migration. Winthrop wrote "Reasons to be Considered for . . . the Intended Plantation in New England" while still in England. As commander-in-chief of the forthcoming expedition his hesitancy is doubly significant. He proffers, as reasons, a tissue of wishes, hopes, conditionals; "who knows but that God hath provided this place"; "what better work can there be than to go [to New England]?" (p. 71). "What can be a better work and more honorable?"; "It appears to be a work of God for the good of his church" (p. 72). For text, see Heimert, pp. 70–74.

12. Samuel Danforth, in *The Wall and the Garden,* A. W. Plumstead, ed. (Minneapolis: University of Minnesota Press, 1968).

13. John Cotton, perhaps New England's "official" apologist, explained the form of church government as "congregational," since individual congregations would contain full authority for their governance and continuance. See *The Puritans in America: A Narrative Anthology,* Alan Heimert and Andrew Delbanco, eds. (Cambridge: Harvard University Press, 1985), esp. pp. 26–27.

14. Michael Walzer, "Puritanism as a Revolutionary Ideology," cited in *The Morality of Terrorism: Religious & Secular Justification,* David C. Rapoport & Yonah Alexander, eds. (New York: Columbia University Press, 1989), p. xiv.

15. John Winthrop, "A Model of Christian Charity," *The Puritans In America: A Narrative Anthology, op. cit.*, Alan Heimert and Andrew Delbanco, eds., pp. 81–92.

16. "The Terror of History and the Fear of the Lord," *Encounter*, vol. 42, no. 4, Autumn 1981: 377.

17. "America, after all, is one of the few countries in which a sense of a particular destiny was prescribed at its origin: if this is true, the relation between origin and aftermath must be peculiarly tense. We interpret an origin as if it marked a principle." See Denis Donoghue, *Reading America* (New York: Knopf, 1987) [uncorrected proof; np].

18. In "The Imagination of Disaster," Susan Sontag finds in modern science fiction an extension of this sensibility: "The lure of such generalized disaster as a fantasy is that it releases one from normal obligations." See *Against Interpretation* (New York: Anchor Books, 1990), p. 215.

19. In *Regeneration through Violence*, Richard Slotkin suggests that the "natives" the colonists found already inhabiting the land that would be their new home were powerfully emblematic of the possibilities of declension: "The strangeness of the Indian was a threat to the outer man and to Puritan society; the Indian's familiarity, his resemblance to the primitive inner man, was a threat to the Puritan's soul, his sense of himself as English, white, and Christian" (p. 55). See the discussions of the captivity narratives for elaboration.

20. Cotton Mather, *The Wonders of the Invisible World* (Boston: 1693; rpt. John Russell Smith: London, 1862), p. 91.

21. See "Where Have All the Tulips Gone?: Being a Brief Treatise Discovering the Causes of the Decline of the Calvinistical Religion in New England Between 1630 and 1776," Samuel T. Logan, Jr., *Westminster Theological Journal*, vol. 50, 1988: pp. 1–26.

22. See no. 92, p. 268, in David Hall, *Worlds of Wonder, Days of Judgment: Popular Religious Belief in Early New England* (New York: Knopf, 1989), for a discussion of the publishing history of "The Day of Doom."

23. So for a complicated mixture of religious, civil, and personal reasons Mather continued the process by which Winthrop's inchoate communal memory was transformed into a fully self-aware, performative nationalism. Following Winthrop's example, Mather reinvented a necessary past by means of which he could reinterpret, even remember, the present: "Whether New-England may Live any where else or no, it must *live* in our History!" (*Magnalia Christi Americana* (1693–1702), I, 27)

24. Naturally, Wigglesworth and Mather (among others) brought their endless zeal for reformation in the interest, of course, of "higher reasons." More was at stake in the fortunes of the New England "plantation"—as Winthrop wistfully terms it (the first example of domestic sentimentality?)—than the collapse of religious hegemony: "The mountains smoke, the hills are shook, / the earth is rent and torn, / As if she should be clean dissolved." Wigglesworth's text can be found in *The American Puritans: Their Prose and Poetry*, Perry Miller, ed. (Garden City, NY: Anchor Doubleday Books, 1956), p. 286.

25. As a case in point, Nathaniel Ward, noted for drawing up the first codification

of Massachusetts' statutes, and minister at Ipswich from 1634 to 1648, pithily denounces, as one of "four things" he detests, "tolerations of divers religions, or of one religion in segregant shapes. He that willingly assents to the last, if he examines his heart by daylight, his conscience will tell him he is either an atheist or a heretic or a hypocrite, or at best a captive to some lust. Poly-piety is the greatest impiety in the world" (Miller, *The American Puritans, op. cit.*, p. 98).

Ward's distoleration, evident here in his "The Simple Cobbler of Aggawam," adds a measure of dramatic irony to this story of culture that we are telling. One of the "four things" Ward detested—ranking even *before* "tolerations"—is "foreigners dwelling in my country to crowd out native subjects into the corners of the earth" (p. 98). One wonders if he ever spoke to the people from whom he borrowed the title of his diatribe—Aggawam was the Native American original name for Ipswich. Ward's text is found in Miller, *The American Puritans, op.cit.*, pp. 95–108.

26. Moore, *Dark Eros: The Imagination of Sadism* (Dallas: Spring Publications, Inc., 1990).

27. For a discussion of "witnessing" and church membership in New England, see Edmund S. Morgan, *Visible Saints: The History of a Puritan Idea* (New York: Cornell University Press, 1965).

28. Samuel Sewall's *Diary*, mentioned above, is representative of the tradition, especially the anxiety that seems a necessary part of the spiritual work: "labouring more constantly and throwly to Examin my self before sitting down to the Lord's Table" [1:258, cited in Hall, *Wonder*, p. 228]. At this point religious orthodoxy becomes social power, since only those visibly "saved" were permitted at the Lord's Table, and, all other arrangements with the civil arm notwithstanding, those present at the Supper wielded visible social power. And yet precisely here lay the rub, the ancient ambiguity: who or what was the self? Did it consist of private acts of love or public (and social) acts of power? For further insight into the diarists see the Preface to Gordon O. Taylor's *Studies in Modern American Autobiography* (New York: Macmillan, 1983); Lawrence Rosenwald, "Sewall's *Diary* and the Margins of Puritan Literature," *American Literature*, vol. 58, no. 3 October 1986: 325–41; and David D. Hall, "The Mental World of Samuel Sewall," in *Saints and Revolutionaries, op cit.*, pp. 75–98.

29. Indeed, there were important social reasons (other than the delights of chewing-the-soul with a friend) for supporting this public soul-baring. Personal evidence of private intimacy with God was becoming more and more common—even enjoined in some communities—as a criterion for admission to the communal (public) table. In *Visible Saints, op. cit.*, Edmund S. Morgan writes, "A person seeking admission to the church first approached the elders who in a personal interview examined both his knowledge and his religious experiences (p. 88). After various public scrutinies, the candidate "was expected to make a narration, perhaps fifteen minutes in length, of the way in which God's saving grace came to him" (p. 89).

30. Again, see Patricia Spacks, *Gossip*. Etymologically, *gossip* means "god-

related": "As a noun, the word originally designated a godparent, of either sex; then its meaning enlarged to include any close friend—someone belonging to the group from which godparents would naturally be chosen" (pp. 23–26).

31. The gradual publication of the diary proved especially popular, not to say gratifying and timely, to the colonists, who often found themselves perhaps bored by the daily grind and the lack of visible distraction. Although Jonathan Edwards may not have realized it at the time, his use of the metaphor of captivity—"Sinners in the Hands of an Angry God" (1741)—reflects, as we shall see, his own entrapment in a specifically American Christian discourse. You might say that John Bunyan's metaphor of the Journeying Pilgrim—*The Pilgrim's Progress*—was an old-world conception, while surprisingly entrapment and stasis would be metaphors associated with the new. One would think the wide open spaces of the new land would be better suited for the *pilgrim* metaphor.

32. For an account of "The Publication, Promotion, and Distribution of Mary Rowlandson's Indian Captivity Narrative in the Seventeenth Century," see Kathryn Zabelle Derounian, *Early American Literature*, vol. 23, 1988: 239–61.

33. For helpful studies on the captivity narratives see "Living on the Edge: Indian Captivity Narrative and Fairy Tale," Jules Zanger, *Clio*, vol. 13, no. 2, 1984: 123–32; "Puritan Orthodoxy and the 'Survivor Syndrome' in Mary Rowlandson's Indian Captivity Narrative," Kathryn Zabelle Derounian, *Early American Literature*, vol. 22, 1987: 82–93; Captain Greg Sieminski, "The Puritan Captivity Narrative and the Politics of the American Revolution," *American Quarterly*, vol. 42, no. 1 March 1990: 35–56; David L. Greene, "New Light on Mary Rowlandson," *Early American Literature*, vol. 20, 1985: 24–38; and Melvin J. Thorne, "Fainters and Fighters: Images of Women in the Indian Captivity Narratives," *Midwest Quarterly*, vol. 23, 1981–82: 426–36.

34. It was, as Patricia Caldwell demonstrates, the original, and obsessive form, of the American Dream, in which the "fact of America" was "inextricably bound up with" a hope for salvation (p. 26). See *The Puritan Conversion Narrative: The Beginnings of American Expression* (Cambridge: Cambridge University Press, 1983).

35. Other examples of the working out of the genre could include Frederick Douglass's *My Bondage and My Freedom* (1855), for instance (or even from a completely different critical point of view, *The Confessions of Nat Turner* [1967], William Styron, or *The Autobiography of Miss Jane Pittman* [1971], Ernest Gaines). Henry Louis Gates, Jr., implies the continuity of genres when he speaks of an "authentic black printed voice of deliverance . . . ". See "James Gronniosaw and the Trope of the Talking Book," in *Studies in Autobiography*, James Olney, ed. (New York: Oxford University Press, 1988), p. 57. In that same volume see especially "Is the Slave Narrative a Species of Autobiography?" by John Sekora. Sekora argues that early slave narratives "do tend to be shaped into familiar, popular patterns of criminal confession, spiritual pilgrimage, gospel labors, and Franklinesque success story, as well as captivity tale" (p. 106). See *Subjects of Slavery, Agents of Change: Women and Power in*

Gothic Novels and Slave Narratives, 1790–1865, Kari J. Winter (Athens: University of Georgia Press, 1992). See Jane Tompkins's reading of the feminine Uncle Tom in *Sensational Designs: The Cultural Work of American Fiction, 1790–1860* (New York: Oxford University Press, 1985). See *My Bondage and My Freedom,* ed. by William L. Andrews, (Urbana: University of Illinois Press, 1987).

36. *The Varieties of Religious Experience: A Study in Human Nature,* Martin E. Marty, ed. (New York: Penguin, 1982), p. 131.

37. And perhaps suggesting the actual reason why she takes pen in hand: "I have felt real poverty these past few years, and I've been on welfare" (*Ordeal,* p. 260).

38. Abraham Lincoln, "Second Inaugural Address," in *Lincoln: Speeches and Writings 1859–1865* (New York: Library of America Press, 1989), p. 687. For an instance of how easily private intimacies of theological abasement could fit— even clarify and explain—the civic mood, consider the millenarian triumphalism of "The Battle Hymn of the Republic," or the somber eschatology of Abraham Lincoln's "Second Inaugural." To refer to my opening discussion of cultic memory: Lincoln created out of raw memory new ideological parameters. He refocused fears of declension and a sense of necessary expiation into permissible civic ideology, thereby realigning the limits of the believable, the thinkable, and certainly the do-able.

Lincoln's "Second Inaugural" is a relatively late—though famous speech and formative example—of the ironic conflation between the discourses of religion, and *civitas.* Lincoln's quite conscious use of the language of transgression and punishment for the purposes of unification—civility—is, like Winthrop, earlier, and Reagan, later, in this regard, an appeal to religious myth for social purposes. It is ironic, because while it is in no sense a traditional Jeremiad, by invoking the rhetoric of transgression Lincoln, like Hawthorne, re-presents as moral allegory a debased religious cosmology. In Lincoln's address its evocation is all the more powerful because it has ceased to be merely "real." In the continuing argument in American letters between the discourses of aesthetics and morality, aesthetics—art—represents the "real" and is always ideological.

CHAPTER TWO

"Entertaining Satan": The American Rite of Deviancy

Your conscience you must keep or it must be kept for you.
—GOVERNOR WINTHROP TO ANNE HUTCHINSON,
BEFORE THE COURT AT NEWTOWN, NOVEMBER 1637[1]

[Witchcraft] was but a shadow, a nightmare: the nightmare of a religion, the shadow of a dogma.[2]

A novel of a girl possessed of a terrifying power.
—FROM THE COVER OF STEPHEN KING'S *CARRIE*

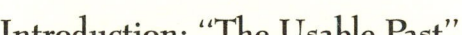

Introduction: "The Usable Past"

We must first rid ourselves of the illusion that penalty is above all . . . a means of reducing crime.
—FOUCAULT, *DISCIPLINE AND PUNISH*, P. 23–24

The captivity narrative and its many variants is an essentially Christian, perhaps even Protestant, genre. The form rehearses again and again a primary cultural *agon*—the ambiguity of being chosen, for better or worse, by a God whose affections to the righteous were as much a captivity as any bondage they had known before, because this God's love provoked an equally overwhelming terror. The complexities of the divine favor, however, are not new, as anyone familiar with the history of mysticism knows. Traffic with gods of any sort was generally dangerous. Even Robert Frost, always circumspect about the Divine, agreed: "If you should rise from Nowhere up to Somewhere, / From being No one up to being Someone, / Be sure to keep repeating to yourself / You owe it to an arbitrary god / Whose mercy to you rather than to others / Won't bear too critical examination" (*The Poetry*, p. 385). Frost's critique could be directly applied to early colonial religious history. Studying the texts emerging from the Salem witch-hunts, for example, one senses the profound confusion of citizen and cleric alike when confronted by a demon whose marks of "bewitchment" so resembled the "signs" of those captivated by the visible throes of religious transports. If, then, God could "possess," as in the case of the so-called enthusiasts, so, surely, could Satan "convert." In either case the Self was in danger of effacement and loss: private religious ecstasy was indistinguishable from public terror.

We have already considered how spiritual and civil proscriptions crossed in early colonial polity. Yet Winthrop's use of a rhetoric of dispossession and religious anxiety to create political identity was not a new strategy in 1630, nor, since, was it an isolated instance. Let us consider, for example, a particular form of Christian charity—the way the normalizing tactics of a moral imperialism played out in New England's social polity, and then, in these latter days, as those same imperatives speak in a tradition of horror and fantasy texts. I am speaking about the rite of witch-hunting, in Salem and elsewhere, and its representation as perennial American myth and unifying rite of deviancy. Consider, for example, Stephen King's *Carrie,* which echoes the national cult myth of the Salem witch trials. Like Mather's own witch crying, *The Wonders of the Invisible World* (1693), King's text points toward a spiritual order that transcends, authorizes, and *normalizes* this temporal order.

1992 marks the 300th anniversary of one of the "three most shameful occurrences in New England"[3]: the Salem witch hysteria of 1692–93. From the vantage point of three hundred years, it is evident that the discourses generated by Salem—whether in apology, defense, or explanation, and whether historical, social, fictional, or autobiographical—demonstrate that numerous pressures intersect at that quite tangible New England site. Metaphysics comes to ground in culture's necessary repudiations. This results in a complex staking out, often quite literally, of the witch's body. In her corporeal *figura*, those early metaphysicians in the dark read allegories of revelation. Thus Salem is in so many ways the point at which American culture comes of age and claims its peculiar tensions. At Salem, for instance, we see the careful negotiating of religious power in a civic site; because of this conflict alone one could say that American "public" or "popular culture" begins where Salem's leadership repudiates, in the body of the witch, social nonconformity. The events of 1692–93 were to be an initial instance, following Anne Hutchinson and the antinomian affair, of what would become an essential civic mechanism. Similar rites of social expiation would be thereafter invoked whenever the body politic felt the need, as it were, for moral exercise or for gestures of self-definition and muscle toning.[4] The issues here, as Foucault reminds us, are two-fold: the socially necessary cultivation of deviancy, and the equally necessary display of "ceremonies of power."[5]

Civic energy for ritualizing normalcy, then, is as old as the nation.[6] As early as 1636, John Cotton and other first-generation Puritan divines, pursuing a provisional and largely ad hoc polity, used the language of witchery to condemn Anne Hutchinson's specifically religious challenge to their civil authority.[7] Said one participant in the trial of the outspoken woman, "therfor we should sine agaynst God if we should not put away from us soe Evell a Woman, guiltie of such foule Evells" (Hall, *Antinomian*, p. 385). The old-world theologies by which Cotton and others established Congregational polity did not—could not—admit Hutchinson's claim of religious equality. The bill of her excommunication read: "Therefor in the name of our Lord Jesus Christ and in the name of the Church I doe not only pronounce you worthy to be cast out, but I *doe cast you out* and in the name of Christ *I doe deliver you up to Sathan* that you may learne no more to blaspheme to seduce and to lye" (Hall, *Antinomian*, p. 388). Some years later in the Quaker challenge to civil authority, Massachusetts authorities used similar tactics of repudiation and exile—and even capital punishment—to enforce their laws. In *The Devil in the Shape of a Woman*, Carol Karlsen writes, when "the first Quaker preachers arrived in Boston Harbor in 1656, the authorities were prepared. Ann Austin and Mary Fisher were arrested as witches before they even reached shore." The women were "stripped naked on board ship and their bodies examined for signs of Devil worship. Their possessions were searched for books containing 'corrupt, heretical, and blasphemous Doctrines' " (pp. 122–3).

The Hutchinson controversy anticipates the repudiation of the Quakers, and then, some thirty-five years later, Salem's witch hysteria. All three represent parallel efforts at righting the body politic; indeed, all three events were a symbolically linked, civic repudiation of Satan.[8] In each, the raggedy society that was to become the Commonwealth of Massachusetts—as yet fluid in concept and external boundary—began systematically to map itself according to a metaphysical topography of hierarchies and proscriptions. In an effort to establish its identity more securely, the *civitas* ordered its scrutinies and surveillances according to biblical precept. In such a system, as Stout explains, "there was no inherent contradiction between civic loyalty and godly sanctification" (p. 21); further, "a willful rebellion against the social order was indicative of an endangered soul" (p. 24).[9] Hall elaborates, "From the preachers' point of view, then, the lesson of the Quakers . . . and Anne Hutchinson was exactly this: they allowed Satan entrance to the self" (*Worlds of Wonder*, pp. 146–7). Consequently, for residents of Salem in 1692, beleaguered by internal conflict and international confusion, the witch's body served the same symbolic social function as did the execution of the Quakers (Boston Commons, 1656), and before that, Anne Hutchinson's exile.

Metaphorically speaking, witches, Quakers, and other freethinkers established a site, a wilderness ready for settlement and domestication. Their bodies were places on which to inscribe the imperial authorizations of the society's religious imperatives: enter the land and possess it in nostalgia; divide, subdue, and occupy it. Confess it. Textify it. Read it in terror.[10] Clearly more was at stake at Salem than just the witch's physical person, and for that matter, even the *stake* was ambiguous, useful for burning as well as for demarcating possession of the land. What Anne Hutchinson and the Quakers had learned the unfortunate victims of Salem would also learn: in this brave New World neither the theory of freethinking *nor* its practice extended inward; mental witchery must be repudiated, conventionality must be protected against the enthusiasm of the particular. The *real* (i.e., the outwardly conformable) must be buttressed against the fantasies that threaten it. Thus do social constructions embody metaphysical assumptions and symbolic repudiations shed real blood. Maps of earth did, after all, affect those of Heaven, which is why John Calvin's theological *Institutes* remain important documents in social theory as well.

Discussions of Salem usually prompt mixed expressions of guilt, relief, and silence: a sheepish surprise that such "old-world" atavistic emotions could sway "enlightened" new-world citizenry, as well as relief that Salem is, after all, years behind us. Yet we shouldn't be so surprised at its ghosts. For while the demons Salem sought to extirpate were invisible, they were nonetheless this-worldly—inevitable shadows cast by a human order. As Hugh Trevor-Roper concludes, the "bizarre mythology" leading to European witch-hunts resulted from "social struggle" (p. 165): "We have here to deal with a mythology which is more than a mere fantasy. It is a social stereotype: a stereotype of fear" (p. 165).[11] And while witchcraft had been generally disavowed in the Old World, it could not escape the gravity of the new. In *Entertaining Satan*, John Demos argues that the witch hysteria served Salem in a rather traditional manner. The articulation of witchery—both accusers and accused—provided a point by which one could judge the intersection of social forces. Witchcraft was the visible fissure where an overlapping series of discourses (religious, civil, ecclesiastical, personal, institutional) failed to hold. In the words of M. G. Marwick, witchcraft served as a "social strain gauge" (Demos, p. 276).[12]

The witch-hunt in effect was a necessary part of communal life, "an integral part of social experience." The witch-hunt organized the group by "sharpening its boundaries, reinforcing its values, and deepening the loyalty of its membership" (Demos, p. 14). Even the term "witch" in seventeenth-century New England was a weapon; it "functioned as a label people used to control or punish someone" (Hall, *Witch-Hunting*, p. 6). Thus "anyone who threatened established authority—that is, anyone who threatened social order—could be perceived as engaged in witchcraft" (Hall, *Witch-Hunting*, p. 6). The symbolic construction of the witch, therefore, encompassed a variety of often divergent ends. As an act of communal finger-pointing, it defined the abstract, ideological boundaries of a community. In the witch's person—on her body itself— the *telling* of the witch wrote out a complex grammar of society's exclusions and its fears.[13] Thus the witch's spells would be countered by the society's own "spelling." In addition, witch-hunting constituted an approved ritual, in a climate generally suspicious of ritual, for maintaining religious control; for shaping the civic imagination; and paradoxically, for transgressing that imagination as well. The rite was both expiatory as well as explanatory, a ritual of guilt and repudiation that in the Calvinistic civic cosmology functioned at the same time as a ritual of identity. Finally, witch-hunting pointed inward as well as outward: "The worst work of the Devil they looked for—and found—among their own kind" (Demos, p. 71).

But these rather dry abstractions had harsh consequences for particular persons. Symbols *could* kill. Indeed. And Salem, for a variety of reasons, is a symbolic site for more reasons than just its memories of witch-hunting.[14] Let me turn for a moment to Cotton Mather's 1693 Miltonesque rendering of "the Fiend's descent on Salem Village" (Starkey, p. 242). If staking the witch was a kind of spell by which to "right" the body politic, Mather concluded that "telling" the witch—"writing it"—was also a reforming action. In *The Wonders of the Invisible World* (1693), intermingled with "sermons and philosophizings," Mather presents "a full and accurate account of the examination and trials of five representative witches, George Burroughs, Bridget Bishop, Susanna Martin, Elizabeth How, and Martha Carrier" (Starkey, p. 238). Mather declares that his account is a "true History . . . respecting the *witchcrafts* wherewith we are at this day persecuted" (p. 107).

Mather insists that he reports "matters not as an *Advocate*, but as an *Historian*" (p. 110). At the same time, however, Mather ingenuously admits that he "was not present at any of [the trials]" (p. 109). This notable omission may explain why his anxiety about how to read the Salem affair constantly intrudes upon the narrative: "The whole business is become hereupon so *Snarled*, and the determination of the Question one way or another, so *dismal*, that . . . *We know not what to do*! (p. 84).[15] The dilemma, however, was less metaphysical than practical, since Mather's main problems, of course, were social and political rather than theological. Mather had set out to write moral narrative, necessary he felt to stem what Porte calls, in another context, a "generalized atmosphere of moral entropy" (Porte, "Sinners," p. 54). Mather makes it clear that the trials were more important as eschatological history—as *exempla* of the moral life—than as history. Indeed, in his hands they were a bit of each. Mather needed to fictionalize what he had not seen; like the witch who was his subject, he needed, in a manner of speaking, to "entertain Satan" for the good of his townspeople.

In the end, the good that Mather intended was a complicated business. First, the staking and claiming of boundaries was a necessary political act for Salem. Salem had been caught up in Massachusetts' international battles for legal definition; the town's boundaries and its legal status had been thrown into disarray when the Crown revoked the Massachusetts Bay Charter in October, 1684. So, while witch-hunting deflected public anxiety of a political nature, at the same time, however, the witch-hunt proved to be an important private gesture—a way for the townspeople to explore and test other sorts of internal boundaries. As Stout explains, "the witchcraft episode was an exceptional response to social change and political insecurity" (*The New England Soul,* p. 114). In short, the metaphysical proscription prohibiting witchcraft (usually derived from Leviticus) also functioned, implicitly at first, as a way to "manage" interior worlds of the imagination. This interior policing had the salutary effect of stabilizing social and sometimes geographic maps as well.

Still, as Hawthorne was later to intuit, witchery was not just a matter of politics; it was aesthetics and drama as well. The *exempla* that Mather gathered about the possessed witches of Salem and their lurid ways enabled a reader to enjoy (surreptitiously, of course) the exotica of the immoral life while obediently repudiating them at the same time.[16] For instance, the bookseller printing Deodat Lawson's account of the Salem possessions advertised the document by saying the "curious will be entertained with as rare a history as perhaps an age has had" (Hall, *Witch-Hunting,* p. 282).[17] Cotton Mather, then, learned from his father that witchcraft was a source of unflagging social interest. John Demos reconstructs such an event:

> Meanwhile a triumphant Cotton Mather is working long and late in his study to complete a book that will soon be published under the title *Memorable Providences, Relating to Witchcraft and Possessions.* A

central chapter presents some carefully selected "examples," and includes the events in which Mather himself has so recently participated. The Goodwin children will be leading characters in a local best-seller. (p. 9)

As Demos suggests, the "metaphor of theater suggests itself quite naturally; every witchcraft case was, in part, a public drama" (p. 117). Thus, for people unaccustomed to power, fame, or its usages, witchcraft made celebrities, not always fortunately, of those accused of witchery, while bringing fame and notoriety to those victims who shared the spotlight. The "possession" of Margaret Rule, for instance, in which Mather was involved, was for a season the "major theatrical attraction in Boston" (Starkey, p. 243), and not always to Mather's credit.

Whatever their theological implications, witch trials provided life and color, however perversely and voyeuristically, to an otherwise bland and colorless life. Mather's breathless accounts of the "Witches *Extasies*" (*sic*, p. 35) served as a diversion and distraction, a "scarlet thread" (Starkey, p. 239) in life's otherwise mundane tapestry.[18] Nor was Mather himself above catching a thrill on the side. His "righteous indignation that such things could be was unconsciously submerged in the thrill of having been present as spectator at a collision between heaven and hell" (Starkey, p. 239). So it was that for the townspeople of Salem witchcraft was *news*, and, additionally, although covertly to be sure, the suggestion of witchcraft was an accepted form of social distraction—a diversion or "entertainment."

From *news* to spectacle, theater, and entertainment, or was it the other way around? Indeed, witches were entertainment even in places where there *were* no witches. Printing made invisible worlds readily available to the far-flung provinces; in effect publishing *doubled* the presence, and power, of the witch. Entertainment, then, stood in curious relation to the actual facts of a matter. In fact a vestige of that ephemeral purpose inheres in the wonderful ambiguity of the language used to bring the witch to law. A witch was brought to trial accused with "giving entertainment to Satan" (Demos, *Entertaining Satan*, p. 10).[19] Although couched in conventional religious language as *maleficium*—doing harm—witchcraft was not considered a religious offense, per se. On the contrary, it constituted a social indictment, a charge tantamount to disturbing the social peace. David Hall writes:

> It is important to note that witchcraft was not formally considered heresy, or a crime against religion. In New England, as in old, trials for witchcraft took place in a civil court. The means of execution was death by hanging, and *never* that of being burned at the stake (*Witch-Hunting*, p. 11).

Thus, the word used today to signify "innocuous" diversions has a rich, politically significant, and sometimes lethal shadow life. Further, the word itself speaks more than a little history in its evident erasures and the slippage of discourse, and in the traces of erotic tension it presumes: is Satan entertaining? Are we entertaining Satan? Who is at dalliance with whom, and why? In *The Wonders of the Invisible World*, Mather himself uses the word "entertainment" in a variety of contexts: as information (p. 79); and as evidence ("with which the Court was newly entertained"); finally as diversion: Mather writes that his "Remarkable and Memorable Instances of Wonders" will be the "chief Entertainment which my Readers do expect and shall receive" (p. 107). Shades—or rather a foretaste—of Stephen King, who, like Mather, "designed for your entertainment" (p. 79). Indeed, so customary already is the genre or contract that Mather's readers "expect" it to "do" something in a conventional way. What might this be? Inform? Arouse? Correct? Admonish? Already we can see the constraints of formula begin to appear, constraints which are also directives, of course. The "contracts" or "literary institutions" (Jameson, *Magic Narratives* p. 135) between author and hearer already begin to dictate the text. Such a formula established a "set of tacit assumptions on the nature of human experience, on human and divine motivations, on moral values, and on the nature of reality" (Slotkin, *Regeneration through Violence*, p. 20). We can see in Mather's narrative, then, qualities which will one day emerge in the tabloidesque features of Stephen King.

In late 1693, Cotton Mather's *Wonders* was to have been an interim report to the public about the goings-on in Salem, then six months old. And while Mather's ostensible topic was the "late Stupendious growth of *Witches* among us" (p. 97) and the "whole plot of the Devil, against *New-England*" (p. 4), Mather believed that he was charged to protect the body politic, since as a minister he was most responsible for clarifying its metaphysical allegiances. Even the title betrays his intentions. Mather was to be a cartographer of the spirit, drawing a boundary, by way of narrative, which would separate this world from the next. Mather hoped thereby to keep these worlds tidily distinct, although he knew that by showing forth the "wonders" of a world that was invisible and (thus) terrifying, he would, in addition, be concretely specifying the limits of this mundane but visible world. Further, *The Wonders of the Invisible World* "made visible" by Mather would also delineate this world's social and imaginative boundaries. Perhaps, finally, theology is all about boundaries. Victor Sage comments that theology, as a "social cement" is "conservative: it must preserve itself and its limits" (p. xiii). Anyway, Mather shows his own explicit conservative leanings in the degree to which political metaphors like boundaries and borders possessed him (if I may use the word). Speaking like a military strategist, Mather claims Satan to be a royal force, a "King of Terrors" (pp. 55–6), and the "appearance" of the "Evil One" to be an "Invasion" (p. 101) for which the citizenry as a whole is responsible: "but indeed, all the *Unreformed* among us, may justly be *cry'd out* upon, as having too much of an hand in letting of the Devils into our Borders" (p. 95). Everyone, that is, was at least implicitly guilty of "the great Transgression" (p. 95). A page or two later he shifts the conceit slightly, revealing more clearly the term's political (rather than theological) content: "Has there not also been a world of *discontent* in our Borders?" (p. 97).

A fissure had appeared in the body politic; as an "agent of the norm" (Stephen King's helpful expression; see *Danse Macabre*, p. 58), it was Mather's task to police the boundaries and to "watch for the mutant" (again, as King would put it). For Mather, the witch was such a limit, the boundary where the inhuman broke through the human as *exemplum*, as the Divine admonishment to an unregenerate community—as *monstrum* and sign. Yet however scandalous and troubling to the average citizen was the revelation of witchery, in addition, by its very existence the witch's dark, inverted world confirmed to believers the necessity—and sanctity—of the *other* revelation. In fact both revelations were often spoken of in the same breath, perhaps by way of contrast. In one description, a ship captain is described as "an Athest beleving that there was nither god nor Devell hell or heaven" (*sic*; cited in Hall, *Worlds of Wonder*, p. 286). The witch's power reflected dimly upon God's, and that was the point. The mapping of the heavens had made necessary a mapping of Hell and those who inhabit that infernal place. Yet the reverse was true as well, since the map of Hell admonished and clarified by directing attention toward the map of Heaven. Thus was born the witch, the devil's familiar, just as the minister was God's. Not for nothing did Salem's Reverend Samuel Parris take it upon himself to organize the outcry against Ann Putnam and others whom he suspected of witchcraft. At a perhaps unconscious level he realized his livelihood was at stake.[20]

Increase Mather's *Illustrious Providences* (1684) and Cotton Mather's subsequent narratives were "meant to reduce the Devil's influence by holding him up to public scrutiny." John Demos observes, "as in so many things 'Puritan,' the issue of *exposure* was central here" (p. 99). Following Reformation precedent, Mather had therefore needed the witch to exist as a sort of negative *exemplum*. No wonder he could say, without irony, recounting the trial of Bridget Bishop, that there "was little occasion to prove the *Witchcraft*, it being evident and notorious to all beholders" (pp. 129–30). Since he had invented (or theologized) the "swarmings of *Witch crafts*" (p. 102) in the first place, it would be almost inevitable that Mather would find evidence of a "major conspiracy" of witches. However, Mather would have been horrified to learn that his metaphysical vigilance had other consequences as well; that in his efforts to glorify God's power he *also* advertised God's limits. By establishing the witch's actual physical presence in Salem, Mather also unwittingly undercut the Divine. By showing where the devil *was*, he also revealed where the Divine *wasn't*—whether because of lack of divine will or a failure of divine power was yet another question to be answered. Also, Mather may not have sensed—or at least he pretended not to sense—what his audience intuitively knew. He may not have understood why eager readers devoured edition after edition of *Wonders*. Yet why would they not? His breathless narrative of witches' "extasies" offered a lurid, dramatic narrative of social violation, in which the demonic was portrayed as erotic and seductive—a presence who (that?) could send individuals as well as cultures into palpitating swoons. Of course, this was not unusual in itself. Indeed, did not the troublesome history of the mystics show this very thing about the Divine?

Historically, then, God's loving embrace was all-prepossessing, problematic in itself and certainly disruptive of other loyalties. The documents from Salem underscore an ancient anxiety that had much to do with the central metaphor of conversion. Whether possessed by God or by the demonic, behaviors were extreme, unpredictable, and finally unacceptable to the social welfare. Thus, the history of religious discourse—and terror, its hand-maiden—can be read as the struggle of human cultures to protect themselves against the eruption in history of the unregulatable Divine. God, like snakes and other demonized creatures, must be handled with respect. The author of all law, by definition God would therefore be the greatest antinomian, and so, in a culture of the law, the greatest lawbreaker to be feared.

By suggesting that witches existed as part of "the Vengeance of God" (p. 51), and thus, only at God's sufferance, Mather might have been hedging just a bit, perhaps even denying God's power slightly. Yet another possibility remained, one ultimately more troubling than these, and this was the suggestion of Divine Connivance—a *divine* maleficium that made possible human ma-leficium. This would be a harrowing, not of Hell, but of earth: God, like Satan in the Book of Job, walking to and fro upon the earth, seeking whom He might devour. Stephen King's Carrie White, gifted with telekinesis, would reach similar conclusions as she muses about the wreck of destruction she leaves behind her in Chamberlain. The town's ruin was as much "His fault" as the fault of her retributive outburst. It seems Mather didn't stop the gap between Heaven, earth, and Hell, after all. Maybe he only made things worse here in *"the Devils Country"* (*sic*; Mather, p. 67).

Interlude: The House That Hawthorne Haunted

> *The mythology of the witch-craze . . . was the articulation of social pressure. In a religious society such articulation generally takes the form of heresy.*[21]

I observed earlier that on January 14, 1697, Samuel Sewall directed his pastor to read Sewall's apology for the witch-hunts. Sewall was the first of the Salem community publicly to acknowledge the wrongness of the witch-hunts and to apologize for his role in them. In a similar confessional moment, however, Nathaniel Hawthorne moves in another direction entirely. He remembers rather than repudiates. Hawthorne astutely recognized the multiple possibilities, for memory *and* its subversion, afforded by the witch trials. After all, as a writer, dealing in the unreal of romance and fantasy, he was a sort of witch himself. (Mary Rucker observes that Hawthorne's "association of art and witchcraft" is a critical commonplace.)[22] So within thirty years of one of the last recorded witch trials of New England (in Bristol, Connecticut, 1800–10; see Demos, *Entertaining Satan*, p. 388), Hawthorne is already busy transmuting the tropes and symbols of witch-hunting into the usable past of romance, narrative, and ideology.[23] In "The Custom-House" Hawthorne explains that the "old town of Salem . . . possesses, or did possess, a hold on my affections, the force of which I have never realized during my seasons of actual residence [there]" (p. 10).[24] Guilt was surely one of those holds, as it had been for Sewall, since Judge John Hathorne, Nathaniel's grandfather, had sat with Sewall in judgment upon the Salem witchcraft proceedings. Yet behind the judge Hathorne sees the shadow of another "haunt[ing]" figure, and this one his "first ancestor": "Soldier, legislator, judge; he was a ruler in the Church; he had all the Puritanic traits, both good and evil" (p. 11). As a writer, Hawthorne then will assume the double burden bequeathed him by the "bitter persecutor" of the Quakers and by that man's son, the Salem Judge: "I, the present writer, as their representative, hereby take shame upon myself for their sakes" (p. 11). In the context of Hawthorne's "neutral territory" (p. 31), the imaginative topography of his romances, Hawthorne echoes Sewall's apology. In Sewall's words, he takes "the blame and shame of it" upon himself. He completes history by remembering it in fiction.[25]

Yet whatever might have been his personal motivations Hawthorne also felt profound imaginative and artistic sympathy for the *literal* (even literary) dilemma of the Puritans. They were a people to whom "religion and law were almost identical" (Hoffman, *Form and Fable in American Fiction*, p. 171), and Hawthorne was able, as Philip Gura explains, "to translate the widespread concern over the crisis in religious language and doctrine into the realm of imaginative fiction" (Clark, *op. cit.*, p. 136). In the 1849 sketch "Main Street," Hawthorne describes the early colonists this way:

"the zeal of a recovered faith burned like a lamp within their hearts" (*Tales*, p. 1030), although the society could pass on only "its religious gloom, and the counterfeit of its religious ardor, to the next" (*Tales*, p. 1038). In *The Scarlet Letter: A Romance,* published the next year, Hawthorne provides an example of the resulting conflict. In the person of Hester Prynne, Hawthorne draws the intimate connection between the *polis* and the private, lawless utterances of the Self that had troubled the colony from its earliest days. In her very person, like the witch, Hester becomes the site in which a community enacts its policies—and policements—of revelation.

For New England, of course, Hawthorne's tale is an old one. Michael Colacurcio argues convincingly that Hawthorne's drama-tization of Dimmesdale and Hester Prynne was intended to recall the conflict between Anne Hutchinson and John Cotton.[26] But Hawthorne is not simply writing allegory. On the one hand, he poses the ambiguities of revelation in both its public and private aspects; on the other, he positions a society's first imperative—its necessary management of memory and myth. How to balance, how to interpret: how to judge between the various readings? And herein, for Hawthorne, for Hester, for the community, lay the terror: right reading, the ability to interpret the signs correctly, indeed, was the thread (threat) upon which hung one's soul, and of course, the challenge upon which early church founders had constructed the society. Yet as Hawthorne intuited, reading can occasion misreading, as well, upon which the social order can founder.[27]

In *The Scarlet Letter,* Hawthorne examines more fully the emo-tional and socio-religious intensity of the metaphor of literacy.[28] So simple an emblem as a single letter of the alphabet could be con-strued in numerous ways. Hoffman observes that Hawthorne "makes the letter itself a supernatural providence; yet instead of evoking allegorical certitude it produces ambiguity on every side" (p. 171). He understood that an emphasis upon right reading only underscored the possibility of "multiplicity," in Henry Adam's word. Such a result could only cause terror in a social order increas-ingly committed to denying ambiguities of any sort. Ironically, of course, such vigilance only perpetuated the crime.[29] However, from another point of view, Hawthorne's private remembering of his family's past (in "The Custom-House") is a social venture, too, a national and a mythic maneuver. The need to remember a past that didn't exist, and the need to nationalize and claim that past, were parallel moments for Hawthorne and his generation, as they had been for Winthrop and his. Hawthorne's private spelunking and excavations into New England's culture-dense memory permits him to transmute nationalist materials—confessions, conversions, and the "folklore of the supernatural" (Hoffman, p. 170)— into a theme which, ever since, has been viewed as particularly American. Why it should be so viewed is perhaps one of the underlying questions about this whole business.

It is astonishing to hear Perry Miller argue in *The New England Mind: From Colony to Province* that the "intellectual history of New England can be written as though no such thing [as Salem] ever happened. It had no effect on the ecclesiastical or political situation, it does not figure in the institutional or ideological development" (p. 191).[30] Miller did enough work in the early colonial tradition to know better. To the contrary, as John Demos argues, New England never "got over" its witch hysteria. Although legal proceedings initiated against witches terminated after the Salem debacle, Salem was not to be the end of the affair:

> In all its *unofficial* aspects that history would long continue. As a matter of individual and collective preoccupation, and even of informal *action*, witchcraft was part of New England life well into the nineteenth century. Its vestigial remnants could almost certainly be discovered not far from our own time (p. 387).[31]

Thus while "witches disappeared from view, other figures were obliged to take their place. Blacks, Indians, immigrants of various kinds; Jews, Catholics, Mormons, atheists; masons, anarchists, Communists" (Demos, *Entertaining Satan*, pp. 399–400). Although the players have changed, so to speak, the exclusionary rites remained—and, lest we forget, so did the entertainment value. Texts like Mather's *Wonders*, or Increase Mather's earlier *Illustrious Providences*, or even the occasional sermon served a variety of routine, prosaic purposes: to teach, to admonish, to astonish. Mather's eager transcription of the Salem affair certainly accomplished what he set out to do, which was to inform the clergy about the awfulness of demonic visitations. However, it also whetted their appetites about just *how*, and in what ways, and to whom, the visitation was awful. Mather helped his readers imagine the socially unimaginable, while at the same time reaffirming for them the socially acceptable and imaginable. His *Wonders*, then, could be considered as a trial run for his later work, *Bonifacius: Essays to Do Good* (1710). It is this moralistic aspect of the "unofficial" history of the witch-hunt that I address—shall we say, its popular, or memorial aspect.

Despite Miller's contention, it is certainly clear from Hawthorne's example alone that the literary history of New England could not be written without taking into account Salem. Some of the earliest precolonial texts, ones that anticipate the "psychological and spiritual loss" (DeLamotte, p. 15) characteristic of the Gothic tradition derive from the Salem affair. These texts— notably Mather's *The Wonders of the Invisible World* (1693) and Deodat Lawson's *A Brief and True Narrative* (1692)—easily conform to at least one definition of the Gothic sensibility: they affirm a "sense that the danger exceeds any that human agency alone can bring about" (Delamotte, p. 16). And, as we have seen, Hawthorne's transposition and resymbolization of once-religious material suggests that Miller is incorrect, and that the ghost of Salem returns precisely as ideology. In other words, culture has a long memory for its privileged Unspoken.[32]

Further, contemporary echoes of Salem (the repeated invocation of "witch-hunt" at times of civic unrest) demonstrate that the language of religious terror and strategies of repressive political discourse intersect most naturally in times when the *polis* is threatened, whether by actual external, historical event or by some perceived internal, ideological threat. For instance, recall the McCarthy era, or, more recently, the rhetoric of Family Values and the politization of the religious right. Of course, there is nothing "natural" about the alignment of political teleologies, social goals, and theology. More to the point, there is something willfully obfuscatory about the linkage of "family values" and the language of "natural"; as there is, conversely, between the linkage of familial depredation and social monstrosity. For example, witches from the time of Socrates through the witchification of Gay people (and other repudiated groups) have been accused of preying upon children.[33] But thus it is that memory, in the name of nostalgia, invents the tradition it needs in order to survive, while at the same time it creates the monsters it needs to hate. This is true for individuals and true for cultures as well. For this reason Salem is an early preparation for the later political dramas of inclusion/exclusion by which a socializing theology of transgression becomes normative cultic narrative, a ritual of self-conscious remembering. To the religious mind that has forgotten itself, there is something satisfying to the formula, expiation is explanation.

Hawthorne's ability to render this process fictionally is instructive. Consider *The Scarlet Letter* again, briefly. In Hester's relations to the community, Hawthorne symbolizes (and enacts) her relations to the Divine, as well. The reader first observes Hester Prynne, an unmarried mother with child, incarcerated in the village jail. As the opening image of the jail, the crowd, and the rose is allegorical, so Hester Prynne is likewise allegorical. She is, multivalent, capable of diverse, even contradictory readings. As husbandless mother, she *embodies* a threat to the social order. Uncontrolled, embodied (unguarded), she suggestively fits the demographic type of a person likely to be accused of witchery. As a witch she will be de-ciphered; decontexted. It is arguable that her term in prison is intended precisely to remove the textual ambiguity—to eliminate the "A"dulteress and to expiate it in favor of the "A"ngel. Further, as noted earlier, the figure of Hester owes a great deal to the historical Anne Hutchinson. Each woman set herself against the received, cultic myth; each woman faced exile as a result. Kristeva argues that society begins at the place of its abjections. Hawthorne understood the point I wish to make, that in a theologically based democracy, even as late as the nineteenth century, grace, often, was communally dispensed. Exclusions can be both real and symbolic at the same time.

Finally, the transformation from theological imperative to fictional narrative shows the extent to which religious materials no longer *directly* controlled popular motivation, although they remained nonetheless present and active. Hawthorne carefully distances himself and his real, historical society from the "neutral" world of his fiction, only, in the end, to join them again, "remembered" in a different way. He connects the original theological tropes to their subsequent social reflections in such a way that their "Ghosts might enter . . . without affrighting us" ("The Custom-

House," p. 31). Theology itself had become memory, reworked as myth. The question, however, is how directly this process occurs. Hawthorne's oblique revisiting of the drama of Salem was an early instance of what would be an irrepressible impulse—to remember and revise the history that was and to invent a history that wasn't. Finally, if Mather could find monsters everywhere, so could Hawthorne. In "Alice Doane's Appeal," Hawthorne remembers Mather as "representative of all the hateful features of his time; the one blood-thirsty man, in whom were concentrated those vices of spirit and errors of opinion, that sufficed to madden the whole surrounding multitude" (*Tales*, p. 216).

This is not a place to discuss Hawthorne's artistry, save to say that his Gothic fantasy/romance mode, his political mode, and his narrative instincts are all conjoined. To the extent that Hawthorne was a social writer, he was a political author; to the extent that he sought a distinctly American mode, he helped re-establish the Gothic as a new-world genre. Not for nothing did Lovecraft and King return to Hawthorne for inspiration and source. And not for nothing did Hawthorne turn to Salem to mine the discourse of the powerless, and to re-member it to the national psyche. In "The Custom-House," Hawthorne imagines his "stern and black-browed" ancestors murmuring in dismay to each other: "What is he? . . . A writer of story-books! What kind of a business in life . . . may that be? Why the degenerate fellow might as well have been a fiddler!" (p. 12). Yet a very significant business, as it turns out, since this writer remakes the past to connive with present needs. The fear of ghosts is in general a fear of time, a fear that the past has escaped our control. Hawthorne, one hundred and fifty years ago, already knew what Stephen King would teach: the dead, never dead, return. Their ghosts do not so much haunt us as they signal how they are trapped *with* us, unable, as it were, to escape our gravity. As the narrator in Hawthorne's "Alice Doane's Appeal" reflects, after using the site of Gallows Hill and the memory of the witch-hunts to elicit a romantic feeling from his companions, "and now the past had done all it could."[34]

But *had* the past done all it could? For it keeps working overtime. Like Hutchinson, the Quakers, even Hester Prynne, then, the witches of Salem were communal offerings. Rewritten as icons, they became, each in his or her time, an approved focus for community energy, a tacitly pleasurable and slightly voyeuristic religious memorial. Hawthorne writes about the significance implied by Hester's letter A: ". . . giving up her individuality, she would become the general symbol at which the preacher and moralist might point, and in which they might vivify and embody their images of woman's frailty and sinful passion" (p. 59). Ironically, the witch embodies a community's symbolic rejection of itself—one made in the very terms by which the community defined itself. That is, a society authorized by an *implicit* relationship with the Divine condemned the witch precisely for making that relationship *explicit*. Thus an ideology of Christian obedience—since Saint Paul, a complex matter of submission to the law (captivity) and paradoxical freedom from it (release)—continues to rewrite historical discourse, as an obvious example (Lovelace's *Ordeal*) makes clear. I have been arguing that important thematic, social, and even literary links can be made between the discourses of Salem and those of contemporary horror. One sees traces and overlapping shadows connecting say, Elizabeth Knapp—the "demoniac-girl" of Groton (Demos, p. 111) and (to name one) Regan, William Blatty's demon girl. I will turn to *The Exorcist* in a subsequent chapter. For the moment I wish to consider another oblique connection—Stephen King's *Carrie*, which shows what happens when the originally theological discourse of witchcraft becomes paradigm of civic imagination, manufactured as ideology and fantasy.

Carrie: Working the Mother Lode

> *Giving up witchcraft is, in effect, giving up the Bible.*
> —JOHN WESLEY, *JOURNAL*[35]

Religious imperatives still echo in places presumed to be unimportant. Let us consider for a moment the genres of the horrific sublime. At age twenty-six, Stephen King was working in a laundry and "writing *Carrie* in the furnace room of a trailer" (*Danse Macabre*, p. 372). Selling *Carrie* to Doubleday in 1973 was his first major break as an author. *Carrie* was also King's first experiment in the genre of horror. So King's meteoric publishing career begins with

his serendipitous discovery that Cotton Mather *was* right: the
devil—or at least deviltry—*did* sell.[36] And with that discovery, as
King puts it, life "began to move at Concorde speed" (*Danse
Macabre*, p. 372).[37] King may have stumbled into success accidentally with his story of Carrie White, the socially inept girl troubled
by (or gifted with) talents. As we have seen, the genre of the captive
woman is almost a cultural cliché, and King adapts the formulas of
the captivity narrative and spiritual autobiography to the darkly
parodic ends of social horror. Carrie White is a sixteen-year-old
social outcast in the small town of Chamberlain, Maine. Even her
physical appearance suggests an interior dis-ease, an inability to
conform to social standards. She is "a chunky girl with pimples on
her neck and back and buttocks, her wet hair completely without
color" (p. 4). Her plain appearance renders her socially invisible.
Carrie, who "looked the part of the sacrificial goat, the constant
butt" (p. 4) always stood "dumbly in the center of a forming
circle" (p. 7). Even Carrie notes the seeming inevitability of her
fate. The other girls "always *stared*" (p. 4); "they've *always*
laughed" (p. 17). "They all hate and they never stop. They never
get tired of it" (p. 21). About Carrie the narrator reflects, at
"sixteen, the elusive stamp of hurt was already marked clearly in
her eyes" (p. 7), and even her gym teacher, usually sympathetic,
reflects Carrie has "always been a group scapegoat" (p. 19).

Carrie's powerful talents are triggered by an abrupt and public
passage into menstruation. Carrie has a history of being singled
out as different at the hands of her classmates and townspeople,
and her public menstruation is both chaotic and humiliating for
her. The community's visceral repudiation of Carrie, and her subsequent use of telekinetic energy to revenge herself upon the
townspeople, drive the plot of this fairly short (for King) novel.

A socially punitive image of the woman is the real monster in
Chamberlain, and so Carrie becomes a convenient token for the
community's intense strategies of repudiation. She is the bodied
form of social self-hate, the witch-woman among girls. Her presence in the community is a powerful threat to their purity (a
traditional charge against witches, of course, is the threat they pose
to children). The community's response to Carrie is three-fold:
she is repudiated as woman, citizen, and finally demonized, she is
repudiated as human. The novel's opening scene graphically por-

trays the social exclusionary tactics at work. Carrie is in the shower following gym class when she begins to menstruate for the first time. Her dark menstrual blood flowing on the shower floor signals that she has come of biological child-bearing age. The scene is darkly luminous with a variety of cultural anxieties: blood, women, witchery; fear of difference. To Carrie's shock and embarrassment, the other girls surround her, throwing tampons and yelling vulgarities. By distancing themselves from her they establish their own "girlish" purity more securely, although they are clearly more sexually experienced than Carrie.

The girls' largely thoughtless and spontaneous repudiation of Carrie's vulnerability re-enacts the adult community's more studied institutions of denying what it fears, since the girls' drama plays out in miniature the culture's systematic rejection of Woman. Biologically powerful Carrie—like other women in this respect— must be rendered ideologically powerless. What differentiates Carrie from other women and what makes her socially dangerous is her freedom from internal constraints—and, consequently, her inability to be properly socialized. She is an antinomian like others in the tradition. Her power exceeds the laws designed to contain it. Carrie's body is itself the prime source of her power and mystery, and her blood flow symbolizes the various metaphysical uncertainties against which the community must arm itself. Carrie's passage to biologically mature womanhood means, most simply, that her powers do not easily lend themselves to management, either personally or socially. Neither tampon nor the coercions of ideology effectively constrain her for very long.

Stephen King commented that *Carrie* "is largely about how women find their own channels of power, and what men fear about women and women's sexuality. . . . The book is, in its more adult implications, an uneasy masculine shrinking from a future of female equality" (*Danse Macabre*, p. 170). This confirms King's general sense that horror American-style is constructed around cultural anxieties about the power and place of women. Carrie White, says King, is "Woman, feeling her powers for the first time and, like Samson, pulling down the temple on everyone" (*Danse Macabre*, p. 170). King's portrait of "woman" of course is hardly value-free; nor is it completely transparent. Nonetheless, the anxiety-of-power he foregrounds is a crucial American metaphor, even myth. In *Carrie*, we see power as it is wrested back from an inscrutable God and from the less-scrutable social systems originally in the service of that God. Bodies—especially women's bodies—have historically signified weak points of the social order. As evidence, one can cite traditional efforts expended for the regulation and policing of the female body's complex mysteries. Theological metaphysics are not dissimilar from political myth in this respect. As the Inquisition knew well, the body is the soul's guarantor, and control of the body is tantamount to managing the soul.

With this in mind, then, King could hardly have chosen the girl's name by accident. For one thing, "White" evokes a tradition in American letters in which whiteness and inscrutability are two points of a hermeneutic triangle, one whose third point is the futility of interpretation—a theme central to the metaphysical puzzlings of Poe, Melville, even Frost.[38] In addition, the name "Carrie" echoes in America's checkered history of social violence. Martha Corey was the first Salem woman cried out as a witch by the young Ann Putnam, and the name also recalls Martha Carrier, likewise executed at Salem for witchcraft. Parenthetically, Cotton Mather, who did witness Carrier's execution, called her the "Queen of Hell" (*Wonders*, p. 159). Further, White etymologically echoes witch, and, at least derivatively, both words suggest "wit," "knowledge." Like Hawthorne's Hester, Carrie's fatal difference from other people is her knowledge and her vulnerability. She knows too much and disowns too little. Less possessed by demons than by her own dark self, Carrie's social sin—if I may be permitted the overlapping of metaphors—is, again like Hester's, the power she refuses to give over to society, and so she becomes, for all practical purposes, its witch—a word whose Old-English roots show traces of its cognate connection to "victim." Her tragedy, like the earlier social traumas in New England history, is prompted, and sustained, by the hidden center of Calvinist metaphysics— power and its systems of authorization and policement. King's tale permits a highly moralized glimpse into the socially deterministic cosmology of Chamberlain. *Carrie* charts the dynamic, transgressive oppositions of a derivatively Calvinist ethos, where, in Mary Douglas's terms, an insistence upon boundary, purity, and law organize and actually create the conflict they enact; and where transgression and scrutiny, rather than love, establish the community; and where orthodoxy and heresy depend upon each other for definition.

Carrie's mother is a religious fanatic—King's own favorite sort of monster. Margaret White is preoccupied by things of the spirit while obsessed by things of the body. Her religion, though couched in the language of sentimental love, is to the contrary, organized as a hierarchy of bodily pain. Mrs. White is a woman to whom fear, guilt, and faith are synonymous, and she has brought her daughter up accordingly—to worship, to placate, and to fear an inscrutable, inescapable deity. The real issue between Mrs. White and her daughter is obedience and loyalty rather than demonic agency, and Carrie's menstruation precipitates a conflict that the mother symbolizes in metaphysical terms.[39] David Skal writes, "menarche, to Margaret White, is nothing less than the beginning of an apocalyptic war between the spirit and the flesh" (*The Monster Show*, p. 355). Mrs. White, of course, can only read Carrie's maturing power as disloyalty to herself, dramatized and heightened as disloyalty to God. The young woman's growing acceptance of her power, then, threatens not only a perverse family unit based upon absent patriarchy and repression, but also a social system similarly based on absent authority—in this case a spirituality of absence that depends upon a quixotic, Barthian *Deus Absconditus*.

Nonetheless, Carrie White is as much burdened by innocence as she is by the guilt of others. She is innocent of knowledge concerning her body's disruptive physicality (she thinks that tampons are for applying lipstick), guilty because she lives out her mother's pathological religious denials and her society's social repudiations. As a result of these pressures, Carrie finds herself trapped in a cage formed by symbolic communal needs—for exclusion, justification, and later, for voyeuristic piety. This cage had been "building slowly and immutably, in accordance with all the laws that govern human nature, building with all the steadiness of a chain reaction approaching critical mass" (pp. 3–4). In a moment of sudden stress, Carrie transforms from victim, innocent of knowledge, into the powerful Other whose ungovernability (her "secret") threatens community stability just as Carrie literally threatens to destroy the town.

Carrie, however, is not the problem; rather she is the victim whose body, witchlike, must *articulate* the problem and make it visible. Around her crystallize the strategies a society wields to buttress and support its metaphysical preconceptions, and by means of which certain exclusions are authorized as socially necessary—approved as they are by a presumptively "right" reading of revelation. As witch, like Martha Carrier, Carrie White is both victim and expiation; transgressor and exemplum; witch and messenger of a dark god. As a witch Carrie will, with and in her own blood, inscribe a society's need to repudiate at all costs that which it can neither understand nor manage. Carrie is the sacrifice, blooded and cut like the pig the boys kill in preparation for her humiliation: "Pig's blood for a pig" (p. 114). She plays out the role of the "angel with a sword" countering the sentimentality of the "savior Jesus meek and mild" (p. 22) to whom Mrs. White prays.

The speed and the thoroughness of the change from virgin to dark destroying Mother, along with the speed of the town's alignment against her, indicates that in King's Chamberlain, as at Salem, witchcraft is functional rather than personal. Indeed, the personal is deflected, erased, subsumed in the deceptive rhetoric of a socially determined fate: Carrie, after all, is different and so punishable. The cruelty of this fate, however, is disguised beneath theological, communitarian sanction. The Martha Coreys and Carriers in Mather's text are dismembered as persons, only to be reconstructed as monstrous through a mythopoetic rhetoric ("Queen of Hell"); the same fate awaits Carrie. Carrie stands in the center of an interpretive storm, a "gaping, whistling hole" (p. 41). She is an emptiness, vulnerable to the powers of society in whose interests she will be "read" and made over—first as the "frog among swans" (p. 4), then society's "butt," then, as a dark Cinderella, the glamorous Other. Finally, as "Typhoid Mary," empowered by her telekinetic strength, she is "capable of destroying almost at will" (p. 102). Her presence highlights, and energizes, a society's politics of interpretation, including those that pass, often without subtlety, as techniques of coercion, as various discourses of social defense—complementary rituals of transgression and victimization—merge to defend a civic order of convention and conformity.

Carrie is a text in the apocalyptic tradition of Mather, in which a war between invisible and visible worlds is rewritten as private obsession and narcissism. Carrie embodies, in the most literally unspeakable way, the jeremiad. She is a communal narrative of self-hate, a text drenched with the rhetoric of responsibility and the energy of denial. King's method of narration in *Carrie* shows how Carrie is vulnerable not only to the functions of myth but also to the displacements of social discourse. King's text, like Mather's, is a hermeneutic document, a polyphonic and problematic text of knowledge, silences, and omissions.[40] Its fragmented structure includes bits and pieces of cultural selfspeak: gossip, narrative, texts of scientific commentary, sensationalist news accounts, and Carrie's own intuitions. Out of these emerge a series of concentric instabilities, ranging from personal to civic: Carrie's identity; her schoolmates' insecurities; her mother's religious pathologies; the town's threatened sense of self; the wider problems of discourse—scientific and theological, even historical—problematized by Carrie's presence. Against these forces Carrie cannot stand alone, and as a result her ostracization is made to seem almost inevitable, even fated, as personal, individual repudiations are transposed to, and hidden in, the bland pronouncements of scientific discourse. So, while Carrie's telekinetic abilities are actually out of place in the metaphysical symmetries of scientific discourse, when explained *in* its measured, supposedly objective, cadences, they become effectively certain and lawful. Carrie, then, is as anomalous and as inoffensive as Bridget Bishop, whose flagrant red cloak was perceived as such an affront to the sumptuary laws of Boston, or Anne Hutchinson, whose theological acuity seemed to equal John Cotton or Winthrop's—or even Martha Carrier, whose silence before the authorities of Salem could only be broken by death. These women were perceived to be powerful to the extent they threatened the legitimacy (that is, the stability) of reigning discourse. And each, to a woman, must find her power broken. Each somehow must be *illegitimated*. Their traffic, whether with the scientific unknown or the theologically unnameable, must be declared illegal. The best way, of course, to do this is to *legitimize* their negative presence—to work them into the system, as it were, negatively.

By extracting Carrie from a purely local situation and resituating her as a freakish but nonetheless scientific case, the various scientific documents interpolated alongside Carrie's self-perceptions confirm the prior, perhaps unreflected, apocalyptic repudiation made by the townspeople. As Mrs. Simard says, testifying about the night of Carrie's destruction: "What happens if there are others like her? What happens to the world?" (p. 206). Thus in final analysis the texts justify and repudiate as much as they explain or rationalize, in the same way that the generally hearsay "proof" introduced by Mather *(The Wonders of the Invisible World)* confirms what the townspeople of Salem already knew—that witches or no, the Ann Putnams and Martha Carriers were necessarily guilty. They needed to be, in order that society's rituals of power might be deployed.

In *Natural Symbols: Explorations in Cosmology*, Mary Douglas argues that witch beliefs flourish under certain conditions, whose structure she metaphorically calls cosmologies. In such societies,

> the body politic tends to have a clear external boundary, and a confused internal state in which envy and favouritism flourish and continually confound the proper expectations of members. So the body of the witch, normal-seeming and apparently carrying the normal human limitations, is equipped with hidden and extraordinarily malevolent powers. The loyalty of the witch, instead of being committed firmly to his group, flies out loose. He goes alone to contend with alien personifications of lust and power. The witch himself has no firm anchorage in the social structure. In appearance he is present, but only bodily; his real inner self has escaped from social restraint.[41]

Douglas's comments are applicable to Salem and Chamberlain; to the fictionalized history of Mather and to the historicized fiction of King. Transgression establishes a central axis, or *ritual* of identity, a set of approved separations and divisions by which the normative center is identified and maintained *along the edge* of its denials and in terms of its repudiations. In such a taxonomic system, as Douglas argues, dirt is function rather than material. It is matter in the *wrong* place, needing to be removed, re*placed.* Analogously, the witch functions in a similar fashion, breaching the line, crossing the categories. In terms we will explore in a later chapter, the witch (or wizard) lets the Outside In—and conversely, permits the Inside Out.

But which comes first, the witch or the system in whose terms the witch is identified and repudiated? My point in this chapter is that Carrie White is a commonplace, a cliché well-worn and as old as

Anne Hutchinson or Ann Putnam. Indeed, Carrie is well-named. She is the carious point of the society, its ingress/egress, its boundary line. So, while she trespasses the line, perhaps, she is also the place of trespass. She functions as a common ground of contention and conflict, a place where visible and invisible worlds intersect. She is the point where the social order defines itself by rejecting what it *will not* permit. Like the clergy in this respect (who, it must be noted, are witches in that they, too, traffic with powers and principalities) Carrie assumes a role prepared for her by her community; she enacts and affirms community ritual. As such she shares another function with the clergy: she is social regulator, a measure of the normal, and finally, its judge. Ironically, of course, she is also the victim of the town's normalizing judgment: "Plug it up, plug it up, plug it up" (p. 8) the girls in the shower scream at Carrie as they fling tampons at her, symbolically enacting their own rite of purity, policing the orifices of the society.[42]

Carrie is not only, or principally, a moralistic story about an isolated case of repressed telekinesis. It is also a telling of a culture's ghosts, and how actual cultural repression organizes a society symbolically. David Skal writes, "The religious fanaticism of Carrie's mother . . . had its origins in a more secular American obsession: the strike-it-rich fantasy of rescue and transformation, of magical entitlement" (p. 356). Carrie plays out a variation of the "recurrent American nightmare" (Winter, p. 2), a kind of Cinderella, doomed to ash. Carrie represents metaphysics come to ground, apocalypse rendered as personal metaphor, shattering not only her ill-fated individual life but also the various civic discourses designed to contain (and conventionalize) individual extravagances. Carrie embodies a society's need to authorize and justify itself through a hierarchy of pain and victims—one that in this tradition, at least, is sanctified in the name of Jesus.[43] Obligingly, her community *reads* her, interprets and confirms her, in the role of the blooded victim, if only to prevent themselves from occupying it. By erasing Carrie and situating her as the pivotal icon of communal ritual, the townspeople draw a line between her and themselves; thus, at least temporarily, they escape her fate.

Nonetheless, hunger for victims seems a divine logic, and having forced the opposition of Carrie and her community, the urgencies of a debased Christian imagination will continue implacably to seek victims. In its inscrutable and deterministic spiritual universe, communal annihilation and personal narcissism go hand in hand. In this symbolic order of power there will always be a victim by which a social order validates its authority. Alive, Carrie is that proof; dead, she enters a different symbolic order altogether. Carrie intends the meaning her community needs for itself, but which it cannot read or interpret clearly. Erased as herself, like Hester, Carrie achieves a dark resurrection in the symbolic order, in which she signifies the meaning of transcendence from which her society derives its authority.

While doctrine might be debased over time, religious metaphors remain constant, though shifting, centers of symbolic energy. No wonder the cross in the White's home had "given Carrie endless nightmares in which the mutilated Christ chased her through dream corridors, holding a mallet and nails, begging her to take up her cross and follow Him" (p. 39). Carrie is the new Jesus, as there will be others after her. Before her final cataclysmic walk home, Carrie pauses for a moment in the Congregational church. There in the dark, she has an insight into the cipherlike emptiness at the center of religious practice. In her misery, like Jesus in the garden, she prays, and reflects: "No one was there—or if there was, He/It was cowering from her" (p. 200). And "why not?" she wonders, no longer intimidated by her own power; Carrie, like Mather before her, then concludes that she was not responsible for the events of the evening. This "horror was as much His doing as hers" (p. 200).

In the final bloody conflict with her obsessed and paranoid mother, Carrie—fatally wounded by her mother's knife—offers her, in return, she says, a present: "What you always wanted. Darkness. And whatever God lives there" (p. 211). Using her paranormal powers, Carrie then stops her mother's heart and kills her. Carrie's reflections emphasize the real experience behind theological abstraction; that however heretical it might be as doctrine, the thought is somehow comforting that somewhere the all-powerful God of love has his all-horrorful equal—or is, as Whitman suggested, Himself such an equal, the "Square Deific." For theologies, no less than fantasies, are accountable to the urgent need of the human imagination which dictates that no scrap of usable memory—pain or pleasure—goes wasted. Carrie herself "did not know if her gift had come from the lord of light or of darkness," and now, finally finding that she did not care which, she was overcome with an almost indescribable relief . . ." (p. 98). For the community and for her mother, it was similarly a matter of indifference; both had long ceased to distinguish the imperatives either of love or its varieties of terror. So far as Mrs. White can reason, there probably is not much practical difference between Carrie's "devilspawn, demon-power" and the "kind, vengeful hand" (p. 55) of the deity she keeps locked in the closet. There she keeps enshrined a portrait, "Derrault's conception of Jonathan Edwards's famous sermon, *Sinners in the Hands of an Angry God.*" Not for nothing does Margaret White lock up Derrault and Carrie "below a hideous blue bulb that was always lit" (p. 54). Both need vigilance; both need to be watched. So alone and locked in the closet, Carrie becomes an ironic reflection of "Momma's angry God" (p. 57). If the apocalyptic imagination gets what it imagines, Carrie becomes for her society the Apocalypse uncovered: one point of an unholy trinity, whose other points are the "crucified Jesus, and . . . Momma" (p. 52).

Mary Douglas writes that the "reasons for any particular way of defining the sacred are embedded in the social consensus which it protects."[44] What is important about Carrie—indeed, about the discourse of the demonic from the New Testament forward—is the "social consensus" which the rituals gathered about her encourage. To her mother, Carrie signifies that "the devil has come home" (p. 210). To Mr. Quillan, her presence likewise signals that "the Devil came to Chamberlain" (p. 181)—an invasion that Mather would have understood. For the demonic is less object or agent than function, and Carrie's function is to facilitate, even justify, a process of exclusion. She is the prohibition and the taboo—the ritualized effacement by which a community, however haltingly and imperfectly, sets its boundaries and comes to self-knowledge. When she attends the prom in her deep red dress, and stands before the assembled community, she resembles Hester Prynne, who similarly is the *meaning* behind a communal convocation. Carrie's humiliation in and exclusion from the social fabric is thus a communal event, a darkly carnivalesque moment in which the threat of change, social upheaval, is made visible and its agent effaced.

Conclusion

Violence is the secret heart and soul of the sacred.[45]

Pilgrims unhouseled by Geneva's night / They planted here the Serpent's seeds of light.
—ROBERT LOWELL, "CHILDREN OF LIGHT"

Salem's effacement of its witches enacts as civic ritual the crucial beginnings of an Anglo-American religious community. It was to be a "People of the Word" governed almost obsessively by rituals and by texts; an order of governance where allegory is privileged meaning; and where secrets and their revelations are chief motivations of public scenes. Two concluding observations about Salem are in order. A society of transgression takes its identity from the gods it worships. And, as at Salem, the witch is always the disposable body upon which the body politic nourishes itself. Salem lives on, its vigilante energies ritually repudiated and discredited, yet just as often reinvoked and remembered. Listen, for example, to Supreme Court Judge Clarence Thomas on nationwide TV deftly recontextualize racial politics by invoking the near-sacred taboo of the witch-hunt. Or, for another example, in the publicization of sex, whether the harrowing of President Bill Clinton or the public bloodying of the Bobbits. (Many other public—or *publicized*—persons could be cited who were urged in various contexts to put their private selves—even private parts—on display.) Or feel the palpable energy in any of these cases, fueled by the media, for a confession. (It seems not to matter whose, or what they were confessing: the secret was the thing; if sexual, all the better, especially in a Don't Ask; Don't Tell social order.) National dramaturgics is that all-expansive, co-optive liturgy by which individuals become socialized and learn their place first, by the articulation of secrets, and second, by publication of those secrets. Salem is a primary commemorative site in this public drama of self-identity and horrific intimacy. Why? For clarity, certainty, identity. Salem's patterns of worship—the exhilaration of fear, moving from theology to polity to fantasy—establish a cultic rhythm for social cohesion. Fear first, and foremost, is the eye of the Divine, ever upon us.[46]

Finally, the Salem witch-hunts offer a civic gesture in which the cycle of transgression, exposure, and expiation, reinstated, becomes national cult. If it is true that bodies go where words cannot, it is also true that where bodies have been, words will follow. Transgression, built into the civic repertoire, becomes a condition of civic self-speaking. As only one of many instances of the recurring American mania for political correcting—if not correctness—Salem remains emblematic of how the awe-ful and the terrible connive with political order and religious memory at particular historical points. In the end, someone dies—silenced, consumed, purged—a pattern, not surprisingly, now ritualized in civic practices and media representations. For this reason, Salem remains an inassimilable *exemplum* in the discourse. Its burden is unredeemable, inarticulateable. No wonder its memory causes us to wince. It *is* monstrous. Indeed, the rite of displaying burning crosses indicates that Salem is never distant from the presumptively Christian center of cultural valuation. The narratives of exclusion in the name of a surely savage God, and the anxiety of being this deity's "specially chosen people," continue to sound from pulpit, presidential speech, Gothic text. They span genres and years, echoing most recently from the media-spawned (though no less tragic for that) apocalypse in Waco, Texas.

To end where we began. The charge of witch-craft in the Massachusetts Code represented a specific civil violation, a rending of the social fabric. Yet it is clear that for all the display of civic energy and rhetoric in repudiation, "entertaining Satan" was a weaving *together* of the fabric, a construction of the body politic on the dismembered bodies of its victims. Salem's almost immediate representation as ideology, memory, and as voyeuristic entertainment reflects upon a ghostly past. Once originally holy ghosts have turned upon themselves, becoming unholy, demonic reminders of a religious discourse so imbedded in social forms that laws had to be enacted to separate it out. But the presence of religion could not legally be unwritten or obscured; its force is nonetheless strongly felt in its absence, just as the argument for prayer in schools remains often louder than the prayers themselves. Finally, in the flaming cross symbolic of at least one normative American political ritual, we can see the final commodification of Christianity. As the metaphor of Jesus seems to give warrant, suffering has been divinized, victim has become God. Salem shows us how, and, partly why, there will always be a victim in American social polity. While Weisman argues that "secular and ecclesiastical concerns were synthesized in the social regulation of witchcraft" (p. 10), so, too, were less tangible concerns of the imagination. Thus it is that dismembering is a remembering, after all—a schizoid process of rending/mending continued through consumer-based machineries of terror. The great silenced text of religious discourse, a society's grammar of worship, continues to speak, principally in this late-capitalistic society's theological repudiations. So there is no little irony in the fact that Jonathan Edwards anticipates both a market for terror and its motive. Edwards, Master of the Divine, also fathered the Perverse, and it is to him that we turn.

N O T E S

1. David D. Hall, *The Antinomian Controversy, 1636–1638* (Middletown, CT: Wesleyan University Press, 1968), p. 313.
2. G. L. Burr, "New England's Place in the History of Witchcraft," p. 192, cited in Richard Weisman, *Witchcraft, Magic and Religion in Seventeenth-Century Massachusetts* (Amherst: University of Massachusetts Press, 1984), p. 7.
3. Cited in Thomas Pribek, "Witchcraft in 'Lady Eleanor's Mantle,' " *Studies in American Fiction*, vol. 15, no. 1, Spring 1987: 95–100, p. 98. The other two "shames" were the persecution of the Quakers in the mid-seventeenth century and the campaign for smallpox inoculation early in the eighteenth.
4. "Antinomianism in its root sense means 'against or opposed to the law.' In theology it is the opinion that 'the moral law is not binding upon Christians, who are under the law of grace.' " David D. Hall explains that the significance of the events surrounding Anne Hutchinson was "plain." It was, he writes, "a struggle for control of Massachusetts, and when control was assured the victors showed little mercy to the vanquished." See Hall, *The Antinomian Controversy*, op. cit., p. 3.
5. In *Discipline and Punish: The Birth of the Prison* (New York: Random House, 1979), trans. Alan Sheridan, Foucault argues that one ought not study "punitive mechanisms" and their "punishment" aspects; that one ought to regard "punishment as a complex social function . . . as a political tactic . . ." (pp. 23–24).
6. The connection between the *articulation* of the soul—theology—and the description of the *polis*—politics—thus makes itself still heard. See, for example, Sacvan Bercovitch, *The Puritan Origins of the American Self*, op. cit.; and Garry Wills, *Under God: Religion and American Politics* (New York: Simon and Schuster, 1990); also, more recently, Harold Bloom, *The American Religion: The Emergence*

of the Post-Christian Nation (New York: Simon and Schuster, 1992). Other interesting, although dated, studies include *An Almost Chosen People: The Moral Aspirations of Americans*, Walter Nicgorski and Ronald Weber, eds. (Notre Dame: University of Notre Dame Press, 1976); and *The Broken Covenant: American Civil Religion in Time of Trial*, Robert N. Bellah (New York: Seabury Press, 1975). See Bellah's recent *Habits of the Heart: Individualism and Commitment in American Life* (Berkeley: University of California Press, 1985).

7. For background on the contest of authority and power that centered on Anne Hutchinson's self-declared (though civilly presumptive) ability to read the Scriptures, see Stout, *The New England Soul*, pp. 24–27, Heimert, *The Puritans in America*, pp. 149–63, and Miller, *Errand into the Wilderness*, esp. "The Puritan State and Puritan Society," pp. 141–52. Her particular relevance to the issues discussed in this chapter David Hall makes clear in *Witch-Hunting in Seventeenth-Century New England*: "It is possible to interpret witch-hunting as a means of reaffirming this authority ["legal, political, ideological, and economic"] at a time when some women (like the charismatic spiritual leader Anne Hutchinson) were testing these constraints . . ." (p. 7). Carol F. Karlsen argues similarly in *The Devil in the Shape of a Woman: Witchcraft in Colonial New England* (New York: Random House, 1987), pp. 14–19. The ironies of the Hutchinson affairs are many; one in particular I will note here. Though essentially accused of relying upon the "immediate voice" of the spirit (Heimert, p. 160) rather than upon the authoritative voice of the ministry for her understanding of Scripture, in the end, as Deputy Governor Dudley complained, Hutchinson's "*Repentance* is in a paper" but "not in her countenance" (Heimert, p. 156).

8. In *Wayward Puritans: A Study in the Sociology of Deviance* (New York: Wiley, 1966), Kai Erickson argues that witchcraft fulfills a crucial social function: it is, he says, a ritual by which a society oversees the "creation of social meanings" (p. 10) — specifically the exclusionary politics encoded around social deviancy. Richard Weisman likewise concurs. See below. As D. H. Lawrence observes in *Studies in Classic American Literature*, America has been "the land of *Thou shalt not*" (p. 5). Thus, the trials served as a socialized rhythm by which a community defines the parameters of the acceptable: the limits, that is, of "thou shall." In *Entertaining Satan: Witchcraft and the Culture of Early New England* (Oxford: Oxford University Press, 1982), John Demos writes, "Witchcraft beliefs (and accusations) are thought to perform functions, confer advantages, impart strength and resiliency to the social fabric as a whole. . . . Hence witchcraft is an aspect of 'social control,' and its effects are profoundly 'conservative' (p. 277).

    For a discussion of the Puritan-Quaker sectarian hostility and its relation to the witch hunts, see Christine Leigh Heyrman, "Specters of Subversion, Societies of Friends: Dissent and the Devil in Provincial Essex County, Massachusetts" in *Saints and Revolutionaries, op. cit.*, pp. 38–74.

9. In "Jonathan Edwards as Great Man: Identity, Conversion, and Leadership in the Great Awakening," Richard Bushman draws a portrait of this same society some years later: "The whole society suffered from a painful confusion of identity. People were taught to work at their earthly callings and to seek

wealth; but one's business had to remain subservient to religion and to function within the bounds of seventeenth-century institutions. The opportunities constantly tempted people to overstep both boundaries, thereby evoking the wrath of the powerful men who ruled society. Even relations with neighbors deteriorated as expansion multiplied the occasions for hard feelings," *Soundings*, vol. 52, Spring 1969: 15–46, p. 40.

10. See Michael Clark, "Witches and Wall Street: Possession Is Nine-Tenths of the Law," in *Herman Melville's Billy Budd, "Benito Cereno," "Bartleby the Scrivener," and Other Tales*, Harold Bloom, ed., *op. cit*. Clark argues that in the witchcraft trials "authority performs the same hermeneutic function that interpretation performs for Mather. In the trials that knowledge ["right interpretation" of often contradictory evidence] was constituted not by providence, but by power, the very channels of social hierarchy through which evidence emerged" (p. 133). In *Witch-Hunting in Seventeenth-Century New England: A Documentary History, 1638–1692* (Boston: Northeastern University Press, 1991), David D. Hall similarly observes that "Witch-hunting was thus a process of interpretation that began at the village level before moving to the courts" (p. 10).

11. In "European Witch Craze," Hugh Trevor-Roper argues that witch hunting was a "social movement" that could be extended "deliberately, in times of political crisis, as a political device, to destroy powerful enemies or dangerous persons" (*The European Witch-Craze of the Sixteenth and Seventeenth Centuries and Other Essays* [New York: Harper and Row, 1969], p. 189). He continues: "At best, the myth might be contained as in the early sixteenth century. But it did not evaporate: it remained at the bottom of society, like a stagnant pool, easily flooded, easily stirred." (p. 191)

12. See also Richard Weisman, *Witchcraft, Magic, and Religion in Seventeenth-Century Massachusetts* (Amherst: University of Massachusetts Press, 1984). Like Kai Erikson's *Wayward Puritans*, Weisman organizes his study around the study of deviance and the creation of social meanings—see his introductory chapter, esp. pp. 2–3, pp. 10–11.

13. For a provocative discussion of the Body-as-Text see Robert Detweiler, *Breaking the Fall: Religious Readings of Contemporary Fiction* (San Francisco: Harper and Row, 1987), esp. "Sacred Texts/Sacred Space," pp. 122–58.

14. The congregation at Salem, gathered in 1629, was literally emblematic of the religious ordering; its gathering formula served as the prototype of later church covenants.

15. Mather comments on the ambiguities he faced: "If the *Evil One* have obtained a permission to *Appear*, in the Figure of such as we have cause to think, have hitherto *Abstained*, even from the *Appearance of Evil:* It is in Truth, such an Invasion upon *Mankind*, as may wee Raise an Horror in us all" (*Wonders*, p. 101).

16. In *Entertaining Satan*, Demos writes, "the *qualities* of witchcraft are at the heart of the story. In one broad aspect they are everywhere similar: they express a tendency to 'project,' to 'scapegoat,' to extrude and expel that which individuals (or groups) define as bad. . . . Diversity is the rule in the fantasies, the generative circumstances, the contingent values, the interper-

sonal structures—which support and reflect any given 'system' of witchcraft belief" (p. 13).

17. Benjamin Harris's note, "The Bookseller to the Reader," deserves to be reprinted in full: "The ensuing narrative being, a collection of some remarkables, in an affair now upon the stage, made by a credible eyewitness, is now offered unto the reader, only as a taste, of more that may follow in God's time. If the prayers of good people may obtain this favor of God, that the mysterious assaults from hell now made upon so many of our friends may be thoroughly detected and defeated, we suppose the curious will be entertained with as rare a history as perhaps an age has had; whereof this narrative is but a forerunner" (Hall, *Witch-Hunting in Seventeenth-Century New England,* p. 282).

18. It is important also to note that the charge of witchcraft offered power and individuality to witch and victim alike—who found themselves, accused and accuser, for the first time the center of public attention and control. As Keith Thomas explains in *Religion and the Decline of Magic, op. cit.,* witches "were the persons whose position in society was ambiguous or insecure" (pp. 168–69).

19. For examples of the language see Hall, *Witch-Hunting in Seventeenth-Century New England*: "thou art indicted by the name of John Carrington of Wethersfield carpenter, that not having the fear of God before thine eyes thou has entertained familiarity with Satan the great enemy of God and mankind and by his help hast done works about the course of nature for which both according to the law of God and of the established law of this commonwealth thou deservest to die" (p. 27); "Elizabeth Seager thou art here indicted . . . for not having the fear of God before thine eyes thou hast entertained familiarity with Satan the grand enemy of God and mankind, and by his help hast acted things in a preternatural way beyond the ordinary course of nature, as also for that thou has committed adultery, and hast spoken blasphemy against God, contrary to the laws of God, and the established laws of this corporation for all or any of which crimes by the said laws though deservest to die" (p. 139).

20. For background of the relationship of "social change" to "declining ministerial status" see Stout, *The New England Soul,* pp. 19, 76ff.

21. Hugh Trevor-Roper, "The European Witch-Craze of the Sixteenth and Seventeenth Centuries," p. 115.

22. See Daniel Hoffman, *Form and Fable in American Fiction* (New York: Oxford University Press, 1965), for an extensive study of Hawthorne. Also Michael Colacurcio, "In the Footsteps of Anne Hutchinson: The Context of *The Scarlet Letter,*" *ELH,* vol. 39, 1972: 459–94; Gabriele Schwab, "Seduced by Witches: Nathaniel Hawthorne's *The Scarlet Letter* in the Context of New England Witchcraft Fictions," in *Seduction and Theory: Readings of Gender, Representation, and Rhetoric,* Dianne Hunter, ed. (Urbana: University of Illinois Press, 1989); Mary E. Rucker, "The Art of Witchcraft in Hawthorne's "Feathertop: A Moralized Legend," *Studies in Short Fiction,* vol. 24, no. 1, Winter 1987: 31.

23. Of course, Herman Melville is at least as obsessed as Hawthorne with the subject. I cited earlier his (possible) reading of Cotton Mather. More directly,

in "The Apple-Tree Table," Melville critiques the "credulous and all-too-credible" Mather. See Levin, *The Power of Blackness: Hawthorne, Poe, Melville* (New York: Knopf, 1964), p. 14. Michael Clark speculates that the narrator of Melville's "The Lightning-Rod Man" parodies Mather's language in *Magnalia Christi Americana* (republished 1853). See Clark, "Witches and Wall-Street," p. 135.

24. Nathaniel Hawthorne, *The Scarlet Letter*, Bradley, Beatty, Long, eds. (New York: W.W. Norton & Co., 1961), p. 10.

25. Sewall is cited in Miller, *American Puritans*, p. 242.

26. See Michael Colacurcio, "In the Footsteps of Anne Hutchinson: The Context of *The Scarlet Letter,*" *op. cit.*

27. Philip Gura argues that the argument between literal and symbolic readings of the Bible, though exhausted as a theological topic by Hawthorne's generation, nevertheless persisted as "a topic of public anxiety." For this reason, as Clark explains, Gura attributes the prominence of Hawthorne and Melville as "practitioners of the symbolic mode" to their ability "to translate the widespread concern over the crisis in religious language and doctrine into the realm of imaginative fiction" (Gura cited in Clark, p. 136).

28. In *Studies in Classic American Literature,* Lawrence describes *The Scarlet Letter* as "a sort of parable, an earthly story with a hellish meaning" (p. 83).

29. In *My Grandfather's Chair,* Hawthorne remarks about the smallpox epidemic of 1720 and shows the social consequences of the Salem allegory, for such it was, as much as Hester's letter A: "Nobody could be certain that his nearest neighbor, or most intimate friend, was not guilty of this imaginary crime" (*Centenary Edition,* Ohio State, vol. 6: 78).

30. Perry Miller, *The New England Mind: From Colony to Province* (Boston: Belknap Press, 1961).

31. As a matter of statistics, the incidents of witchcraft in New England were abnormally high, Demos argues (234 indictments or complaints filed, and 36 executed persons). The panic in Salem of 1692 to 93 was the highest concentration (19 persons executed), after which, effectively, the witch craze *in itself* died out. See Demos, *Entertaining Satan,* pp. 10–13, and his "Appendix: List of Known Witchcraft Cases in Seventeenth-Century New England" (pp. 401–09). See also Carol F. Karlsen, *The Devil in the Shape of a Woman: Witchcraft in Colonial New England, 1620–99, op. cit.,* chapter 2 and "Appendix 5: Witches Accused in New England, 1620–99."

32. Eugenia C. DeLamotte, in *Perils of the Night: A Feminist Study of Nineteenth-Century Gothic* (New York: Oxford University Press, 1990), argues, further, that Hawthorne, and Brockden Brown "wanted, at least in some sense, to use the Gothicists' techniques, if not all of their materials . . ." (pp. 7–8).

33. See, for example, "Home Repairs: Parents, Work and the Durability of the Family," by Ann Hulbert, *The New Republic,* 16 August 1993, pp. 26–32.

34. In "Alice Doane's Appeal," Hawthorne examines critically the narrative functions of nostalgia, as history and fiction are placed directly, it must be said, into the service of [emotional] seduction. The narrator, at the site of the witch executions, reads a "wondrous tale of those old times" (p. 207) by

which he hopes to elicit the "well-spring" of his two female companions. There, on the now pastoral Gallows Hill, the narrator makes "a trial whether truth were more powerful than fiction" (p. 215). In the end, it is the narrator's imaginative reconstruction of the real scene of Gallows Hill that moves his companions. *Nathaniel Hawthorne: Tales* (New York: Library of America, 1982).

35. John Wesley, *Journal,* Nehemiah Curnock, ed. (London: Epworth, 1914), V, p. 265.

36. For additional background information on King and his first novel, see David Skal, *The Monster Show: A Cultural History of Horror* (New York: W. W. Norton & Co., 1993). Skal writes, "Although Ronald Reagan was widely touted as the Great Communicator . . . the title more fairly belongs to the novelist Stephen King, who, in numbers and dollars, emerged as the most successful storyteller in human history" (p. 354).

37. King's other four novels were subsequently published under the pseudonym of Richard Bachman. See Bill Thompson, "A Girl Named Carrie," in *Kingdom of Fear: The World of Stephen King*, pp. 29–34. See also King, *Danse Macabre, op. cit.*, p. 372.

38. See Harry Levin, *The Power of Blackness, op. cit.*

39. Margaret White is, like Carrie, portrayed animalistically, like her, too, though for different reasons, always on the far edge of control: she "makes a noise a bull alligator would make" (p. 31); her face is "a gargoyle's face" (p. 31); she bays at the sky; she squats "like a frog" (p. 32).

40. Marion Starkey, in *The Devil in Massachusetts: A Modern Enquiry into the Salem Witch Trials* (New York: Knopf, 1949), comments that Mather's text "had two conspicuous defects: its omissions and its tone." See pp. 238–40.

41. Mary Douglas, *Natural Symbols: Explorations in Cosmology* (New York: Random House, 1970), p. 113.

42. See Peter Stallybrass and Allon White, *The Politics and Poetics of Transgression* (London: Methuen, 1986): The "commonplace" is what is "most radically unthinkable" (p. 27) because, in some senses, it is too close, transgressed so often.

43. Lloyd Rose writes, "[King's] characters live in the worst possible moral universe: you're punished if you do wrong and you suffer if you're innocent. It's like the world of a child with crazy parents—whatever you do, they'll beat you, and you'll never know why. The confusion and rage at the center of this view of the world have a primal power that has nothing to do with King's hokey plots and monsters and that, boiling under them, gives them disturbing heat." "The Triumph of the Nerds," *The Atlantic*, September 1986, p. 103.

44. *Implicit Meanings: Essays in Anthropology* (London: Routledge & Kegan Paul, 1975), p. xv. Bryan Wilson makes the point that in a sectarian society "worship of God is worship of the community" (cited in Douglas, *Natural Symbols*, p. 115).

45. René Girard, *Violence and the Sacred*, cited in introduction, *The Morality of Terrorism*, David C. Rapoport and Yonah Alexander, eds., *op. cit.*, p. 9.

46. For a discussion of New England and ritualism, see *Worlds of Wonder, Days of Judgment: Popular Religious Belief in Early New England*, David D. Hall, *op. cit.*,

especially chapter 4, pp. 166–212. See also Demos, *Entertaining Satan*, who argues, finally, that the religion of New England had much to do with the events at Salem: "The case can be overstated, and sometimes is, but in this respect the Puritans deserve the reputation that history has given them. Simply put: their religious experience was distinctive in its intensity—and in some qualitative aspects as well. They regarded themselves as participants in a cosmic struggle between the forces of God and of Satan for control of the universe. History was, by their lights, a theater of unceasing warfare—grand in scale, terrifying in character, and fraught with the gravest consequences for all concerned" (p. 310).

CHAPTER THREE

Writing the Unholy: Chanting the God Demonic

... all that preserves them every moment is the mere arbitrary will, and uncovenanted, unobliged forbearance of an incensed God.
—EDWARDS, "SINNERS"[1]

The principal appeal of the high Gothic lies in its epistemology and moral ambiguity. It makes us think: How much do we know about reality, about life and death, about the universe and God, about human personality and motivation, and about the course of our own destiny?[2]

... The Scripture is written as we are told, For our Comfort; *but it is quoted by the Devil,* for our Terror.
—MATHER, WONDERS

———— ■ ————

Introduction

... more horrid even from the very resemblance ...
—THE CREATURE TO VICTOR FRANKENSTEIN

Previously I have tried to show how the rhetoric of divinity signifies the outer reach of the human, and that divinity itself was impermissible *in* history except as *monstrum*. Its eruption in the mundane order was a complex and dark moment—a judgment upon the community, usually portending change and conversion. Still, if the manifestations of the Divine were problematic, its language was even more so.[3] We have seen how, at Salem, theological discourse converged with political usage. Jonathan Edwards begins most directly to evidence another alliance, this time the uneasy one between the twinned discourses of theology and fantasy, a blending of the Sublime and the Terrible which will in time consolidate a *mode* of dark fantasy—the genre of terroristic texts loosely termed "American Gothic."[4] A colonial practice of apocalypse, with its conventional language of ecstatic eschatology, eventually prompted, and even facilitated, its opposition: a fertile discourse of fantasy.[5] Theological speech is of course a paradox, a "speak[ing] about the enigma of that which cannot be spoken." By a process of imaginative entropy, theology—the study of ultimates—participated in and even encouraged its ultimate subversion, as first the threat of heresy and then the use of fantasy nudged the Holy one step closer to its impermissible kin, the grotesque (but moralistic) Horrible. Edwards, Master of the Divine, was also a Master of the Perverse. As his biographer put it, Jonathan Edwards made Hell "real enough to be found in the atlas"; in addition he "made those consigned to it personally responsible for being there" (Winslow, 193).[6]

Writing the Unholy

Men need to be terrified and have the arrows of the Almighty in them that they may be Converted.

—SOLOMON STODDARD, *THE DEFECTS OF PREACHERS REPROVED*, P. 14[7]

In my final chapter I intend to discuss in more detail similarities between Gothic and theological discourse. However, it might be helpful at this point to make some preliminary remarks about the term "Gothic" as it used in literary discourse, and to show its usefulness in discussing the practical theologies of Jonathan Edwards. G. R. Thompson suggests that the "Gothic quest is, finally, 'metaphysical' rather than 'religious' " (p. 10). As we have seen, from Winthrop through Wigglesworth and Mather, the issue for at least one school of American theology seems to be cosmological rather than specifically religious in origin. That is, theological language—relations with the cosmos, if you will—often disguised a tangled web of socialized restraints and imperatives that were by definition cultural and aesthetic. Definitions of the Gothic are many, though there is general agreement that the Gothic "signals an immediate attention to terror and fear" (Green, *The Language of Nightmare*, pp. 1–2). Punter observes that the Gothic "has, above all, to do with terror" (*The Literature of Terror*, p. 14), and that "how and why this is the case" needs to be questioned. He further argues that its "central dialectic is a continuous oscillation between reassurance and threat" (p. 423).

So, while Gothicism is usually associated with poorly written formulaic novels, with castles and dungeons and other *arcana*, these are the least important aspects of the genre. In "Gothic Versus Romantic: A Revaluation of the Gothic Novel," Robert D. Hume writes that the crucial "characteristic of the Gothic novel is not its devices, but its *atmosphere* . . . of evil and *brooding terror*" [my emphasis]. Joel Porte, in "In the Hands of an Angry God: Religious Terror in Gothic Fiction," argues, further, that Gothic terror "is usually at bottom theological . . ." (p. 45).[8] This is why, he says, a conventional Gothic setting is "attenuated or eliminated" in the "American school generally" because,

> the atmosphere of psychological or theological distress has become so pervasive and profound that it scarcely needs to be reinforced by the overt presence of a ruined abbey; like the pestilence, it can be tasted in the surrounding air itself (Porte, p. 45).

I agree; although Gothic texts—the tales of nightmares walking abroad by day in their endless revenants and deformed varieties—can be dismissed as an antiquarian's bad dream, still, they ought not to be tossed aside as literary aberrations. To Gothic, and gothicized, texts are committed matters of ultimate, even grave cultural concern (if I may be permitted the pun). How best to scare the Hell out of a community—as the contentious history of theologies suggest—than by telling the tales of God?

Gods and the cultures they reflect are indissolubly linked—particularly, as we have seen, in the particular practices of religious ritual. We have discussed how the ritualization of scrutiny, transgression, and expiation in civic forms, for instance, provides badly needed metaphysical buttressing to a social order while at the same time lending authority to its civic practices. I will later have occasion to cite Porte again; for the moment I wish to consider his cogent observation that "theological distress" is, in "the American school generally," "pervasive and profound" (p. 45). There are at least two reasons for this, as I have been suggesting. First, theological distress is so pervasive because this religiously based culture, struggling for self-possession and identity, inscribed its theologies into the minutest aspect of daily life. The gradual declension of American theological discourse into its darker negation began in the task colonial ministers and magistrates set themselves. Desiring to speak the Holy in society, they defined that society in terms of a grammar of the Holy. Reading the Divine into the very flesh of the community, as it were, in turn produced the paradox of Salem—exposure of the witch was necessary to confirm the revelation of the Divine. Secondly, so intertwined were social and political narratives in New England that the rituals and theological anxieties of the first generation had become questions of civil polity, even social mythology, by the second and third generations. As Victor Sage observes, in its "social and political aspects" Protestantism is "notoriously hydra-headed" (*Horror Fiction*, p. xiii). Whatever religious practice and ideology might have once signified soon became allegorized, either as history (in Matherian nationalistic fantasies), or as fantasy in a theologically based cosmic determinism (particularly by Poe, Twain, and Lovecraft).

The original Puritan settlements in the New World could be seen as an effort to clarify through actions what had remained dogmatically contentious and politically murky—that is, the Great Migration was to provide the practical answer to the nature of human relations with the Divine. Abstract and theological issues of holiness remained yet to be tested in the *praxis* of politics: to what extent is the individual soul public property? Recall that John Winthrop urged Anne Hutchinson to "keep" her own conscience lest it "be kept" for her. Hutchinson, of course, understood the contradictory language; she knew that by "keep" Winthrop meant rather that she should "give away" her conscience—that is, conform it to the magistrates' civil sense of things. This she would not do. Jonathan

Edwards faced similar problematic questions. For example, to what extent is language of the soul public speech? Indeed, can the soul be spoken at all? Further, beyond these questions lay even more troubling ones. How, indeed, do words contain the wordless? How does grammar express the ineffable? To what extent is language—the corrupt instrument of corrupt men—capable of speaking the Divine, given its "dangerous capacity for misrepresentation, inadequate description, and rhetorical deception"?[9]

In *The Language of Nightmare,* Gary Green suggests that Puritan historiography "creat[ed] a rhetoric of avoidance of the actual in favor of that of potential." This rhetoric, says Green, "introduced the power of the rhetorical negative to the American sensibility, a power which could and would have ambiguous consequences" (p. 58). Yet the power of the negative all along had been a major buttress of the Holy. Scholastic theologies had matter of factly, if somewhat confusingly, described the Deity as the "negation of imperfection"; and early in the tradition it had become clear that the Holy could not be expressed in language at all except by way of negation: as absence, as ineffable—or by contrast and inversion, as demonic.[10] In New England something of the same sort seemed to happen, as the daily sermons, broadsides, and theologies of the early divines declined more and more to the excoriation of human frailty rather than inclining toward divine sublimity. In the end, Original Sin and its woeful effects, dwelt on at length, served to obscure original grace. Consider some of the titles of Edwards's sermons: "The Eternity of Hell Torments"; "When the Wicked Shall Have Filled Up the Measure of Their Sin"; "The End of the Wicked Contemplated by the Righteous"; "The Future Punishment of the Wicked Unavoidable and Intolerable"; "The Justice of God in the Damnation of Sinners"; "Wrath Upon the Wicked to the Uttermost." This slippage from the sublimities of Heaven to the grotesqueries of Hell presented a curious state of affairs. If, after all, the point of religious discourse was to meditate upon God's perfections, why then spend so much time hectoring the instability of the Self? Yet even Calvin understood that the very act of religious reflection was somehow a participation in Original Sin, and that consequently all spiritual speech was to some extent transgressive. Michael Wigglesworth makes the point in "The Day of Doom" (1662):

That tongues of men (nor angels' pen)
cannot the same express,
And therefore I must pass it by,
lest speaking should transgress.

(MILLER *AMERICAN PURITANS*, P. 286)[11]

Puritan texts reflect the frustration they experienced trying to wrestle the protean Holy to the ground, as it were: "Permanent self-doubt was built into the system," says David Levin, and the legal codes and theologies of the community likewise reflect this difficulty of expression.[12] Yet as we have seen, the problem of spiritual entropy was not merely human inadequacy. The problem with divinity, then—and the prospects for human holiness—is partly hinted at in the circumlocutions used, if not to deny or unspeak the divinity, then at least to control it in discourse. The Divine, in a quite literal sense, is anomalous, even above the law; it is ineffable, unnameable, unspeakable. At the very least then, divinity remains unsympathetic to the constraints of grammar and certainly unsympathetic to any legal governance of the heart. In an extreme articulation of this position, Karl Barth argued that the deity exists beyond and outside of human history as *totaliter aliter*—a position not unlike Edwards's own.

Since language itself was a fallen instrument, it often twisted back upon itself, with foreseeable results: the very attempt to write the Holy pointed not to God's perfections, nor to the fragile Self, but to the instability of discourse and the frailty of language. Of all horrors attending the spiritual project, this *last* was the most horrible. It was one thing to have the society at large and the private Self threatened by human frailty and spiritual entropy. It was quite something else to realize, as Edwards did, that while the language of the Holy provided a *boundary* site at which one could invoke the ineffable God, language could not do more than that. Indeed, at that paradoxical intersection of speaking and unspeaking the Divine also suffered a kind of sympathetic declension, transgressing the boundary of sense, and slipping into its demonic opposite. Edwards's preaching would be a case in point; the more fervent the attempts to articulate and express the Holy, the more thoroughly the Divine converted into the unspeakable demonic.[13] Further, the example of the mystics attests that the Divine reveals itself as *negativa*; and that such an experience can only be described in *figura*—that is, in the collapse of sensible language. In summary, then, the Divine could only be spoken obliquely in one of two ways, by negation or by metaphor. Language moves toward its ultimate confusion in two directions—at the limit set by propriety and convention, and at the limits of grammar itself. Propriety governed what *might* be permitted; grammar what *could* be spoken. At either of these limits the text collapses in upon itself, like the individual self at the limits of speech, undergoing a kind of annihilation. At this limit, in effect, waited the Divine.[14]

This last point would be crucial to New England's experience of spirituality. In addition to the many variables inherent in writing the Holy—the fragile Self, the failure of language, and the inexpressible experience of the Divine—one other factor needs to be considered. New England politics added a twist to its practice of divinity, as the Antinomian crisis and the later Quaker controversy made evident. Expression of the Divine was evidently a matter of legality as well as holiness; a matter, really, of license, in all its meanings, as moral speech. Winthrop had observed long ago that the "care of the public must oversway all private respects, by which not only conscience but mere civil policy doth bind us" (p. 89). In effect, this meant New England had to construct a discourse to contain that which could be neither grammatically circumscribed nor legally expressed. They sought a language with dominion over the grammars of the soul as well as one that would control its expression in public. No wonder, then, that the errand into the wilderness seemed doomed before it began. The New Israel the Puritans might well be, their tent pitched in a New English Canaan, as Thomas Morton termed it. However, the direct address of the deity formerly enjoyed by the Israelites seemed not to be part of the inheritance.

Jonathan Edwards's "Strange Crew"

> *'Tis a reasonable thing to fright a person out of an house on fire.*
> —*DISTINGUISHING MARKS*, P. 248

In "The Day of Doom," Wigglesworth recognized the potential of imaginative language to scare the Hell out of slip-sliding believers. Nonetheless, Wigglesworth was minor leagues compared to Jonathan Edwards, who set himself the task of seriously imagining the awfulness of the awe-ful. One might say that Edwards was the first to stare unblinking into God's darker face and return to write about it.[15] Singlehandedly, writing out of the wilds of western Massachusetts, Edwards attempted to do for theology what Robert Frost said Edward Arlington Robinson had done for poetry. That is, he tried to find the "old-fashioned way to be new" (*Selected Prose of Robert Frost,* p. 60). For Edwards this meant shaping a theological tradition consistent with Calvin, but one that would also be appropriate to the new world of the American spiritual experience. In particular, Edwards's sermons and private papers provide a fascinating example of how theology produces its ap[parent] opposite, the Unholy. Although, as the word suggests, does the process work in reverse? Edwards's enthusiasm for the "awful sweetness" of divinity shows how the rhetoric of Divine Love, in its linguistic excess, seems by its very nature to encourage a transgression of boundaries by which the rhetoric of love creates a parallel rhetoric of terror.[16] So as a result, when Joseph Campbell wished to consider the "ogre aspect of the Father" as figured in various mythologies, it is to Edwards he turns as example.[17] Whitman makes much the same point in "Chanting the Square Deific," and he certainly would understand. Does fantasy produce theology after all?

In his own implacable way Jonathan Edwards was a man possessed by words and their implications, though whether possessed angelically or demoniacally, his critics could not agree. Wayne Lesser writes that any assessment of Edwards's "spiritual belief and practice must recognize" that his life was as "much a life verbalized as spiritualized" (p. 287).[18] A "textuary in an age of textuaries" (Kimnach, "Jonathan Edwards's Pursuit of Reality," p. 112), Edwards nonetheless found language and words to be philosophically troubling and not always reliable instruments[19]:

> Language is indeed very deficient, in regard of terms to express precise truth concerning our own minds, and their faculties and operations. Words were first formed to express external things; and those that are applied to express things internal and spiritual, are almost all borrowed, and used in a sort of figurative sense. . . . But

language is much less adapted to express things in the mind of the incomprehensible Deity, precisely as they are.[20]

While language might be the "occasional" cause of grace, nonetheless it was not the "efficient" cause. All the words in the world would not provoke a hearer into a change of heart; sermons alone could not move to conversion. Only God's grace could do that. This realization, of course, did not stop Edwards from figuring away in sermon after sermon. If the word as a sign is dead, Edwards said, "we are put to the trouble of exciting the actual idea and making it as lively and as clear as we can."[21] But while God might be illimitable, the resources of language used to describe him are not. Edwards pushed language to its reasonable limits, with an occasionally unexpected result. Not only did its objects become "lively" and "clear," they also became unspeakable in polite society, as Oliver Wendell Holmes would later note with some heat. Edwards's theology, Holmes said, was rooted in "the deepest depths of hell."[22] Holmes notes, in particular, the "plans and machinery of his 'Inferno' " (p. 384) and his "Dante-like descriptions" (p. 386); he charges that Edwards's language "shocks the sensibilities of a later generation" (p. 384).

Edwards was born into a preacher's family, the son of two generations of Protestant ministers. The Word was in the blood, and Edwards spent his life working it out. His father and grandfather would have presented him with two differing visions of religious boundaries. His grandfather, Solomon Stoddard, was famous for his theological flexibility, while his father, Timothy Edwards, was a rigorous preacher whose psychological effect on Jonathan was perhaps less liberating. Ola Winslow, Edwards's biographer, suggests that "instead of quieting childish fears," Timothy Edwards "raised them, as though parental guidance consisted in advance notice of potential disaster" (*Jonathan Edwards*, p. 43). About this passage, Richard Bushman comments that the father's anxieties would have "reinforced in the children the ordinary apprehensions of violent destruction" ("Jonathan Edwards as Great Man," p. 22). Perhaps, then, along with the more traditional virtues of theological rectitude, at home Edwards learned the values of melodrama.

Later, as a student at the newly founded Yale, Edwards was

exposed to the quickening religious sensibilities of the culture around him. He became caught up in a popular anxiety of religious emotionalism that by Edwards's time had rigorously formalized spiritual experiences into a "morphology of conversion." For this reason, Edwards would have been concerned both about the appropriateness of his inner religious experience as well as its conventional or outward "form." In "Personal Narrative," Edwards offers a retrospective description—as well as covert evaluation—of the spiritual movements leading to his conversion. The first sentence of the "Narrative" reflects Edwards's eagerness to fulfill the expectations of conventional calls to grace: "I had a variety of concerns and exercises about my soul from my childhood; but had two more remarkable seasons of awakening, before I met with that change, by which I was brought to those new dispositions, and that new sense of things, that I have since had" (Levin, p. 24).[23] Edwards's version of the customary spiritual autobiography, is, like Mary Rowlandson's in this respect, personally effacing. It reads like a hymn to God's inscrutable and glorious intervention—but, thank you, an intervention that was nonetheless dramatically timely, at least as viewed in retrospect. Yet considered as spiritual autobiography, the "Personal Narrative" is also Edwards's apology for a conversion experience that in fact seems to have been neither typical nor conventional.

Like other spiritual diarists before him, throughout the "Personal Narrative" Edwards finds himself trapped between the conventional and the inexpressible. What he wishes to articulate, in effect, beggars description. Edwards repeatedly emphasizes that he knows not "how to express" (Levin, p. 27) what he feels, and that the Divine falls short of the sayable. So inexpressible is his subject that Edwards finds himself reduced to the conventional and bland, even limited to the formulaic. Thus he will resort to a sort of spiritual synesthesia, repeatedly characterizing his experience as "sweet" ("sweet" or its derivatives is used at least twenty times in the first few pages of the "Narrative"). Nonetheless, despite Edwards's self-advertised inabilities to speak, Wilson Kimnach argues that his "power of specification is one of his most prominent traits" ("Jonathan Edwards's Pursuit of Reality," p. 111). Although Edwards himself repeatedly insisted that he did not know "how to express" the truths that lay behind his words, nonetheless Edwards marshals the forces of rhetoric in his self-declared war against the inexpressible:

> My wickedness, as I am in my self, has long appear'd to me perfectly ineffable, and infinitely swallowing up all thought and imagination; like an infinite deluge, or infinite mountains over my head. I know not how to express better, what my Sins appear to me to be, than by heaping infinite upon infinite, and multiplying infinite by infinite (Levin, p. 37).[24]

In extremis, as it were, Edwards finds himself repeating words almost as an incantation, ritually hoping to conjure up an otherwise absent and recalcitrant spirit. In so doing, Edwards makes psychological and semantic links between the Holy and the Horrible: his wickedness is "ineffable"—like the Divine, one supposes. Further, Edwards confides that the "doctrine of God's sovereignty. . . . used to appear like a horrible doctrine . . ." (Levin, p. 25). However, a few lines later, Edwards reverses himself, saying that what he formerly objected to now seemed "an exceeding pleasant, bright and sweet doctrine" (Levin, p. 26). In expressions like "awful sweetness" or "majestic meekness and sovereignty of God" (Levin, p. 27), Edwards begins to float terror free of its didactic intent, placing it in the service of sensation.[25] His example would not be without consequences.

So, in pursuit of being lively and clear, the sheer psychic torque of Edwards's emotional range is noteworthy. Hyperbole—like metaphor, a bit of linguistic fantasy in disguise—forces Edwards to an awareness "of the barely thinkable" (Kimnach, "Reality," p. 114). His heart "looks like an abyss infinitely deeper than hell" (Levin, p. 37) while a few lines later he says, "I should appear sunk down in my sins infinitely below hell itself" (p. 37). The images Edwards uses are "barely thinkable" in more than one sense, and the "abyss" opened up would eventually almost swallow him. His metaphoric range is as muscular and as enthusiastic as Mather's, and, often, as explicitly erotic. Edwards registered in his sermons a depth of passion perhaps unequaled in other areas of his life. In the "Narrative," for instance, Edwards's recollections of the "ravishingly lovely" Holy prompt him to a rhetorical legerdemain uncharacteristic of his more analytical theological texts. In the space of one short paragraph, for instance, he replicates the experience of his religious culture, covering the spectrum from exaltation to abasement. First he ascends to the "ravishingly lovely"(p. 30), the "highest beauty and amiableness, above all other beauties . . . far purer than any thing here upon earth. . . ." And then he drops precipitously, noting that "everything else, was like mire, filth and defilement, in comparison of it" (p. 30).[26] Such pyrotechnics are, of course, not necessarily unusual, except that Edwards here employs them in pursuit of the Divine, which he himself indicated—perhaps as apology for his own wordiness— was "inexpressible." For a moment compare Edwards with the original "personal narrative" of the Christian tradition. Edwards's chattiness here contrasts with Saint Paul, who lapsed into silence rather than into metaphor when discussing his own moment of conversion. Or compare Edwards to a rather more secular mystic, Walt Whitman. When Whitman finds himself caught up in mystical transports, he, too, is momentarily without words:

> Backward I see in my own days where I sweated through fog with
>   linguists and contenders,
> I have no mockings or arguments, I witness and wait.[27]

Edwards's struggle to remain balanced between the conventional and the particular, between the formal and the grotesque, reflects a split between external appropriateness and internal necessity that establishes the general tenor of religious address from Winthrop onward. While accounting for some of the tension of the "Personal Narrative" and of "Sinners," this split also reflects a wider cultural opposition between the formalists of the spirit and those less concerned about such conventionalities— revivalists, for instance. Indeed, the debate between revivalists and formalists also reflects the enduring uncertainty about trafficking with the Divine, whose apprehension gave one good cause to be apprehensive, since to have a direct vision of the Divine was, by historical warrant, a tumultuous experience. Often it was culturally transgressive, even sometimes illegal. Ask the Quakers who tangled with the Divine in Massachusetts, and who did not live to tell about it.

Throughout Edwards, this tension between the public and the

private recurs. To what extent, indeed, is the language of the soul public discourse? To what extent is its grammar translatable into public forms? In the "Personal Narrative," Edwards describes his "pursuits after holiness" as "eager and violent" (p. 33). The incongruity of the two adjectives seems an important register to an underlying sense of disjunction, a "devout violence," as Peter Gay observes, that "marks all his work."[28] Edwards writes that his spiritual anxiety "has made me some times since to question, whether ever it issued in that which was saving" (Levin, p. 25). His private torment leaves a shadow upon the very public text, a document in which he attempts to speak what must remain, finally, unspeakable. In this gap, then, between the literal and the spiritual (or "figural") use of language, Edwards leaves open the possibility that theology might undergo a conversion of its own. Green explains that between these two uses of language a "gothic sensibility . . . emerges, one trapped in uncertainty of perception and its relation to knowledge, primarily a knowledge of self" (*The Language of Nightmare*, p. 20).

Consider one last—and, for Edwards, characteristic—example of this semantic fracture. In "Personal Narrative," Edwards writes that after perceiving the sublimity of the Divine, his heart "as it were, panted . . . to lie low before God, and in the dust; that I might be nothing, and that God might be all" (pp. 30–31). Edwards's image here is curious, animalistic, or even, as Edwards himself might say, "viperish." The image of abasement, of course, is all too typical, even conventional. But Edwards must have thought it *too* revealing because he subsequently backs away from its implications. Retreating from the horrific and inexpressible to the bland and sentimental, he concludes by mixing the metaphor with a moralistic biblicism: "that I might become as a little child" (p. 31). Surely the disjunction between the abasing imagery of lying low "in the dust," on the one hand, and the vulnerability of the "little child," on the other, is a poignant reminder of the polarizing imperatives of an Americanized theological imagination. Specifically, Edwards poises on the edge of the dark wilderness, fully realizing its potential for savagery and spiritual slippage. Yet it is precisely at *that* dark place that he suddenly recalls the helplessness of being a child—implicitly, an experience of being "in the hands of" someone else.[29]

"Sinners in the Hands": The Maze of Grace

"Refine/Thyselfe from thy Declentions. Tend thy line."
—EDWARD TAYLOR QUOTED IN HEIMERT, *THE PURITANS*, P. 275

Edwards's use of entrapment and captivity metaphors in his [in]famous Enfield sermon, "Sinners in the Hands of an Angry God," reflects his own entrapment in the American Christian discourse, which by 1740 had already undergone an internal conversion into a public speech of sentimentality, on the one hand, and grotesquery, on the other. We have seen that Edwards considered language itself a kind of primary entrapment—indeed, wasn't language the "supreme manifestation of original sin"?[30] But one senses that Edwards slipped into cliché or linguistic excess out of desperation rather than out of thoughtlessness, as he forced his language beyond "those things for which language was chiefly contrived."[31] Thus the problem of speaking what convention and propriety dictate as unspeakable resulted either in the formulaic use of abstractions "infinite upon infinite" or in an alternation between the blandly conventional ("sweet") to the (sometimes) grotesquely particular ("filth"). Despite the fact, as Daniel Shea observes, that "formulary expressions . . . were quickly emptied of meaning" (p. 30), Edwards uses words vigorously, hoping that one could in fact speak of the "awful majesty" yet "lovely" sovereignty of God (*Religious Affections*, p. 265).[32]

Edwards preached his "spider sermon" (as a recent biographer calls it) at Enfield, Connecticut, July 8, 1741.[33] And while Samuel Hopkins, Edwards's first biographer, did not deem the sermon worth mentioning, it is now the text by which Edwards is known, and misknown, best.[34] Captivity and release; being held and being dropped; a sense of slippage and imbalance—all are themes easily distinguished in "Sinners in the Hands of an Angry God." Edwards's "prelude" gives a foretaste of things to come: "Their foot shall slide in due time" (Deut. 32:35). Throughout the sermon one feels a vertiginous sense of failure and slippage. The ground is not steady; the bottom does not hold: "That the reason why they [sinners] are not fallen already, and do not fall now, is only that God's appointed time is not come" (*Works*, p. 451).[35] Throughout

"Sinners," Edwards will appeal to an almost visceral sense of precarious balance; he emphasizes a fear of falling as he works and reworks the metaphor of "defile," transforming its geographic significance into a moral allegory. In the third paragraph of the "Application," for instance, Edwards says "Your wickedness makes you as it were heavy as lead, and to tend downwards with great weight and pressure towards hell; and if God should let you go, you would immediately sink and swiftly descend and plunge into the bottomless gulf . . ." (*Works*, p. 456). The focus here "is on the predicament of the sinner, how dreadfully he dangles *just before* he plunges to eternal agony" (Cady, "The Artistry of Jonathan Edwards," p. 69). Further:

> O sinner! Consider the fearful danger you are in: it is a great furnace of wrath . . . that you are held over in the hand of that God, whose wrath is provoked and incensed as much against you, as against many of the damned in hell. You hang by a slender thread, with the flames of divine wrath flashing about it, and ready every moment to singe it, and burn it asunder; and you have no interest in any Mediator, and nothing to lay hold of to save yourself, nothing to keep off the flames of wrath, nothing of your own. . . (*Works*, p. 458).

Edwin Cady remarks that if "one had to guess the place where Edwards was forced to request silence from 'a breathing of distress, and weeping' as Eleazar Wheelock remembered, it would be here. . . " ("Artistry," p. 68).

Edwards seems to have come by his imagistic roughhousing naturally, or at least early, just as he probably made the connection between theology and transgression at his father's knee at home. For example, we find Edwards as a youth at Yale excoriating his classmates for their "monstrous impieties and acts of immorality."[36] This is an interesting example of Edwards's later habit, a rhetorical strategy of confusing, or at least entwining, the fantastically "monstrous" with the theologically conventional. Implicit connections linked them both in Edwards's understanding. For example, in another instance in which morality entangled with monstrosity, Edwards pillories the Roman church, likening it to a "viper or some loathsome, poisonous, crawling monster" (cited in Stein, *Apocalyptic Writings*, p. 11).[37] Edwards must have had a special fear of reptilian creatures, so often does he evoke them. Take this line, for instance: "You are ten thousand times more abominable in his eyes, than the most hateful venomous serpent is in ours" (*Works*, p. 458). In the most notorious passage of Edwards's famous sermon, the preacher intones: "The God that holds you over the pit of hell, much as one holds a spider or some loathsome insect over the fire, abhors you, and is dreadfully provoked: his wrath towards you burns like fire" (*Works*, p. 458).

Yet Edwards's use of creepy-crawly insects to make theological points did not represent a sudden new interest; as a boy he had studied spiders with fascination. One of Edwards's earliest publications was an essay called "On Spiders," which he sent to the Royal Academy in London, in which he characterizes spiders as "little collections" of "corrupting nauseousness." Spiders were designed, so he thought, to cleanse the air of noxious materials before blowing away to their deaths at sea. Thus Edwards's repeated use of insects or "crawling" creatures as means of theological repudiation, then, casts an interesting light *backward* upon his earlier, pseudoscientific interest in insects. Richard Bushman notes that the young Edwards's essay,

> is most useful to a biographer if it is read as an unconscious allegory of human existence. Such an interpretation is not far-fetched considering that later Edwards consciously made a spider the emblem of man's plight. Aside from purely scientific curiosity, something held Edwards' attention on spiders hour after hour ("Jonathan Edwards as Great Man," pp. 28–29).

To anticipate a bit, Edwards's facility with a language of grotesquery, negation, and creaturely depredation will find a surprising companion in Lovecraft's twentieth-century taxonomy of the Unholy. So while Edwards may indeed have been a theologian of the high Divine, he was also well-practiced in the arts of popular fear.[38] Read Edwards as he attempts to describe the Divine by negation: "innumerable and inconceivable"; "uncovenanted, unobliged"; "inexpressible and inconceivable"—all this in the one sermon, "Sinners in the Hands of an Angry God." One can easily understand how Lovecraft achieves some of his greatest effects merely by imitating the earlier theologian's nay-saying. In effect Lovecraft will invert Edwards and chart a downward transcendent, using materials, strategies, and language gleaned from early American theological history.

Edwards came to his maturity in an expansively figurative tradition, accustomed to the broad, allegorical reaches of type and antitype. He would have been familiar with conventional images of the demonic, of brute power and hapless captivity. His main genius as a preacher, then, was an ability to raid the popular cupboard, so to speak, where he found images fresh enough to convey to his auditors the "eternal anguish" (Carse, "An Urgent Now!" p. 221) of God's love that he himself could hardly express.[39] For example, the threat of imminent disaster traceable to the whim of an implacable sovereign was a social commonplace.[40] The lore of terror from which Edwards derived his prosaic images of entrapment, slippage, and vulnerability reflect how central were these anxieties (powerlessness, boundary-loss, and instability) to the society at large. We have not here a lasting city, preachers had been saying for years—and no matter that it is to be a city on a hill for all to see. Following Edwards's sturdy example, the dire possibilities of annihilation, attributed to the "mere pleasure" and "arbitrary will" of God (*Works*, p. 451), or again, to God's "hand of arbitrary mercy" (*Works*, p. 452), would become fantasy conventions—just as before Edwards dire crisis had been the American way of writing the Holy. In this slow transition from theology to fantasy, we can find directly spoken at last an awareness of the awfulness of the Deity that had gone unspoken in earlier formulations. In this regard, Edwards best captured the difficulties as well as the contradictions of the spiritual project: God had fixed an "eternal and immutable rule of righteousness . . . between Him and mankind" (*Works*, p. 452). As a consequence, "there is no fortress that is any defense from the power of God" (*Works*, p. 451). Edwards's Hell "is a strong prison: it is beyond any finite power, or the united strength of all wicked men and devils to unlock . . ." (Carse, "An Urgent Now!" pp. 221–22).

As various reports attest, Edwards was largely successful in conveying God's power. He gave his auditors Hell, even when he thought he was saving them from it. Edwards was noted to be a reserved preacher; Hopkins says his "delivery [was] easy, natural, and very solemn," and although he "had not a strong, loud voice," he preached with "gravity and solemnity" (Levin, p. 47). Yet notwithstanding Edwards's sense of presence and gravity, Reverend Stephen Williams noted in his diary that during the Enfield Sermon "a great moaning and crying out through the whole house could be heard" (Stuart, "Jonathan Edwards at Enfield," p. 46.)[41] Perhaps then one understands the response of another awed listener who commented that Edwards "used no gestures, but looked straight forward," and "looked on the bell rope until he looked it off" (Miller, *Jonathan Edwards*, p. 51).

The Gothic and the Holy: Private Woe and the Public Weal

"Woe to him who seeks to please rather than to appall."
MOBY-DICK, CHAPTER 9[42]

The discourse of divine things had been slipping into fantasy since the earliest days in the New World. In "The Day of Doom" (1662), Michael Wigglesworth was one of the earliest Puritan writers to connect the discourses of "moral entropy" (Porte, p. 54) and civic instability to the formal rhythms of poetry. Perhaps his instinct was correct; as experience wore colonial ideals more and more ragged around the edges, only the rigors of poetic structure and the aesthetics of language could "stay" the moral decline of the community. Mather's *The Wonders of the Invisible World* may well have developed to new heights the public uses of perfervid religious bombast. But Edwards normalized the demonization of the Divine; his language of repudiation would find a welcome home in the clichés of Gothic condemnation. Yet there are some differences between earlier theologians and Edwards. Set "Sinners" against Mather's bizarreries, for example. If the narrative voice in "Sinners" is distant and dispassionate, Mather, some years earlier, was less controlled. Says Gary Green: "Mather's scathing condemnation of his own generation and his own fears of inadequacy collide in a narrative voice which borders on a complex combination of sadism and masochism" (*The Language of Nightmare*, pp. 52–53). Perhaps Green has in mind passages like the following:

. . . what *Woes* indeed must we expect from such a Devil of a *Moloch*, as relishes no Sacrifices like those of Humane Heart-Blood, and unto whom there is no Musick like the bitter, dying, doleful Groans, ejaculated by the Roasting Children of Men" (Mather, *Wonders*, 50–51).

This passage sounds very much like Oliver Wendell Holmes's critique of Edwards! One wonders what Clarence Darrow would have made of all this; he was already on record charging that Edwards's "main business . . . was scaring silly women and little children and blaspheming the God he professed to adore."[43] In "Sinners in the Hands of an Angry God," however, with a single rhetorical sweep, Edwards accomplishes something altogether different from Mather. Mather's forte was turning theological energy into the public, typological allegories of political history. While Mather fulminated against the devil, Edwards addressed the deity in the same terms, or at least so it seemed. To a careless listener it might appear that the devil and God were one, or at least of one mind—as Holmes, Twain, and Whitman (just to name three) would later argue.[44] In "Chanting the Square Deific," Whitman writes the image into poetry, describing Satan as one of the four faces of God. Whitman specifically notes the "new-world" genesis of the complex image: "Aloof, dissatisfied, plotting revolt" / . . . "Defiant, I, Satan, still live, still utter words, in new lands duly appearing, (and old ones also,) / permanent here from my side, warlike, equal with any, real as any . . ." (p. 445).[45] Holmes, too, would employ a similar image: "The God of Edwards is not a Trinity, but a Quaternity. The fourth Person is an embodied abstraction, to which he gave the name Justice" (*Pages*, p. 368). Of course, Whitman may have given the idea to Holmes, who then used it as additional ammunition against Edwards and his whole school of strict-observance Calvinism.

It was precisely in their efforts to speak the Holy in propaedeutic ways that the topographers of the Puritan interior invoked horrible catastrophe, hoping thereby to safeguard against individual and communal failure. Their moralistic *horrors* were collective exercises, their jeremiads rhetorics of nationalistic woe. Yet something happens in the decades between Mather and Edwards as the discourse begins to veer into the undiscovered countries of the soul. To see the difference between Edwards and his predecessors, recall for a moment his sermon on Job 31:3, where Edwards describes the "torments" awaiting the unjust at the Day of Judgment. After an increasingly baroque explication of God's wrath, Edwards exclaims that sinners "will have a strange and wonderful sensation of misery under God's wrath" (cited in Kimnach, "Reality," p. 113). The word "strange" returns again, as again Edwards conjures the ineffable by iteration of the effable:

> The bodies of the wicked, after the Resurrection, will be strange, hideous Kinds of bodies; there will be a strange crew at the left hand of Christ at the Day of Judgment. . . . Such a strange punishment as being suitable to such a strange and monstrous evil . . . the torments being principally spiritual and consisting in the horrors of the mind makes it appear like some strange fable or dream . . . (cited in Kimnach, "Reality," p. 113).

To compare Edwards with his predecessors, then, is to realize how the language of moral limits has changed and how terror has been interiorized. Colonial writers—Hooker and Winthrop, for instance—catalogued such punishments and horrors as dispossession or dismemberment at the hands of Indians, infestation by plague or witches, or on occasion, violation by the French or other political (or religious) enemies. A century later, Edwards offers his ingenuous suggestion that the wildly imaginative torments he so painstakingly details are, as we have seen, "principally spiritual and consisting in the horrors of the mind." Edwards has reversed the focus of what was once a public act of scrutiny. He inverts the typical metaphors: dispossession is internal, and the language of physical terror, imaginative. This interiorization, in turn, permits the accommodation of terror to private rather than to public rhythms, which helps push the rhetoric of the communal Holy over the edge into sentimentality and nostalgia. In the end, then, Edwards undid himself. It is almost as if Edwards had declared himself defeated by the antinomians, conceding to their unspeakable habits of speaking the soul whenever, and in whatever way, they wanted. Henceforth God would be more tyrannous—perhaps even more manic—than before: the divine whimsy now beholden to private, unregulatable, and thus presumptively unrational inner lights, rather than to the formal, legal, and linguistic constraints of the Covenant.

Another point needs to be observed. Edwards's "horrors of the mind" are only a step away from a different sort of language of moral limits. It closely resembles the Gothic allegories of psychomachia, the telling of the rended soul. If, as Harry Levin suggests, American fiction "sprang from religious allegory" (*The Power of Blackness*, p. 20), Edwards probably gave it a terminal push in that direction. For this reason, Calvin's systematic mappings of the Divine were to become guideposts into another interior, creating a kind of "internalized Calvinism" that could be "pressed naturally into the service of a common Gothic fable of total decay" (Porte, p. 54).[46] That "fable" was a theological tale "of inexpiable guilt and unremitting punishment—in which many Gothic writers saw an image of their own condition and fate" (Porte, p. 50). Within a few years, the iconography of fallen man, with its roots in the "Age of Faith," would become conventions of the Gothic. In *Perils of the Night: A Feminist Study of Nineteenth-Century Gothic*, Eugenia DeLamotte argues that Gothic romance "offers a symbolic language congenial to the expression of psychological, epistemological, religious, and social anxieties" that, in addition, establish the "boundaries of the self" (pp. 13–14). DeLamotte's observation helps us read Edwards and his theologies better, as texts perhaps less directed at the Divine than at the human.

Joel Porte remarks, "It is surprising, particularly in view of the evidence that lies readily to hand, how little systematic consideration has been given to Gothic fiction as the expression of a fundamentally Protestant theological or religious disquietude" ("In the Hands," p. 43). "Gothic mystery," Porte insists, functions "as a substitute for discredited religious mystery" (p. 43). Barton St. Armand makes a similar point:

> . . . given the Gothic's stiff anti-clerical and anti-catholic bias, profoundly inward, even "religious" in the broadest sense . . . the religious impulse in Gothicism soon galloped from a concern with talking pictures and bleeding nuns to a consideration of man's position in a terrifying and inscrutable universe, an obsession with individual destiny and damnation, and a determined exploration of the mysteries of the soul itself.[47]

So in the study of American theological history, if the Holy was not always what it seemed, it was partly thanks to Edwards's dogged pursuit and eventual revision of it. In the very Protestant earnestness of his attempt to speak the Divine, Edwards pushes the Holy as far as it can go—to the point, in fact, where theology becomes fantasy, where deity becomes demon, and where the ineffable cannot be addressed except in unspeakable terms. Edwards himself was aware of the dangers of words. Words, he knew, were "formed to express external things"; when turned toward expression of the "internal and spiritual" they are "almost all borrowed, and used in a sort of figurative sense" (in Ramsey, *Freedom of the Will*, p. 376). Edwards ruefully observes, "No wonder, therefore, that the high and abstract mysteries of the Deity, the prime and most abstract of all beings, imply so many seeming contradictions."[48] No wonder, indeed. Although a thin line separates the Holy and the Horrific, it also joins them. The sacred and the taboo are necessarily linked at the edge, or beyond the edge, of speech. There culture sets up night watch over its boundaries.

Edwards's exercise in writing theology, then, involves him in some cross-boundary skirmishing; he makes extended forays beyond the walls of the cultural permissible into the land of the nonconventional. The spiritual anxieties Edwards focused upon were real enough; as we have seen with the images of entrapment and dispossession, they epitomized a wide range of social vulnerabilities.[49] Two themes, in particular, will recur in American culture with the sturdy rhythm of a Charles Wesley hymn: self-encounter that becomes annihilation; and second, the revelation of God's love that is at the same time an experience of divine scrutiny and judgment.[50] In this respect, Edwards's "horrors of the mind" reshapes an eschatology of disaster into a new genre. Rhetorical pandemonium had been used rather conventionally to scare the devil out of people, but after Edwards, into the sentimentalized Christian piety of the nineteenth century, fright separated off and went its own way, becoming a business—or at least an appetite—in its own right. Shaken loose of its ostensibly theological and didactic context, terror becomes endlessly manipulatable— for reasons, among others, of social control, and, simply, for the voyeuristic delights of lurid narrative. For example, in "The Poetics of Horror: More Than Meets the Eye," Dennis L. White charts an "aesthetic of horror" (p. 7) that would certainly not be foreign to Edwards. Horror, White says, describes the "continual revelation of

random, but at the same time, inevitable forces asserting themselves," whose "lack of comprehensible causation is clearly inten-
tional." Death, in the horror aesthetic, is the kind "from which
there is no protection, no warning, and no escape" (p. 7); and
typically, horror shows a "continual loss of means of escape until
there is no safety and no hope of safety" (p. 8). It manifests a fear of
"being under someone else's power, of losing control over not just
the *id* but the entire self" (p. 10). Edwards has, as the expression
goes, been *there* and done *that.* Finally, White's concluding
observation—"God-mania is also a common element in the horror
film" (p. 10)—could go without saying.[51]

So although David Punter has argued that the Gothic is not a
"native growth" to America (*The Literature of Terror*, p. 198), this is
not altogether true. Nor should we be diffident about calling
Edwards a "crypto-Gothicist," since Edwards was writing in the
tradition decades before Brockden Brown, who is generally considered America's first "Gothic novelist."[52] One can hear Edwards
ask Brown, echoing Hawthorne's gloomy elders: "Ah, you're a
storyteller. But can you write Gothic *sermons?*" *That* is the real test
of the Gothic imagination.[53] So as we map the various terrains of
American culture, whether locating them high or low, or defining
them as spiritual or political, it should be clear by now that Edwards is *more* than just a minor figure in one or another tradition.
Rather, one might call him the fissure king, since his work shows
forth so many of the contradictions and fractures of a spiritually
hegemonic culture. He was philosopher, theologian, preacher of
the Holy, teller of the terrible: all in all, he was reader of the
American psyche and creator of an important American myth. He
drew for the culture a religious portrait of itself that would assume
increasing importance to the degree it was denied and deflected,
inverted and sentimentalized. Edwards is "key to understanding
the emergence of distinct 'American' culture" (Hatch and Stout,
p. 8). His theology, as William Scheick notes, was "transmitted to
our time without interruption" (*Critical Essays*, p. xiii), although
surely, as we have seen, changed and in ways that still surprise.
While seeking to reform the strict theological boundaries effaced
by popery and other forms of liberalism, Edwards gave secret aid
and comfort to America's vibrant strain of lawless, irreverent dark
fantasy.

Wigglesworth, Winthrop, Cotton Mather, and Edwards—each in differing ways anticipates the thematic and categorical excesses of contemporary moralistic horror. It can be argued, additionally, that their shadows fall over much of the literatures between them. So effectively do these writers efface the line between fantastic theology and theological fantasy that for all practical purposes the two genres would never be separate discourses again. Indeed, the pungent language of Mather and Edwards working the invective of Heaven gives us a foretaste of Poe, Lovecraft, King—all those who would raid theological cupboards to find a suitably "red and hideous" language for Hell (Twain, *Letters*, pp. 719–20). In particular, Edwards's earnestly unironic demonization of the Holy was to darken religious mystery to a degree that would profoundly affect later generations of writers, whose culture offered them rather the opposite—a sentimentalization of the Divine. Porte notes that the Anglo-American school of Gothicists "distilled the pure essence of a tradition of religious terror which was to find its true culmination in the theologically obsessed romances of Hawthorne, Melville, and Poe" (pp. 50–51). Yet individual authors resisted Edwards's heavy theological pressure in differing ways. Hawthorne, for example, is fairly self-aware of his religious borrowings, especially in his allegorical pieces. So was Melville, whether one wishes to consider *Moby-Dick* or "Benito Cereno."[54] In fact, Melville was so conversant with Edwards's writings that he often argued them, for and against, in his fiction and essays. In "Hawthorne and His Mosses," for instance, Melville catches an Edwardsean echo:

> Certain it is, however, that this great power of blackness in him derives its force from its appeals to that Calvinistic sense of Innate Depravity and Original Sin, from whose visitations, in some shape or other, no deeply thinking mind is always and wholly free.[55]

More directly, Melville introduces Edwards as a foil in "Bartleby the Scrivener." Melville's narrator, at a loss as to what direction to take regarding the perplexing, silent Bartleby, turns to theology and philosophy for help. He "looked a little into 'Edwards on the Will,' [*sic*] and 'Priestly on Necessity'." These books, the narrator says—not without some irony, one supposes—"induced a salutary feeling" in the anxious office manager.[56]

Less-direct links connect Edwards to Poe ("The Jingle Man," in

Emerson's dismissive phrase), although there are intriguing infer-
ences to be made. A century before Poe, Edwards had formalized
the conjunction/opposition of the awe-ful and the awful that anticipates many of Poe's themes—for instance, entrapment, epistemological despair, cosmic disequilibrium.[57] Thus, while Poe's
Eureka represents a different form of cosmological critique than
Edwards's posthumous cosmologies, it is similarly motivated. Marion Montgomery writes that "seemingly antagonistic surfaces can
distract from the underlying similarities between Poe's mind and
that of a Jonathan Edwards" (p. 352).[58] Recall how Poe himself
distinguishes the "terrors not of Germany but of the soul" (Poe
refers here to Continental Gothic narrative conventions) and the
linkage between Edwards and Poe may not seem so strange. Indeed, what Poe described as the "terror of the soul" is not, says
David Hirsch, "man's fear of death; it is the dread ensuing from a
confrontation with the possibility of his own immortality" ("The
Pit and the Apocalypse," p. 652). Joel Porte, further, reads Poe's
"William Wilson" (1839) as demonstrating "the persistent conjunction of Gothic terror and Calvinist theology in Anglo-
American writing." Poe's tale,

> might—with a justifiable pun and a nod in the direction of Jon-
> athan Edwards—be called "Poe on the Will," for it is an all but
> patent allegory describing how the perverse Will of fallen man,
> which is the degenerate offspring of the Divine Will, is pursued
> relentlessly by the righteous Hound of Heaven (p. 61).[59]

Edwards may not have caught the irony of what he had done for
(or to) theological discourse, but others surely did. In "The Deacon's Masterpiece: The Minister's One-Hoss Shay," Holmes pokes
fun at the self-contained determinism of Edwards's theological
system. He allegorizes it as a "One-Hoss Shay," a carriage that
"went to pieces all at once,— / All at once, and nothing first,— /
Just as bubbles do when they burst."[60] And even William James
had opinions about Edwards. In *The Varieties of Religious Experience*,
James writes that Edwards's doctrine of divine sovereignty "appears to us, if sovereignly anything, sovereignly irrational and
mean. Not only the cruelty, but the paltriness of character of the
gods believed in by earlier centuries also strikes later centuries with

surprise."[61] Mark Twain also reacted strongly to Edwards. After reading "Freedom of the Will," Twain wrote his friend Joseph Twichell (also a clergyman). Twain wrote that he felt a "strange and haunting sense of having been on a three-day's tear with a drunk lunatic. . . . The glare of a resplendent intellect gone mad— a marvelous spectacle." In Edwards's thinking, said Twain, "Calvinism and its God . . . show up red and hideous in the glow from the fires of hell. . . ."[62] If that registers Twain's reactions to Edwards's theology proper, one wonders what he would have thought about "Sinners in the Hands of an Angry God."[63]

In summary, Edwards's particular brand of vernacular, narratively organized theology, anticipates a range of fantasy motifs still popular in formulaic American horror. At the same time, it represents Edwards's implacable adherence to an already threadworn Calvinism which he refurbished and Americanized. And, no doubt about it, Edwards missed his calling. Concerning one of Edwards's imprecatory sermons, Carse writes, "If these are the words of man become captive to an extreme religious position, they are also the words of an artist, for Edwards, with a skill as sure as that of any story teller, has collapsed the distance between his subject matter and his listeners by describing a strange and terrifying world in terms of a present and familiar world" (p. 224). Listen, for instance, to Edwards's sermon on Luke 16:24:

> Consider that if you do go to hell, hell is certainly near. How near, you can't tell, but in the general that it is near you may be certain. . . . It would terrify you if you knew you was to burn at the stake, or [be] roasted to death by the Indians . . . (cited in Kimnach, "Reality," p. 114).

Edwards certainly knew his theological tradition, and these lines suggest a particular awareness of Thomas Hooker's "The Danger of Desertion." More importantly, Edwards's images demonstrate his genius—a capacity to shift from theological discourse to political, and thence to the personal. Note how Edwards adapts and Americanizes the conventional "hell" of theological discourse by conflating it with images familiar to the colonial situation—in particular, images of civil control (burning) and civic paranoia (being roasted to death by Indians). Edwards is, surely, proto-

Gothic in his "obsessive images and recurring emblematic figures" and in his "recurring religious undercurrent of meaning." In his ritualistic use of these elements, he blends the "themes of physical terror, moral horror, and religious mystery" (Thompson, *The Gothic Imagination*, p. 6).[64] If Edwards never tried his hand at straightforward fiction, it seems a pity. Were he writing today, he could give Stephen King some competition.

Conclusion: The Language of Nightmare

> *. . . the fantastic is a compensation that man provides for himself, at the level of the imagination, for what he has lost at the level of faith.*
> —MAURICE LEVY[65]

In these preceding pages I have tried to show that examples of linguistic disarray in theological discourse permit one to trace, in its prescriptions and proscriptions, not only the culturally Unspeakable, but the unspeakably Divine, as well. To be alert to these moments in America's desacralized, mystical tradition is to observe how, within the lawful conventions and rhythms of grammar, the unlawful or prelawful makes itself present. The collapse of grammar points to the fantasy brooding darkly within the real. By "desacralized" mystical tradition, I mean, for example, the poets in the theological line of Emerson—including Whitman, Dickinson, Frost, and Robert Lowell.[66] These poets are surely distinct from one another; I claim only that each of them, like other writers of their eras, with some degree of conscious artifice found new ways to refurbish previously theological interiorities.[67]

Why was such aesthetic reformation necessary? A culture continuously threatened by the appearance of antinomians or enthusiasts found mystical encounters of any type uncomfortable, even terrible. Experiences of numinous possibility, either individually (as reflected by Anne Hutchinson) or communally (as at Salem) were rarely welcome; their portent was never clear. Hitched to a rhetoric of the Holy, partly by fortune and, later by policy, the theocracy of New England attempted to write spirituality into communal standards; as a consequence, it never quite escaped a spiritualized fear of the lawless—an anxiety evident even in its rhetorics and political fantasies. Hawthorne, then, had his ancestors dead to rights: what they feared most was the lawless human heart. My point here is that evidences of conflict within systems of speech—whether Mather's grammar of paranoia at Salem, Edwards's earnest gothicization of the Holy in "Sinners," or Emerson's exploding metaphor—the "transparent eyeball" passage of *Nature*—give evidence, in effect, of a struggle to hold a social boundary. The land they patrol is the contested ideological space in which a society charts, and occasionally redraws, its cosmological, theological, and social maps.

The unspeakable Divine and the culturally unspeakable are deeply entangled. Each is interdicted, and forbidden; yet each, historically, has compelled speech, whether in denial or deflection. Indeed, one could say that the Holy and the Horrible alike are construed by negation and transgression; the language of the Holy shapes itself in terms of a "language of nightmare" (Green, p. 21). Additionally, both provoke similar modes of suppression and strategies of silencing. Not for nothing were Anne Hutchinson and her followers exiled to the wild and barbaric lands of Rhode Island.[68] After all, what does one do with an experience that is explicitly ungrammatizable, beyond the limits of human expression, and thus presumptively beyond the limits of experience? To entertain such a possibility is the way of madness. Against it social orders stand vigilant, because it represents the land of unlikeness—*terra incognita*: the land of mysteries and terrors guarding the edges of the mapped and comfortable known.

Lastly, in summary and anticipation: Edwards spent his whole life seeking a symbolic language by which to understand himself and his world. He attempted to relate his experience of that world and himself to another world—a prior, transcendent world of the Divine. Like Mather, he wanted to define, and police, the spiritual place. In the measured and complex logical beauties of reformed Christianity's theology Edwards found the appropriate language. The language of Incarnation, which traditionally confirmed the deity's presence in and through this world, had not, after all, been forgotten as theologically inconvenient. The doctrine had merely undergone a metamorphosis of its own. For if gods can play in the fields of men, as the Book of Genesis assures us, so too could other less-desirable intruders, a theme I shall consider in a subsequent chapter.

Edwards, like others, found that to write the Holy presumes, or at least implies, its own opposition. The Holy can be unwritten, or denied, since to speak the unspeakable *or* impermissible required, very dramatically, the resources of the unspeakable. Second, the gradual transformation of the Holy *into* its opposite—negative fantasy—culminates, finally, in an outright denial of mystery itself. Over time the fantastic theologies of Edwards resurface in the cosmological speculations of another fantasiste (Emerson), as well as in the cosmicisms of Poe and Lovecraft and in the moralistic allegories of Twain and Holmes; that same theological energy can be found, finally, in the high-church, bleakly secular poetics of Robert Frost. What had been perhaps a gesture of dissent for Emerson becomes, later, a wholesale repudiation. Theological meditations upon the end time by Wigglesworth and others would, in due time, shape a contemporary "imagination of disaster."[69] Similarly, customary meditations upon death would anticipate a modern genre. They would become, in Stephen Koch's expression, "the full-fledged pornography of death."[70] Woven together thread by thread, the theological imagination clothed itself in the lineaments of the awful. Power and mystery, entrapment and annihilation, became formalized in civic address and formulaized in a variety of literary contexts.

Wilson Kimnach argues that Edwards's preaching techniques and his verbal mastery became the "ultimate weapon in colonial homiletics, and it established the literary technology of American revivalism."[71] Surely it was to do more than that. It would transform the moralisms of the revival tent, the spectacular displays of sin, into another context entirely. The disciplinary fictions of Edwards, that "eighteenth-century Kafka" (Simonson, *Theologian of the Heart*, p. 126), authorize Edgar Allan Poe and Stephen King to write a literature of interiority, and if horror was first used as homiletic strategy, it became useful in other ways as well. For example, in Stephen King's dark horrors an eschatology of the terrible disguises, while remembering, this older metaphysics—a system in which a rhetoric of *communitas* legitimizes a discourse of violation and endless control. While the Holy may not presume the Horrible, nonetheless the Horrible affirms the Holy. In this way, the intense inwardness of the Puritan diary rediscovers itself in the "unbearable encounter with self that informs so much Gothic literature" (Frank, *Through the Pale Door*, p. 158). But to sort all this out, we really do need to return to the source, since it was the outrageous *sweep* of Calvin's theological vision that Edwards spent his lifetime supporting. In fact, it is Calvin rather than Edwards who most directly anticipates H. P. Lovecraft. Yet it is Lovecraft who in his turn most completely realizes the horrific consequences of Jonathan Edwards. So while Edwards may have taken the first step toward disengaging the Holy from a specific cosmological (and ideological) context, Lovecraft, as we will see, denies the Holy any context whatsoever except in a rhetoric of negation. Following Edwards's example, Emerson rewrites the Holy as rhetorical figure, using the fantasy of metaphor to negotiate some minimal connection with the Holy. To Lovecraft, however, no rapprochement was possible, since the Holy *was* rhetoric and fantasy. Thus, the retreat from a problematic mysticism already evident in Edwards and Emerson will be a nonquestion for Lovecraft. There is no Holy from which to retreat; no mysticism save the appalling solipsism of the Self in a cosmos of incomprehensible, literally unimaginable design. As we will see in the next chapter, even Frost will perform his compulsory figures upon this cosmological theme, although in Frost's hands the supposedly benign cosmology of the Calvinists becomes a darker habit of determinism, its metaphysics stripped of its beneficence.[72]

A final word about Mark Twain, who perhaps better than any other writer bridges Edwards's theology and Lovecraft's fantasy. One can detect in Twain's late fiction an increasing and pervasive sense of guilt, often expressed religiously, as Twain found himself imaginatively trapped in a system of belief from which he could not emotionally free himself. Try as he might, Twain could never fully pry the fingers of divinity from around his neck. In fact, much of Twain's posthumous work reads like an extended answer, in general agreement, to Edwards's sense of the human situation. Edwards wrote "[man] is hateful to his Maker, *ex officio*, as a human being" (cited by Holmes, p. 370). Twain wrote "The Great Dark" in several sittings over a number of years, and in many respects this tale, published posthumously, seems to be a direct parody of Edwards's theology.[73] Twain's claustrophobic tale of a world contained in a microscope slide, is a meditation on the terror of an indifferent cosmology—just as Edwards's theology offers a meditation on the terror of a universe *not at all* indifferent to mortal beings. Twain's tale thus resembles Frost's "Design," and the cosmology common to Twain and Frost could easily have come from a young writer named Howard Phillips Lovecraft. In 1910—the year Twain died—Lovecraft was just abandoning poetry and beginning to dabble in fantasy. He found religious *arcana* congenial to his temperament, although perhaps it is only accidental that he seizes upon the bleak Calvinism of Twain's posthumous vision and makes it one of his central, distaff-theological images.[74]

NOTES

1. "Sinners in the Hands of an Angry God," in *The Works of President Edwards*, vol. 6 (New York: Burt Franklin, 1968), p. 455.
2. Richard P. Benton, "The Problems of Literary Gothicism," *ESQ*, vol. 18, 1972: 7.
3. The language of fantasy served the classics, as well. Servetus, for example, repudiating Calvin's Trinitarian God as a "three-headed Cerberus," found that to speak orthodoxy "plainly" he had to stretch language to its utmost, speaking most unplainly. Talk of certain kinds may be cheap; in theological warfare not so. Calvin responded by condemning Servetus "impious ravings" and later, orchestrating a trial for heresy that eventuated in Servetus' death (Schurr, p. 35).
4. For general studies in the Gothic, see Richard P. Benton, "The Problems of Literary Gothicism," *ESQ*, vol. 18.1, 1972: 5–9; Edith Birkhead, *The Tale of Terror: A Study of the Gothic Romance* (London: Constable, 1921); William Patrick Day, *In the Circles of Fear and Desire: A Study of Gothic Fantasy* (Chicago: University of Chicago Press, 1985); Coral Ann Howells, *Love, Mystery, and Misery: Feeling in Gothic Fiction* (London: Athlone, 1978); Elizabeth MacAndrew, *The Gothic Tradition in Fiction* (New York: Columbia University Press, 1979); Nelson Lowry, Jr., "Night Thoughts on the Gothic Novel," *Yale Review* 52, 1962: 236–57; Robert L. Platzner and Robert D. Hume, " 'Gothic Versus Romantic': a Rejoinder," *PMLA* 86, 1971: 266–74; Victor Sage, *Horror Fiction in the Protestant Tradition* (London: Macmillan, 1988); G. R. Thompson, ed., *The Gothic Imagination: Essays in Dark Romanticism* (Pullman: Washington State University Press, 1974).

　　For studies in the American Gothic tradition see especially Martha Banta, "American Apocalypses: Excrement and Ennui," *Studies in the Literary Imagination*, 7, 1974: 1–30; Leslie A. Fiedler, *Love and Death in the American Novel* (New York: Criterion, 1960); Frederick S. Frank, *Through the Pale Door: A Guide to and*

Through the American Gothic (New York: Greenwood Press, 1990); Gary L. Green, *The Language of Nightmare: A Theory of American Gothic Fiction* (Ann Arbor: University of Michigan Press, 1985); Louis S. Gross, *Toward the American Gothic* (Ann Arbor: University of Michigan Press, 1989); Donald A. Ringe, *American Gothic: Imagination and Reason in Nineteenth-Century Fiction* (Lexington: Kentucky University Press, 1982); Brian Attebery, *The Fantasy Tradition in American Literature: From Irving to LeGuin* (Bloomington: Indiana University Press, 1980); and G. R. Thompson, "Washington Irving and the American Ghost Story," in *The Haunted Dusk: American Supernatural Fiction, 1820–1920, op. cit.,* pp. 11–36.

5. Paul Tillich, "The Word of God," in *Language: An Enquiry into its Meaning and Function* (New York: Harper and Bros., 1957), p. 133.

6. Elsewhere Ola Winslow says that Edwards's verbal portraits of the *arcana* of religion were "as real as though they had been murals painted with a brush on the gray meetinghouse walls." *Jonathan Edwards, 1703–1758, a Biography* (New York: Macmillan, 1940), p. 145. Incidentally, for Calvin, Hell, in whatever "physical metaphors" it is depicted, is: "alienari ab omni Dei societate" (*Institutes,* III, xxv, 12 [p. 1008n in *LCC,* vol. 2]).

7. Original publication: New London, CT: Printed and Sold by T. Green, 1724; reprinted, Worcester, 1963.

8. Robert D. Hume, "Gothic Versus Romantic: A Revaluation of the Gothic Novel," p. 286. Joel Porte, "In the Hands of an Angry God: Religious Terror in Gothic Fiction," in *The Gothic Imagination: Essays in Dark Romanticism,* G. R. Thompson, ed., *op. cit.,* pp. 42–64.

9. Wayne Lesser, "Jonathan Edwards: Textuality and the Language of Man," in *Critical Essays on Jonathan Edwards,* William Scheick, ed. (Boston: G. K. Hall, 1980), p. 294.

10. See David Daiches's 1983 Gifford Lectures, published as *God and the Poets* (New York: Oxford University Press, 1984).

11. See also Wayne Lesser's point that "every verbal act of self-reflection is necessarily a religious transgression" in "Jonathan Edwards: Textuality and the Language of Man," in Scheick, *Critical Essays,* p. 295. In general, my ideas in this chapter are indebted to Jonathan Dollimore's critique of Augustine's "punitive metaphysic." (p. 140) See *Sexual Dissidence: Augustine to Wilde, Freud to Foucault* (New York: Oxford University Press, 1991), especially his chapter entitled "Augustine: Perversion and Privation" (pp. 131–47).

12. David Levin, *Jonathan Edwards: A Profile* (New York: Hill and Wang, 1969), p. xiii.

13. Needless to say, under these conditions, a culture habituated to crisis and annihilation, and used to paying lip-service to conversion, reconsidered its options. Implicitly distrusting any sign of change, it would not therefore be much inclined to trust this inscrutable God Whose Unchangeable Nature seemed nevertheless so unstable.

14. These difficulties have canonical warrant, too, for as early as the Acts of the Apostles and Saint Paul's Letter to the Galatians (1 Gal. 15; but see also 2 Cor. 12:1–6) we see the difficulties inherent in speaking the Divine. Paul, no

stranger to words, is radically converted to silence as well as to Christ. He remains steadfastly wordless about the encounter with the limits of his soul. When on the rare occasion he adverts to his moment of conversion, he is unaccountably reticent, either about describing the event or evaluating it.

15. In a study of Edwards's manuscripts, "Manuscript Problems in the Yale Edition of Jonathan Edwards," *Early American Literature* 3, 1968: 159–71, Thomas Schafer notes that of the more than two hundred and fifty sermons that Edwards composed during the first decade of his career, only nine have been published. Writing two decades later, Nathan O. Hatch and Harry S. Stout, in their Introduction to *Jonathan Edwards and the American Experience* (New York: Oxford University Press, 1988), say that over "fifteen hundred of [Edwards's] sermons" survive; that when they are published, the collection "could extend to as many as fifty volumes of printed text" (p. 9). As a consequence of the skewed vision of Edwards, Roland Delattre, in "Beauty and Theology: A Reappraisal of Jonathan Edwards," argues that the theologian is inaccurately thought to consider "God as a terrifying and arbitrary sovereign whose providential and predestinarian governance of the world is so unbendingly deterministic in its power as to deny to his creatures the least fragment of freedom and to leave them no sure hope but to throw themselves upon the divine mercy in an ecstasy of conversion" (Scheick, *Critical Essays*, p. 137).

See also Conrad Cherry, "Conversion: Nature and Grace," in which he similarly notes: "There is in 'Sinners in the Hands of an Angry God,' the sermon so often taken as representative of Edwards's pathological preoccupation with a God of wrath, a stream of hope and mercy running through the exposition of the wrath of God" (Scheick, *Critical Essays*, p. 85).

16. Commenting on Edwards's posthumous treatise on the Will (1758) Alexander V. G. Allen calls it one of the "literary sensations" of the eighteenth century. In the treatise Edwards seemed to align himself with "infidels and free-thinkers such as Hobbes, and Collins, and Hume . . ." in denying the freedom of the will. In the popular imagination Edwards's treatise "added an element of inexpressible horror to the situation if it was also true that the will was not free to choose between good and evil" ("The Freedom of the Will," Scheick, *Critical Essays*, p. 90).

17. Joseph Campbell, *The Hero With a Thousand Faces* (New York: Pantheon, 1949), p. 126.

18. Wayne Lesser, "Jonathan Edwards: Textuality and the Language of Man," in Scheick, *Critical Essays*.

19. "Jonathan Edwards's Pursuit of Reality," in Hatch and Stout, *Jonathan Edwards and the American Experience*, pp. 102–17.

20. *The Works of Jonathan Edwards: Freedom of the Will*, Paul Ramsey, ed. (New Haven: Yale University Press, 1957), p. 376.

21. *The Philosophy of Jonathan Edwards from His Private Notebooks*, Harvey G. Townsend, ed. (Eugene: University of Oregon Press, 1955), p. 118.

22. Oliver Wendell Holmes, *Pages from an Old Volume of Life: A Collection of Essays 1857–1881* (Boston: Houghton, Mifflin and Co., 1892), p. 369.

23. "The Life and Character of the Late Reverend Mr. Jonathan Edwards,"

Samuel Hopkins, excerpted in David Levin, *Jonathan Edwards: A Profile*. Yet what troubled Edwards was the fact that his experience seemed nonconventional, lacking distinguishing "signs." Nor does this youthful anxiety leave him. In *Jonathan Edwards: Theologian of the Heart* (Macon: Mercer University Press, 1982), Harold P. Simonson observes that an "epistemology of religious conversion" informs Edwards's "whole theology" (p. 12). Edwards was so concerned to distinguish what Shea calls "the sometimes baffling resemblance between authentic and fraudulent spirituality" that he builds his future career on the task, defending the unpopular view of visible and "true" signs (See Daniel B. Shea, "The Art and Instruction of Jonathan Edwards's *Personal Narrative*," *American Literature*, vol. 37, 1965: 17.). Simonson notes, however, that these "true" signs "did not necessarily imply that crying, shaking, fainting, and other apparent aberrations were false signs. Such was the problematic nexus of the religious revivals" (p. 365).

24. Shea observes, "So hideous a view as Edwards reported would have taxed any vocabulary, but his own had so far been richest and most novel when he expressed the affection of love. For this other task he might have been forced to depend entirely upon the communal vocabulary of Calvinists vis-à-vis man's corruption had his sensitivity to language not intervened. Edwards's awareness of the problems involved in verbal self-chastisement compares with that of his fictional fellow minister, Arthur Dimmesdale, who found that he could excoriate himself as the 'vilest of sinners,' not only with impunity, but with the ironic dividend of being revered the more for his sanctity" (*American Literature*, pp. 29–30).

25. Edwards was aware of the dangers of eliciting emotions through words. In "A Divine and Supernatural Light" (1734), he speculates that reactions to Christ's suffering could easily be the same as those provoked by reading a tragedy or romance (*Works*, VI, pp. 175–76).

26. Simonson observes, Edwards leaves no doubt "that his linguistic allegiance was to spiritual affections rather than to aesthetic niceties" (p. 94), and his use of "defilement" is a case in point. Not only does the word convey moral repugnance, but also a sense of its original substantive meaning: "defile," a ditch into which, often enough, one would find filth thrown. In addition, as Kristeva might argue, the word carries with it the sense of the "excluded," "on the basis of which religious prohibition is made up" (p. 65). And, Kristeva adds, the excluded is also, at some reach, the sublime, the sacred, the taboo. Defilement, then, for Edwards, suggests a *place* as well as a moral condition, both of which are necessarily repudiated. For this sort of exclusion, of course, Edwards had warrant of Saint Paul in the Letter to the Philippians.

27. "Song of Myself," 4, p. 32.

28. Peter Gay, "An American Tragedy," in Levin, *Jonathan Edwards*, p. 244.

29. Holmes may have read this passage from Edwards when he comments about Edwards's uncompromising insistence on the total depravity of unregenerate children, "Is it possible that Edwards read the text mothers love so well: Suffer little *vipers* to come unto me, and forbid them not, for of such is the

kingdom of God?" ("Jonathan Edwards," in *Pages from an Old Volume of Life* [Boston, 1892], p. 393).

30. *Errand into the Wilderness*, p. 178. See, in addition, Wayne Lesser: "The writing self, unlike the self engaged in the act of reading Scripture, is constituted by language, is weighed down in a mode of existence named and nameable by discourse, and cannot bring a consciousness of the self as saved to a presence. The language of man is an expression of fallen man..." (p. 290). "The language of man—which strives to define those spiritual things it cannot name, which strives to detach itself from ordinary speech and usage, but which also relies upon such custom for its communicative power (to the self or another audience)—embodies such oppositions and sublations and, therefore, refers indirectly to the existential dynamics of Puritan theology" ("Textuality and the Language of Man," pp. 291–92).

31. "The Mind," no. [35], in Anderson, *Scientific Writings*, p. 355.

32. See William H. Schurr, *Rappaccini's Children: American Writers in a Calvinist World* (Lexington: University Press of Kentucky, 1981). Schurr argues for a mystical interpretation of "Stopping by Woods": "Frost, in this poem, is responding negatively to one of the most profound and typical elements in the American religious experience" (p. 67).

33. See Elisabeth D. Dodds, *Marriage to a Difficult Man: the "Uncommon Union" of Jonathan and Sarah Edwards* (Philadelphia: Westminster Press, 1971), p. 69.

34. For background information on the sermon and a brief history of its reception, see "Jonathan Edwards at Enfield: "And Oh the Cheerfulness and Pleasantness...", Robert Lee Stuart, *American Literature*, vol. 48, no. 1, 1976–77: 46–59.

35. It is this sense of "eerie suspension of the sinner upon almost nothing" that Cady finds "essential to the peculiar success" of the sermon. (p. 69) Edwin Cady, "The Artistry of Jonathan Edwards," *The New England Quarterly*, vol. 22, 1949: 61–72.

36. David Levin, "Edwards, Franklin, and Cotton Mather," in *Jonathan Edwards and the American Experience* (Hatch and Stout, p. 37).

37. Jonathan Edwards, *Apocalyptic Writings*, Stephen Stein, ed. (New Haven: Yale University Press, 1977).

38. John F. Lynen, in *The Design of the Present* (New Haven: Yale University Press, 1969) argues that Edwards was not merely a theologian but a literary artist who fused his theology with his narrative craft. See esp. pp. 93–119.

39. James Carse, "An Urgent Now! for the Languid Will," in Levin, *Jonathan Edwards: A Profile, op. cit.* Carse comments that "Not just once, but with surprising frequency, Jonathan Edwards delivered the most searing maledictions in the memory of the American church. ... The eternal torment of the damned was a subject to which [Edwards] repeatedly and tirelessly turned in his preaching, and even in his miscellaneous notes. There is no item in this vivid explosion of metaphoric carnage on which his imagination could not feed at length. Indeed, we might well argue that his creative powers are nowhere more in evidence..." (pp. 220–21).

40. Cady observes, "to a people who lived long months by the hearth, whose

leisure moments would often have been taken up in playing with the fire, it must have been horrifying to participate imaginatively (on both ends of the web) in the metaphysical *and* physical experience denoted in Edwards's 'Sinners in the Hands of an Angry God' " ("Artistry," p. 67). See also Christopher R. Reaske's "The Devil and Jonathan Edwards," JHI, 33 (1972), pp. 123–38.

41. Without irony, a few lines later he observes, "And several souls were hopefully wrought upon that night. And oh the cheerfulness and pleasantness of their countenances that received comfort" (cited in Stuart, "Jonathan Edwards at Enfield," p. 46).

42. Herman Melville, *Moby-Dick*, Norton Critical Edition (New York: W.W. Norton and Co., 1967), p. 50.

43. Clarence Darrow, "The Edwardses and the Jukes," *American Mercury*, VI (October 1925), p. 153, cited in Simonson, *Jonathan Edwards, Theologian of the Heart, op. cit.*, p. 168, note no. 44.

44. Here is Twain, a few years before his death, reflecting upon God: "The real God, the Supreme One, is not a God of pity or mercy—not as we recognize these qualities. . . . The human conception of pity and morality must be entirely unknown to that Infinite God, as much unknown as the conceptions of a microbe to man, or at least as little regarded." In *Mark Twain's Fables of Man*, John S. Tuckey, ed. (Berkeley: University of California Press, 1972), pp. 110–11.

45. "Chanting the Square Deific," *The Collected Writings of Walt Whitman*, Bradley and Sculley, eds. (New York: W.W. Norton and Co., 1965). Whitman is a special case in all this, of course. Just as he mimicked—or seems to have— Emerson's *Nature* vision in the fifth verse of "Song of Myself," he also turns to a subject near to Edwards's heart. In "A Noiseless Patient Spider," Whitman uses the "flying spider"—the same species that had fascinated Edwards—as an emblem for his soul.

46. Porte writes here about Godwin's *Caleb Williams*.

47. Barton Levi St. Armand, "The 'Mysteries' of Edgar Poe: The Quest for a Monomyth in Gothic Literature," in Thompson, ed., *The Gothic Imagination*, p. 66.

48. "The Mind" [no. 35], in Wallace Anderson, *Jonathan Edwards, Scientific and Philosophic Writings* (New Haven: Yale University Press, 1980), p. 355.

49. Larzer Ziff, "A Reading of 'Wieland,' " says this: "Jonathan Edwards's voice may have been shouted down but America still had to reckon with the realities the old beliefs attempted to explain. This was to be the almost constant theme of Hawthorne and the agony of Melville." (*PMLA* 77, p. 56) Samuel Coale, appropriately, remarks, "In the ruins of Calvinism, Melville discovered darker foundations" (p. 25). See also Paul Levine, "The American Novel Begins," who similarly argues, "Thus if *Wieland* starts out as a rationalist attack on the excesses of religious enthusiasm it ends up virtually as a Calvinist assault on the conception of the universal efficacy of reason." (*The American Scholar*, Winter, 1965–66: 140); also see "Calvinism and Gothicism: The Example of Brown's *Wieland*," Michael T. Gilmore, *Studies in the Novel*, vol. 9, no. 2, Summer 1977.

50. For example, the literature of self-scrutiny and annihilation is extensive. For example, in "William Wilson," Poe writes a parodic tale of the externalized conscience, and Henry James's "The Jolly Corner" is, likewise, a variant of this spiritualized Gothic, exploring what Sage calls the "monstrous nature of absolute self-scrutiny"—a legacy, he says, of Calvinistic theology (*Horror Fiction*, p. xix). In James's tale, Spencer Brydon returns to his childhood home only to encounter his own perverse, literally unacknowledged and dismembered self.

51. Dennis L. White, "The Poetics of Horror: More Than Meets the Eye," *Cinema Journal*, vol. 10, no. 2, Spring 1971: 1–18.

52. See Green's discussion of Michael Wigglesworth's "Day of Doom," whose "dramatic rhetoric . . . was soon channeled into the sermon which, in turn, would be transformed into an overt weapon aimed at social control and construction of identity" (p. 63ff). G. R. Thompson writes, "The early American ghost story is one manifestation of the Gothic impulse of American dark Romanticism." See "Washington Irving and the American Ghost Story" (in *The Haunted Dusk: American Supernatural Fiction, 1820–1920*, p. 32).

53. Edwards's "naked preaching of terror" (Miller, in *Critical Essays on Jonathan Edwards*, p. 132) qualifies him as one of the earliest American Gothicists. Charles Brockden Brown's *Wieland* is generally considered the "first" American Gothic text. Larzer Ziff implies a familial, if distantly so, relationship between Brown and Edwards when he suggests that *Wieland* is important because it "recognizes the claims which Calvinism makes on the American character" (p. 51): "Brown rewrites the sentimental tradition and ends his journey through the mind by approaching the outskirts of [Jonathan] Edwards's camp" (p. 54).

54. Discussing dying—"in the highest sense of the word"—Edwards says this is "to die sensibly; to die and know it; to be sensible of the gloom of death. This is to be undone; this is worthy of the name of destruction. This sinking of the soul under an infinite weight, which it cannot bear, is the gloom of hell. We read in Scripture of blackness of darkness; this is it, this is the very thing" (cited in Simonson, *Theologian of the Heart*, pp. 126–270). Robert Lowell, quite evidently, also knew this passage from Edwards: "This is death: to die and to know it."

55. "Hawthorne and His Mosses," in *The Piazza Tales and other Prose Pieces, 1839–1860*, Harrison Hayford, Alma A. MacDougall, and G. Thomas Tanselle, eds. (Evanston: Northwestern University Press, 1987).

56. *Billy Budd and Other Tales* (New York: Signet Classics, 1956), p. 130. Leo Marx comments about the "salutary feelings": the narrator "infers from these theologians that it is his fate to furnish Bartleby with the means of subsistence. This excursion in Protestant theology teaches him a kind of resignation" (*Herman Melville's Billy Budd, "Benito Cereno," "Bartleby the Scrivener," and Other Tales*, Harold Bloom, ed., *op. cit.*, p. 20).

57. Anticipating Whitman's "Chanting the Square Deific" and Lovecraft's monstrous theologies, too. David H. Hirsch, in "The Pit and the Apocalypse"

(*Sewanee Review*, LXXVI, no. 4, October–December 1968) quotes Richard Wilbur approvingly in his explication of Poe's "The Pit and the Pendulum." It is "an account of a nightmare in which the dreamer is spiritually impotent, and cannot free his soul of the temporal . . . and the physical. . . . Finally, it is a horrible vision of Judgment Day, in which a fallen soul is all but sent to damnation or annihilation" (pp. 632–33).

58. Marion Montgomery, *Why Poe Drank Liquor* (LaSalle, IL: S. Sugden, 1983).

59. Porte, further, suggests a "curious confirmation of [the tale's] religious bearing, is suggested by a resemblance between this story and the conclusion to Poe's theodicy, *Eureka*" (Porte, "In the Hands," p. 63).

60. *The Poetical Works of Oliver Wendell Holmes*, Eleanor M. Tilton, ed. (Boston: Houghton Mifflin and Co., 1975), p. 160.

61. *The Varieties of Religious Experience* (New York: Penguin, p. 330).

62. Clemens to the Reverend Joseph H. Twichell, February 1902, in A. B. Paine, *Mark Twain's Letters*, 2 vols. (New York, 1917), II, pp. 719–20.

63. Consider much, if not most, of Twain's last works, especially Twain's #*44*—or Albert Bigelow Paine's "Mysterious Stranger"—puts the matter succinctly: "Strange, indeed, that you should not have suspected that your universe and its contents were only dreams, visions, fictions! Strange, because they are so frankly and hysterically insane—like all dreams: a God who could make good children as easily as bad, yet preferred to make bad ones; who could have made every one of them happy, yet never made a single happy one . . . in *The Mysterious Stranger Manuscripts*, William M. Gibson, ed. (Berkeley: University of California Press, 1969), pp. 404–5.

64. G. R. Thompson, "Introduction," *The Gothic Imagination: Essays in Dark Romanticism*, *op. cit.* Porte suggests as a possible source for Poe the religious/ Gothic fiction of James Hogg—"that egregiously Scotch-Presbyterian *Doppelgänger* story." *The Private Memoirs and Confessions of a Justified Sinner* (1824). Still remaining to be explored is Edwards's possible influence on the strict Calvinist Hogg. In general there might be a case. Oliver Wendell Holmes, in an 1883 essay on Edwards, intriguingly cites the "barbarous theology" of Scotland—in particular, the work of the Rev. Thomas Boston of Ettrick (from whence Hogg hales)—as an antecedent to Edwards's "Dante-like descriptions" and his imprecatory language. Edwards comments in a letter to the Rev. Mr. Gillespie of Scotland that he liked [Boston's 'Fourfold State of Man'] "exceedingly well. I think in that he shows himself to be a truly great divine" (Holmes, in *Critical Essays on Jonathan Edwards*, p. 220). It could be then that Boston provides a source for Hogg and Edwards both.

Harold P. Simonson further notes that the "extent to which Edwards's connections in Scotland reveal similar patterns of revivalism and theological debate" are not "generally recognized" (p. 353). He adds that what "has been known in a cursory way is that Edwards's reputation in Scotland was impressive. No fewer than 44 editions of his separate works were published in Scotland alone . . ." (p. 354).

65. Cited in Porte, "In the Hands of An Angry God," p. 43.

66. These poets (and Edward Taylor, Dickinson, Crane, Frost, Lowell) are espe-

cially useful in examining a tradition of secular mystical poetry. See, for example, Nina Baym, "God, Father, and Lover in Emily Dickinson's Poetry," in *Puritan Influences in American Literature*, Emory Elliott, ed., *op. cit.*, pp. 193–210. For a more general, although dated, analysis of the Puritan roots of American poetry, see Pearce, *The Continuity of American Poetry* (Princeton: Princeton University Press, 1961).

67. Robert Frost, already mentioned in connection with Edwards, indeed shares more than a passing similarity with the theologian of Divine Mystery. Frost however demurred from mystifying "that which must be gone into, / tho not explained." In "Stopping by Woods on a Snowy Evening," however, Frost uses, like Edwards, similar misconjunctions (lovely/dark and deep) to signal a parallel moment of awkward, perhaps unwanted, mysticism: "The woods are lovely, dark and deep / But I have promises to keep, / And miles to go before I sleep . . ." (p. 224).

68. The language of civic alienation here, then, will be written religiously and racially. In American geopolitics proscribed persons—heretics and racially different—will be consigned to the wilderness, a site *extra-domum*, physical or metaphysical. Hawthorne uses the trope in *The Scarlet Letter*, of course, but even earlier and less reflectedly Mather will use this language to alienize the Indian, portraying him as a sort of *native* antinomian, one who was racially different: the "Swarthy Indians" (Mather, p. 85) were of course kin to the "small Black man," (p. 80) the devil: "but [spectators in a witch trial] supposed, the *Black Man* (as the Witches call the devil; and they generally say he resembles an *Indian*)" (Mather, p. 126).

69. Susan Sontag, "The Imagination of Disaster," *Against Interpretation* (New York: Farrar, Straus and Giroux, 1966), p. 224.

70. Stephen Koch, "Fashions in Pornography: Murder as an Expression of Cine-matic Chic," *Harper's*, vol. 253, November 1976, pp. 108–11. Regarding the cinema of the seventies, Koch argues that "sentimentalism finds its outcome in pornography," and that the "invariable companion of sentimentalism" is "sadism" (p. 111). Exchanging terms more in keeping with my argument, one can see just how the "awe-ful" can, in terms of its representation, give way to the "awful." The further possibilities of sadism in such a public theorizing of the Divine are of particular interest in recent New Right alignments of religion and power.

71. Wilson H. Kimnach, "The Brazen Trumpet: Jonathan Edwards's Conception of the Sermon," in *Jonathan Edwards: His Life and Influence*, Charles Angoff, ed. (Rutherford, NJ: Fairleigh Dickinson University Press, 1975), p. 44.

72. See Ingebretsen, " 'If It Had To Perish Twice': Robert Frost's Aesthetics of Apocalypse," *Thought*, vol. 67, no. 264, March 1992: 31–46.

73. Bernard DeVoto writes: "The various ideas that make up the story troubled Mark almost obsessively . . . some of them go back many years in his note-books, all of them were obviously important to him. . . . These facts and the story itself have important implications." *Mark Twain's Letters from the Earth*, Bernard DeVoto, ed. (New York: Harper & Row, 1962), p. 297.

74. It is interesting to speculate on the connections between Twain and Love-

craft, although nothing very concrete can be established. As for "The Great Dark," it was possibly written in 1898, and not published until posthumously in 1962. Chances are slim that Lovecraft actually borrowed the idea from Twain. See *The Devil's Racetrack*, Tunney, and *Letters from the Earth*, Bernard de Voto, ed., *op. cit.*

CHAPTER FOUR

The Shape of the Dark: Robert Frost and H. P. Lovecraft

> *"A man said to the universe:*
> *Sir, I exist!"*
> *"However," replied the universe*
> *"The fact has not created in me*
> *a sense of obligation."*[1]
> —STEPHEN CRANE

> *. . . And through this revolting graveyard of the universe the muffled, maddening beating of dreams, and thin, monotonous whine of blasphemous flutes from inconceivable, unlighted chambers beyond Time; the detestable pounding and piping whereunto dance slowly, awkwardly, and absurdly the gigantic, tenebrous ultimate gods—the blind, voiceless, mindless gargoyles whose soul is Nyarlathotep.*
> —LOVECRAFT[2]

> *[Tone metaphysical]: "If you know any big words this is your chance for them."*
> — *"How to Write a Blackwood's Article," From* Great Short Works of Edgar Allan Poe, *p. 199*

■■

The House That Edwards Built: Spiders and Their Gods

Good gloom on her was thrown away.
—FROST, "THE NIGHT-LIGHT," P. 386

In this chapter, I wish to consider the potential for melodrama implicit in the theology of Jonathan Edwards. Edwards's fearsome cosmology anticipates a range of responses, on the one hand prompting fantasy, satire, and parody, and, on the other, Emersonian, drawing-room poetry. H. P. Lovecraft and Robert Frost demonstrate this split. Contemporaries of a sort, they read like Protestants in denial; both articulate two variations of what, after Edwards, might be called a "providence of terror."[3] Frost enshrines a high-canonical sublime as poetic mysticism, while Lovecraft in effect takes Edwards's cosmology to its logical, if horrific, conclusion. Frost learned much from Poe *and* Emerson, and his cosmological musings, apocalyptic verse, and concern for revelation echoes Edwards.[4] Frost's "dis-ease" with space, and his muscular self-hauntings (in "Acquainted with the Night," for instance) seem like interiorized versions of Lovecraft's baleful metaphysics. In "A Lesson for Today," the poet writes "Space ails us moderns: we are sick with space. / Its contemplation makes us out as small / as a brief epidemic of microbes" (*Poetry*, p. 352). Twain's sentiments, exactly, if you recall "The Great Dark." Lovecraft's, too. Unlike Frost, however, Lovecraft repudiates theistic design, although he appropriates the language of apocalypse as pose and the form of the universe as trap. If Edwards implied that cosmic terror resulted from the too-attentive love of deity, Lovecraft situates terror in the indifference or malignity of the cosmos—as did, in different ways, Robert Frost.[5]

It is a commonplace of Frost criticism to trace his poetical roots to Emerson; Frost himself did so on numerous occasions, although he took care to distance himself from the "cheerful Monist," remarking once that a "melancholy dualism is the only soundness" (Cox and Lathem, p. 112).[6] Yet while it is a commonplace to link Frost to Emerson, an earlier connection must be made—backward from Emerson's idiosyncratic unorthodoxies to Jonathan Edwards's more traditional theologies. For Edwards—

or at least the school of American theology derived from Edwards—is the source, I maintain, of Frost's notorious "dark" mode. That such a link is not made more often only confirms one of the points of this study: theology, discredited, has gone into hiding and so is everywhere present as trace and shadow. Frost once described himself an "Old-Testament Christian," and his verse perfectly exemplifies Joel Porte's thesis, discussed earlier in connection with Edwards.[7] Porte argued that in Anglo-American culture, religious mystery has been emptied of specific religious content and become, instead, merely a habit of dread.[8] Frost remained extraordinarily reticent about his religious beliefs, and they are not really at issue here. What is significant, however, is the way Frost calculatingly distanced himself from this theological heritage—most typically, by reimagining deeply felt theological imperatives as aesthetic questions of form, structure, and design: "Grant me intention, purpose, and design—/ That's near enough for me to the Divine" ("Accidentally on Purpose," p. 425). In other words, an inscrutability that to Edwards would have been a matter of theology becomes, for Frost, a matter of textual competency. In either case questions of reading and interpretation are foremost. Edwards's theological eschatology, then, with its distant, unknowable deity, gives way to the crafty poet whose poetic rhythms reveal and occasionally conceal, keeping the revelation of meaning for "the right ones." One can readily see Frost's gradual conflation of discourses. For instance, in "Education by Poetry," Frost's subject is aesthetics but his discourse is theological. He declares that "the only materialist . . . is the man who gets lost in his material without a gathering metaphor to throw it into shape and order. He is the lost soul" (Cox and Lathem, p. 41). But Frost's most famous dictum of the poetic life—and its relationship to spiritual things—could have come right from Edwards himself: "Every poem is an epitome of the great predicament; a figure of the will braving alien entanglements" ("The Constant Symbol," Cox and Lathem, p. 25).

Frost and Lovecraft, then, in genres seemingly as disparate as fantasy and poetry, find themselves rewriting theology. The tradition most congenial to them would have been those American thinkers for whom religion persisted as imaginative habit long after ceasing to be intellectually significant. Consider for a moment what Frost does with a central image and motif—spiders and entrapment—found in Edwards's sermon, "Sinners in the Hands of an Angry God." A consistent cosmological map governs Edwards and Frost (and Lovecraft as well, as we shall see). The relations and tensions of "Design" and "Sinners in the Hand of an Angry God" reflect a metaphysics of power and scrutiny; of unwitting transgression and expiation. Each presents a cosmos in which human will fails before the ultimate entrapment of cosmic determinism. Yet Frost's deft, ironic poem undercuts Edwards's metaphysics of spiritual power.

In "Design," Frost reflects on the sorts of revelation that one might reasonably divine from Emersonian "natural facts."[9] The sonnet's last few lines ask what kind of cosmic order so arranged the "dimpled" spider, moth, and "innocent" flower that their conjunction traps the unwitting moth:

> *What had that flower to do with being white,*
> *The wayside blue and innocent heal-all?*
> *What brought the kindred spider to that height,*
> *Then steered the white moth thither in the night?*
> *What but design of darkness to appall?—*
> *If design govern in a thing so small.*[10]

Though the poem at first seems to argue a conventional, philosophical sense of design, the mounting tension caused by a series of unanswered interrogations undercuts the consolations typically associated with this argument of divinely sanctioned order. If these interrogatives—"what had" and "what brought"—are more than rhetorical questions, then the more than rhetorical force of the poem's last interrogative pronoun catches the reader off-guard. Looking for comfort, the reader finds none to be had; the poem shows that the argument for universal design conceals possibilities far darker than first perceived. Finally, the closing couplet denies outright any rhetorical comfort offered by a design, and so the poem concludes with an apparently shattering, disruptive sort of revelation. Thus the poem is apocalyptic in a traditional, though limited and derivative, sense of the word. Its intricate design traps the reader in despair as surely as the argument for universal design provides a deterministic trap for the spider.

Frost himself often warned readers against thinking his ostensibly simple verse to lack complexity. "I should like," he said,

> to be so subtle at this game as to seem . . . altogether obvious. The casual person would assume that I meant nothing or else I came near enough meaning something he was familiar with to mean it for all practical purposes.[11]

"Design" underscores Frost's point. On the one hand Frost cleverly manipulates a discourse of fear, highlighting anxieties that are partly cultural and theological, as well as partly psychological. Return for a moment to what easily could have been Frost's model; Frost increases the sense of helpless abjection that in "Sinners in the Hands of an Angry God" is Edwards's main, although submerged, theme. The sinner can do nothing, can save nothing, can hold nothing "unless" God acts for him. In addition, Frost sharpens the irony of the scene by making the spider—Edwards's metaphor for the victim of judgment—the unwitting agent of judgment. The conviction behind Edwards's sermon is congruent with his belief that God "abhors" unregenerate men and women; their sinfulness, Edwards imagines, causes God to be "dreadfully provoked," and so he holds them like "a spider or some loathsome [*sic*] insect over the fire" (p. 458). This graphic image reflects Edwards's belief in the impotency of the human will; like the spider dangling over the fire, human volition is powerless to change its fate and therefore must suffer the "mere pleasure of God" (p. 451). Frost, however, mutes the drama, making it harder to assess responsibility for the tableaux's potential tragedy. Indeed, is it one? After all, asks the poem, what "had that flower to do with being white?" The "innocent heal-all" is typically a blue flower, although in this specific instance by genetic accident it is white. The abnormal coloring in turn provides a haven for the white spider, thus leaving the moth vulnerable to its predations. Frost echoes Edwards in his dark suggestion of unwanted complicity, even cosmic inevitability. The spider, once victim of justice, is now, in its own implacable turn, the agent of a "design of darkness." Driven both by force of its nature *and* chance, the spider can only do, in a manner of speaking, what it is determined to do—and that is to act predatorially. So, in different ways sermon and poem present "designs of darkness to appall." For Edwards the terror was dying under the judgment of God; for Frost, the terror was living under life's judgment, and being held accountable to life—a "trial by Existence," as Frost termed it in an early poem.

It is easy to be lulled into agreement with "Design" because of its formal civility, its comfortable and unobtrusive rhyme. Its design, simply put, renders it benevolent. Yes, agrees the reader, unaware of the trap, what governs here *but* a design of darkness, whose literary design (like the Gothic in this respect) is to appall— *if*, of course, design governs in a thing so small as the eating habits of spiders. But what if design does *not* govern? What might we expect then? What makes for good theology may have terrible, even horrible, human implications, as Lovecraft was to perceive.[12] A draft of the poem that became "Design" was written very early in Frost's career, probably before he had published his first book in 1913. Thus the distinctive dark shadow on Frost's middle and late poetry is not a late accretion to the poetic voice; rather, it is typical of Frost from beginning to end. Hayden Carruth calls this tone of Frost's "the blackest, bitterest despair in three hundred years of the New England tradition" ("The New England Tradition," p. 34). In a review of the New England poetic tradition, Carruth traces the despair he hears in Frost's verse back to Michael Wigglesworth. One must take Wigglesworth's text, Carruth says, "and then abstract the knowledge of salvation from it, to find anything like Frost's vision of the human hell" (p. 35). And although he doesn't mention Edwards directly in this connection, Carruth notes how much Frost's generally self-deprecatory platform manner resembled Edwards's. Carruth cites reports of Edwards's formal and quiet manner at Enfield and concludes that theologian and poet resemble each other in that both report a bleak vision "so quietly . . . that the horror almost skips past us, and that itself adds to the horror" (1971, p. 945).[13] Even Lionel Trilling, who peered into Frost's darkness perhaps earlier than it was fashionable to do so, confessed himself surprised by the Frost he discovered. "He is not," Trilling said, "the Frost who reassures us by his affirmation of old virtues, simplicities, pieties, and ways of feeling: anything but." Frost, said Trilling, is a "terrifying poet" who conceives of a "terrifying universe" (Cox, *Robert Frost*, pp. 156–57). To explain his point further Trilling added, "Read the poem called "Design" and see if you sleep the better for it" (Cox, *Robert Frost*, p. 157).

Frost is a "terrifying" poet partly because he does not repeat pious poetic platitudes, as hasty readers sometimes suppose him to do. Frost's verse holds a potential for terror because Frost is working in a poetics of terror as old as Calvin, whose inscrutable Deity seemed perversely designed for cruelty and anxiety. In the Calvinistic universe, formal design and entrapment seemed one and the same thing. And so, in the American school, as Calvin's severe theologies were increasingly dismissed by mainstream religionists, nonetheless traces of them would remain in other discourses. Thus, while Edwards evoked terror in the service of a God whose "arbitrary" compassion alone stayed his hand, the profoundly dark tone of Frost's poems stems from his steadily neutral response to mystery. So while Frost's "Design" reflects perhaps an unbridgeable philosophical distance between himself and Edwards, the poem also reflects a certain theological congruency, a tacit agreement, if you will, upon first principles: "What but design of darkness to appall?— / If design govern in a thing so small."

"Design" may not help a reader sleep, as Trilling suggests, but then, so many of Frost's poems do not. So much of Frost seems in fact to be written at night, or written *to be read* at night. It sometimes catches Frost's devotional public by surprise, especially those who have not read him well, to consider how much night there *is* in Frost's world. For example, a simple count of the poems themselves reveals an interesting fact. While thirty-seven of the poems in Frost's *Complete Poems* focus on daylight images of roads, forty-five concern themselves with night skies, stars, or various concerns of astronomy. Indeed, darkness is Frost's signature as well as his scene; his poetry constructs a taxonomy of darkness, a darkness no less so because of his complex attitude toward it. If, as Rexford Stamper argues, the dark presents "an ontological view devoid of certainty or comfort," it is also the time at night when one sees the stars—"small hopes" Frost once glossed them.[14] The dark limits vision ("Acceptance") and limit of sight suggests, metaphorically, the imagination's limits ("Into My Own"; "Come In"). The dark represents a state of mind or imagination ("Mending Wall") and a physical location ("A Cabin in the Clearing"). In "Stopping by Woods on a Snowy Evening," the dark extends an invitation, if not to death, then to something forbidding enough to make the usually laconic Frost respond, with reference to the poem, "All I meant was to get the hell out of there" (Greiner, *Centennial Essays*, p. 57).

In many night poems, the dark occasions revelation and insight ("One More Brevity"; "Unstamped Letter"; "Two Look at Two"). Sometimes the dark describes the future ("Acceptance"); at other times it is the past reimagined as the present ("The Trial by Existence"). The dark embodies the complexity of an individual person ("Acquainted with the Night"; "Mending Wall"); represents the entrapment of familial traditions ("Home Burial"; "The Witch of Coos"); of social traditions ("Neither Out Far Nor In Deep"). It signifies the present, existential condition ("The Draft Horse"; "The Wood-Pile"). The darkness, lastly, is ontological—a "design of darkness to appall," the "background [of] hugeness and confusion, shading away from where we stand into black and utter chaos."[15]

This ontological darkness falls everywhere in Frost. For instance, consider the opening lines to the "The Wood-Pile," which in theme and tone are characteristic. A hiker loses his way "Out walking in the frozen swamp one grey day," and he reflects that "The view was all in lines / Straight up and down of tall slim trees / too much alike to mark or name a place by / So as to say for certain I was here / Or somewhere else: I was just far from home" (*The Poetry*, p. 101). The scene is emblematic of Frost's verse. In particular, this image of homelessness echoes Emerson's rapturous metaphysical homelessness wandering alone on Boston Commons. In "The Wood-Pile," the monochromatic tones of a winter's landscape symbolize human inability to differentiate limits, boundaries, or to set them—or to locate the self within them—with any certainty. Frost's poetry offers endless variations on a theme of metaphysical dis-ease, and the many instances of being lost in the dark—generally in the woods—serves as a metaphor for Frost's metaphysical and ethical convictions. That is, human attempts to know and to do the right and the good inevitably fail. Or take another short poem, ironically, the last poem Frost read in public, only weeks before his death:

> She always had to burn a light
> Beside her attic bed at night.
> It gave bad dreams and broken sleep,
> But helped the Lord her soul to keep.

> *Good gloom on her was thrown away.*
> *It is on me by night or day,*
> *Who have, as I suppose, ahead*
> *The darkest of it still to dread.*

(*THE POETRY*, P. 386)

Darkness and gloom; dispossession and homelessness were repeated themes for Frost, and this is obliquely reflected by the titles
of his books, most of which named places or aspects of the land
(for instance, *North of Boston* [1914], his major critical success,
derives its name from a real estate sign).[16] Frost probably never
reflected upon the source of these powerful images, or, if he did,
he would have backed away from any formally theological expression of them. Like Thoreau, and in the words of Keeper (*A Masque
of Mercy*), Frost would "rather be lost in the woods / Than found in
church" (*The Poetry*, p. 513). Indeed, part of the tension throughout his verse reflects, on the one hand, Frost's repeated reference
to the pastoral possibilities of the woods, set against, on the other
hand, a refusal to consider that possibility. A hundred years or so
earlier it had been rhetorically daring, even brash, for Emerson in
Nature to enthuse that he went to the woods when he wanted to be
alone, since in Puritan group-speak only the devil (or, remembering the colonials, the deity?) would dare be alone in that fierce-
some place. Eventually, the habit of solitude as self-expression
cherished by Emerson would become more and more disallowed,
as the spiritual world it portended fell into increasing disrepute.

The difference in the philosophic sensibilities between Emerson and Frost becomes clearer when we consider their attitudes
toward nature. Unlike Emerson, Frost's speakers rarely want to go
into the woods they so much admire. Turn for a moment to Frost's
classic night poem. "Stopping by Woods on a Snowy Evening"
(1923) is the best-known example of what is practically a distinct
genre in Frost's poetry—life imagined from the edge of the woods.
Recall that the opening lines of *Nature* charts Emerson's solitary
and soul-expanding encounter with the Sublime. In Frost's poem,
on the other hand, a similar moment of solitude in the woods
prompts only a reflection that "my little horse must think it queer
/ to stop without a farmhouse near"; the moment of solitude
supports only steady and somber observation for Frost's traveler, a

moment of imaginative shrinkage, even terror. In poem after poem the dark woods—mysterious, dark, alluring, frightening—alternately invite and terrify. Like other poems ("The Onset," for example, its companion piece, or "Desert Places," or "Come In") this poem takes its energy from the pressure of the night and the presence of "dark woods."

That we are to read these woods as an expression of Frost's late-theological, gothicized imagination seems clear. After Emerson, authors like Frost find themselves negotiating around moments of transcendence/mysticism; moments for which their language did not prepare them and against which their culture had increasingly gathered its forces of denial. The difference, then, between Frost and Emerson's approach to the woods is instructive.[17] Emerson's ecstatic vision on Boston Commons could have provided Frost all the warning he needed that mystical experience is perilous and potentially self-annihilating. After all, one ought not go *too* far into the woods. And Frost's speakers rarely go into the woods. They linger on the outside, safely behind fences or in the middle of the road as they peer in. For example, in "Come In," the speaker at "the edge of the woods" reflects upon the invitation he thinks he hears from a thrush "far in the pillared dark." He thinks the bird invites him to "come in" (p. 334); nevertheless he backs away and does not: he "would not come in . . . even if asked"—and, as he realizes more soberly, he "hadn't been." Frost, then, is a reticent heir to a mystical tradition gone secular, and in "Stopping By Woods" the narrator reflects the conflict. Although clearly inter-ested in *something* about the dark woods, nonetheless the speaker admonishes himself, "But I have promises to keep, / And miles to go before I sleep, / And miles to go before I sleep" (*The Poetry*, p. 25). The speaker's somewhat belated admonishment that he has promises to keep means of course that he *didn't* have himself to lose in the cold, clear, boundary-less midnight. Indeed, that the traveler *needed* to remind himself of his promises suggests the effort it took to do so in the first place. Yes, the woods *were* lovely, dark, and deep. Good Protestant that Frost was, private visions both allured and frightened him, and Frost had learned from his theological ancestors not to trust himself in someone else's hands or out of his own sight.

In summary, then, anxiety and a generalized dread replace the religious awe more typical of Emerson and other nineteenth-century writers of nature. If Emerson found solitude a self-possessing experience, one that signaled the approach of the Divine, suggesting a hope of revelation, in Frost's verse such solitude most typically is crushing and annihilating. In this regard Frost resembles Edwards in another way, as well. Frost's speakers wander lost and alone—or they are lost because they are alone—at night, while "at an unearthly height / One luminary clock against the sky / Proclaimed the time was neither wrong nor right" ("Acquainted With the Night," *The Poetry*, p. 255). In the diminishing space of the spirit, the self returns as self-haunt. "One need not be a Chamber—to be Haunted—" as Dickinson put it, and in "Desert Places," reflecting about a snowfall and dark night woods, Frost responds similarly: "I have it in me so much nearer home / to scare myself with my own desert places" (*The Poetry*, p. 296).[18] The "horrors of the mind" appropriate to Edwards's orthodox theology in effect become the chief subject of Frost's verse—the Self, held captive in imaginative thrall. In "A Servant to Servants," for instance, a woman says "There's nothing but a voice-like left inside / That seems to tell me how I ought to feel, / And would feel if I wasn't all gone wrong" (p.63). No longer is there a transcendent order or valuation possible. Yet Frost's housewife here, like so many of his other men and women, are rarely victimized by cosmological forces alone: they, themselves, are Hell, trapped as often by their imaginative impoverishment as by their abandoned or decaying cabins or unhappy intimacies or upstairs cages. This is another way of saying, of course, that Original Sin has ceased being theology and become metaphor, played out again in the constraints of imagination and memory. In Frost's late poem, "Directive" (1946), the reshaping of personal memory seems to indicate a "source"—however minimal—of comfort and "healing," yet overall it is clear that Frost shared Edwards's pained awareness of human consciousness, his acceptance of "gloom" that was, oddly enough, "good." But this is no surprise; in an earlier reading of that paradigm, "culpa" could also be "felix." The habit of religion was more than sin deep.

Reading Frost's poetry with any care one wonders what pressures were at work to establish him, as Trilling commented, as "virtually a symbol of America" (Cox, *Robert Frost*, p. 154). Most

readers know Frost—or misknow him—as a Currier and Ives min-
iaturist, hymning a New England that never was, delighting in a
poetics of Yankee comfort. Yet Frost was truer than the sentimental nostalgia that on occasion held him captive. Consider one last
poem, published months before his death, although reportedly
written forty years before. "The Draft Horse" makes a startling
though appropriate companion piece to "Stopping by Woods"
(1923), and both date from the same period. The pair of poems
surely represent Frost's "darker mood," and the difference in
their public fates is instructive. While "Stopping by Woods" went
on to become one of Frost's most anthologized poems, most critics
abandon any attempt to place "The Draft Horse" in Frost's *oeuvre*
because it seems so "unFrostian." However, it is vintage Frost,
deep, dark, and Calviny. In fact as background and potential
source one hears some interesting echoes—particularly of Oliver
Wendell Holmes's "The Deacon's Masterpiece: or The Wonderful
'One-Hoss Shay'."[19] Frost's "frail buggy" in the "pitch-dark limitless grove," like Oliver Wendell Holmes's poem, pitches the reader
headfirst into Edwards's cosmology of tyrannous inscrutabilities;
Frost's universe is the same dark universe of Edwards's "Freedom
of the Will":

> *With a lantern that wouldn't burn*
> *In too frail a buggy we drove*
> *Behind too heavy a horse*
> *Through a pitch-dark limitless grove.*
>
> *And a man came out of the trees*
> *And took our horse by the head*
> *And reaching back to his ribs*
> *Deliberately stabbed him dead.*
>
> *The ponderous beast went down*
> *With a crack of a broken shaft.*
> *And the night drew through the trees*
> *In one long invidious draft.*
>
> *The most unquestioning pair*
> *That ever accepted fate*
> *And the least disposed to ascribe*
> *Any more than we had to hate,*

> *We assumed that the man himself*
> *Or someone he had to obey*
> *Wanted us to get down*
> *And walk the rest of the way.*

What Lovecraft could do with that vignette! Or even Stephen Crane, whose universe reminds the petulant man that his existence has not created "a sense of obligation." Lawrance Thompson dates Frost's "The Draft Horse" back to the early twenties, just about the same time that Eliot published "The Waste-Land." Like Eliot, Frost here picks over the metaphysical leavings of an abandoned culture and finds them wanting.

"The Draft Horse" is Frost's obituary for a metaphysic, and it turns our attention to Lovecraft, who in 1923, twenty years younger than Frost, was just coming into *his* own—to borrow the title of Frost's first book. Lovecraft would have endeared himself to Frost, among other reasons, because he hailed from Providence, a little north of Boston. The two writers also shared a common set of philosophical beliefs, although Lovecraft's fiction would darken the universe to such a degree that he would have startled even the austere and essentially pious Frost of "The Draft Horse." Cosmology is imaginative destiny, and while Frost appropriated the terms of a Christian cosmology for his poetry, there is no clearer repudiation of Calvin's universe—and of its unrelenting theological determinism as well—than Lovecraft's horror fiction. Like Melville's Hawthorne, Lovecraft says "no in thunder" to the inherent contradictions of a beneficent, inscrutable deity, while repossessing its metaphysical terror in fantasy.

Lovecraft can be read as a sort of taxonomy of the Protestant imagination, in which the pursuit of the transcendent is expressed as a debased titillation of the terrible. Lovecraft's career is paradoxical for a variety of reasons; he blends an eighteenth-century neoclassical prose and diction with the unreasonable phantasmic, yoking twentieth-century principles of physics with the witch-hunting theological discourse of Cotton Mather. He is the doyen of American theological repudiation: the priest of the pulps, the last word and lowest remove from Edwards. If Edwards found that he had to speak demoniacally in order to talk about God, Lovecraft found that invoking the Holy was a most excellent way to evoke

horrific "overtones of the soul" ("Pickman's Model," p. 44).[20] For
example, a favorite expression of Lovecraft's—"soul-annihilating
memory" (*The Best of Lovecraft*, p. 41)—comes ready-to-hand from
the complex depths of Christian mysticism. John of the Cross
would easily have understood the language and the emotion behind it, even if not the use to which Lovecraft puts it. Thus it was
that old-world theologies of abasement found a resonance in the
new-world literary basement, as Edwards's ineffable sublime became increasingly more grotesque the more it was contained in
speech.

"*More* Errands into the Wilderness"

I am Providence.

—INSCRIPTION ON H. P. LOVECRAFT'S TOMBSTONE,
PROVIDENCE, RI

It's probably an exaggeration to claim that Lovecraft is "univer-
sally regarded as the most important American writer of dark
fantasy since Edgar Allan Poe" (Barron, p. 160). He does, however, have his fans—Fritz Leiber called him the "Copernicus of the
horror story" and in a recent collection of horror, Lovecraft is
called the "most notorious throw-away author in modern American literature" (Bleiler, p. iii).[21] Hyperbole aside, Lovecraft is
probably not regarded at all, or if so, is quickly dismissed. Any
attention he gets is likely to be tinged with the guilt or shame
generally associated with the fantasy genre. Yet fantasy is a favorite
mode of American writing, and the examples of Mather, Edwards,
and Emerson showed Lovecraft that the discourse of fantasy, while
appearing to repudiate theology, nonetheless affirms it. Lovecraft's letters acknowledges an interest in Cotton Mather, although
no such direct evidence suggests that he read Emerson's *Nature*.
Indeed, it would be difficult to imagine him reading the Emerson
of *Nature* and *Essays* for long or with much patience. However, one
could imagine Lovecraft saying about Emerson (as he wrote about
Hawthorne) that "the heritage of American weirdness was his to a
most intense degree" (*Supernatural Horror*, p. 61).[22]
Indeed, Lovecraft was as much a theologian as was Emerson,

and his Cthulhu Mythos constructs a "horrific cosmological and historical context for human history" (Barron, p. 137). Further, definite intellectual affinities connect Emerson—the former Unitarian cleric turned cosmologian—and Lovecraft, the cosmologian who had no use for the "cringing Semitic slave-cult of Christianity" (*Selected Letters*, III, p. 45).[23] Therefore a reader must pay attention, since Emerson and Lovecraft sometimes sound like parodies of each other. Consider, for example, this line from the beginning of *Nature*: "But if a man would be alone, let him look at the stars" (p. 9). Read without irony, the sentiment could be Lovecraft's, as it was also Frost's—to whom the wide cosmos signified divinity's absence, if not its outright indifference. Or compare Emerson's bravado in the face of the cosmos to Frost's gloss on his early poem, "Stars": "There is no oversight of human affairs" (*The Poetry*, p. 529). Then, set Emerson and Frost beside Lovecraft's self-declared, equally bravado atheism: "A mere knowledge of the approximate dimensions of the visible universe is enough to destroy forever the notion of a personal godhead" (*Selected Letters*, 1, p. 44).

Read in context, Emerson's meditation about becoming a "transparent eyeball" makes him sound like one of Poe's self-absorbed and self-absorbing narrators:

> Standing on the bare ground,—my head bathed by the blithe air, and uplifted into infinite space,—all mean egotism vanishes. I become a transparent eyeball; I am nothing; I see all; the currents of the Universal Being circulate through me: I am part or particle of God. . . . The greatest delight which the fields and woods minister, is the suggestion of an occult relation between man and the vegetable. I am not alone and unacknowledged (*Nature*, pp. 10–11).

Emerson's overheated prose contains a number of literary echoes. Most importantly it refers obliquely to Calvin's *Institutes* (Book I; chapters 5, 6), in which the theologian uses the image of weak eyes and spectacles to analogize the place of Scripture in discerning Revelation.[24] In addition, as suggested above, Emerson suggests the frenzy of Poe's manic narrators—perhaps from "The Pit and the Pendulum" or "The Tell-tale Heart"—who find themselves trapped within a nightmare that will, if persisted in, leave them certifiably mad. Lovecraft learned the bizarreries of first-person point of view from Poe, and he could have learned from Poe about revelations that could not be spoken within the conventional limits of speech. In Poe, too, Lovecraft would have found narrators to whom madness and verbal collapse was the price paid—or *exacted*—for unspeakable or impermissible knowledge.

But no less an authority than Jonathan Edwards reminds us that madness (of speech, at any rate) shares an oblique kinship with theological discourse, and more than one of Lovecraft's highstrung narrators exhibit signs of an imagination soaked with theology.[25] They obsess about boundaries that shift and slide; fulminate about untold sins and regretted transgressions; decry the awe-ful secret they know but cannot tell; they bemoan the expiatory price exacted by what they know. For example, in Lovecraft's "The Outsider," a story of a dead man returning to the land of the living, the narrator is unaware of this fact until he meets his horrid reflection in a glass. Innocent of self-reflection, he knows peace. Awakened to self-consciousness, he finds himself trapped in his labyrinthine memory. Before that moment of shattering revelation, the narrator naïvely reflects upon his condition:

> So through endless twilights I dreamed and waited, though I knew not what I waited for. Then in the shadowy solitude my longing for light grew so frantic that I could rest no more, and I lifted entreating hands to the single black ruined tower that reached above the forest into the unknown outer sky (p. 38).

The scene here is very like Emerson's. When the epiphanic moment breaks upon the appalled narrator, and he stares at his decay in the mirrorlike glass, he could be Edwards, Emerson, even Frost, confronting the potential enormities of human consciousness and its exploding metaphysics, and maddened by the hardly recognizable, Lacanian nightmare in the mirror. The hapless narrator's quest for a light always receding beyond his grasp, in "a labyrinth of nighted silence" (*The Best of Lovecraft*, p. 38), could easily be read as a Lovecraftian parable of the futility of religious pursuits. The outsider's universe is a place of secrets partly suspected, a maze of revelations dimly revealed; and in the death of God (or, from an orthodox point of view, in His inscrutability and ineluctable distance), the only end remaining the spiritual quest is an "eidolon of unwholesome revelation"—an "inconceivable, indescribable, and unmentionable monstrosity" (*The Best of Lovecraft*, p. 40). Lovecraft's "At the Mountains of Madness" imagines just such a scene, as we shall see.

It is a sign of Lovecraft's intellectual complexity that the God denied so thoroughly by his materialism returns so insistently in the arcane horrors of his fiction. Though he remains largely unknown except to a stalwart and devoted "fanzine" audience, Lovecraft's tales are a representative guide to the American theological imagination in all its bristly contrariness. Post-Puritan moralist, Lovecraft writes in the traditional cadences of religious discourse: salvation and damnation; grace and sin; surface and interiority; faith and unbelief. His is the widening abyss beneath the sheen of appearances, the great fragility of things as they seem. His themes are the endless return of the body, and thus, the haunting of the soul by its own hungers; by time; by memory; finally, its effacement as the consequence of ill-fated love. His obsessions, ghosts—call them what you will—reflect the exhaustion of metaphysics as normative guide to interiority. A first-time reader, however, will find Lovecraft's fiction oddly familiar—largely because he traffics with abandon in unburied (and often unburiable) memories, exploiting fears that are as old as the earliest colonists, and which just as often derive from the same spiritual anxieties ("Dreams of the Witch House," "The Unnameable").

In "The Unnameable," for example, Lovecraft turns the ineffable Divine into a metaphor. He describes a ravening, repining spiritual entity haunting an abandoned house near Salem. Lovecraft carefully works out the chronology of the tale so that it is evident that the creature's origins coincide with the Puritans' Great Migration in 1630. Similarly, in other tales Lovecraft pillages ancient cultural closets for their hidden unspeakables—anxieties about identity and purity ("The Dunwich Horror," "The Shadow over Innsmouth"); generation and transgression ("The Dunwich Horror," "Pickman's Model"); the meaning and value of history ("The Case of Charles Dexter Ward"); the cosmos and the terrors of its teleologies ("The Shadow Out of Time," "The Whisperer in Darkness"). In sum, Lovecraft takes for his subject the hermeneutics of suspicion by which life is experienced in a Christian metaphysic.

Not only did Lovecraft write horrific fiction; he also thought critically about what he was doing, and his insights are instructive. In *Supernatural Horror in Literature*, Lovecraft argues that "the oldest and strongest emotion of mankind is fear, and the oldest and strongest kind of fear is fear of the unknown" (p. 12). However, Lovecraft distinguishes a superior weird tale, that of "cosmic fear" (p. 15), that he sets apart from ordinary literature of fear:

> The true weird tale has something more than secret murder, bloody bones, or a sheeted form clanking chains according to a rule. A certain atmosphere of breathless and unexplainable dread of outer, unknown forces must be present; and there must be a hint, expressed with a seriousness and portentousness becoming its subject, of that most terrible conception of the human brain—a malign and particular suspension or defeat of those fixed laws of Nature which are our only safeguard against the assaults of chaos and the daemons of unplumbed space (p. 15).

Lovecraft's definition here echoes Poe, who a century earlier had distinguished the terror "not of Germany but of the soul."[26] Indeed, Lovecraft acknowledges that "the real weavers of cosmic terror" are the "artists beginning with Poe" (p. 25), and he ranks Poe "as deity and fountain-head of all modern diabolic fiction" (p. 56). Poe, says Lovecraft, possesses a "master's vision of the terror that stalks about and within us" (p. 54). And that vision, the soul-in-terror, is:

> The unknown, being likewise the unpredictable, became for our primitive forefathers a terrible and omnipotent source of boons and calamities visited upon mankind for cryptic and wholly extraterrestrial reasons, and thus clearly belonging to spheres of existence whereof we know nothing and wherein we have no part (13).[27]

Reading again some early New England texts—perhaps Increase Mather's *Remarkable Providences* or his son Cotton's *The Wonders of the Invisible World*—it is clear that similar fears touched less primitive forefathers much closer to home. Lovecraft had read Mather carefully, and the numerous allusions he makes in letters and fiction show that Lovecraft had an intuitive feel for the Matherian, Christian universe of unseen powers and principalities: "there existed amongst educated and uneducated alike a most unquestioning faith in every form of the supernatural; from the gentlest doctrines of Christianity to the most monstrous morbidities of witchcraft and black magic" (*Supernatural Horror*, p. 19).[28]

The "one test" of the successful weird tale, argues Lovecraft, is "a profound sense of dread, and of contact with unknown spheres and powers; a subtle attitude of awed listening . . ." (p. 16). To switch discourses for a moment, Rudolph Otto could easily have said this, writing of the sacred terror of the *mysterium tremendum.* Otto argues, "Taking in the religious sense, that which is 'mysterious' is—to give it perhaps the most striking expression—the 'wholly other' . . . that which is quite beyond the sphere of the usual, the intelligible, and the familiar, which therefore falls quite outside the limits of the 'canny,' and is contrasted with it, filling the mind with blank wonder and astonishment" (*The Idea of the Holy*, p. 26). And although Otto says that the West lacks a "mysticism of horror" similar to eastern religious traditions, St. Armand argues that it was precisely "just this kind of horror mysticism Lovecraft was seeking . . .":

> However, Lovecraft then turns away from the *tremendum* factor of the numinous, which Otto defines in Christian terms as the "abyss," the "night," the "deserts" of the divine nature, into which the soul must descend, in the "agony," "abandonment," "barrenness," *tedium*, in which it must tarry, in the shuddering and shrinking from the loss and deprivation of selfhood and the "annihilation" of personal identity (*Roots of Horror*, p. 84).

Brian Aldiss concurs. In *Trillion Year Spree*, he writes that for Lovecraft, "the abnegation of personality, is his one permanent interest" (Aldiss, p. 171). Or consider "The Outsider" once again, in which, as we have seen, Lovecraft adapts an implicitly religious *dimension* of the unknown and makes it a central epistemological principle.[29] Lovecraft's narrator lives in the aftermath, as it were, of too little knowledge, or perhaps too much. The narrator is, in a word, God-haunted, or at least caged by metaphysical absolutes. His life *is* Original Sin, and his continuing to live a dubious, expiatory grace. As for that, Lovecraft left no doubt as to what he thought of life. In "A Confession of Unfaith," Lovecraft writes, "It is good to be a cynic—it is better to be a contented cat—and it is best not to exist at all" (cited in St. Armand, *Roots of Horror*, p. 22).

Lovecraft's essay on supernatural horror methodically considers all the great names normally associated with the Gothic tradition. His remarks about the origins of the "weird tradition in America" are so curious they need to be cited in full. After first reflecting on the "keen spiritual and theological interests of the first colonists," and noting the "strange and forbidding nature of the scene into which they were plunged" (*Supernatural Horror*, p. 60), Lovecraft warms to his topic:

> The vast and gloomy virgin forests in whose perpetual twilight all terrors might well lurk; the hordes of coppery Indians whose strange, saturnine visages and violent customs hinted strongly at traces of infernal origin; the free rein given under the influence of Puritan theocracy to all manner of notions respecting man's relation to the stern and vengeful God of the Calvinists, and to the sulphurous Adversary of that God, about whom so much was thundered in the pulpits each Sunday; and the morbid introspection developed by an isolated backwoods life devoid of normal amusements ... [;] harassed by commands for theological self-examination, keyed to unnatural emotional repression, and forming above all a mere grim struggle for survival— ..." (pp. 60–61).

There you have it, in a nutshell. It is almost as if Mather or Twain or Holmes had returned from the grave, like a revenant character out of Lovecraft's own tales, and perfervidly taken possession of Lovecraft's pen. All these influences, he says, "conspire to produce an environment ... in which tales of witchcraft and unbelievable secret monstrosities lingered long after the dread days of the Salem nightmare" (p. 61). This environment, of course, would provide fertile ground for the mysticism of horror exemplified by Jonathan Edwards and capitalized upon by Lovecraft.[30]

Significantly, Lovecraft here identifies the twin wildernesses— the "desert places"—that have served as horizons of interpretation in American epistemology and American myth: the varieties of space, inner and outer, the manifest determinisms of geographical and spiritual topographies. Lovecraft's fiction confirms my point that the failure of the Holy as new-world theological model permits its rhetoric to function all the better as an other-worldly theological fantasy. That is, the civilly minded theologies of Winthrop and Mather lead step-by-step to the uncivil civil theologies of Lincoln's "Second Inaugural" and, later, to Reagan's civic sentimentalities. From one perspective, this theological model sketched out a cultural program of aspiration—a sort of spiritual imperialism, as it were. From another point of view this same model elaborated a cultic memory of expiation and abasement. Thus it was that the continuing demonization of the Holy—or at least its estrangement—in the writing of nineteenth-century authors helped transform the covertly fantastic theologies of John Calvin into Lovecraft's final "perfection of the horrible." When a culture of guilt rereads Calvin, for hauntings, it seems, the Divine is nice and would suffice.

It remains a curious fact that Lovecraft spent the better part of his short life (he died at 47) doing little else, as he said, except reimagining his dreams.[31] Lovecraft intersects the wider American theological tradition in two directions, critiquing its Manifest Destinies outward into metaphysical, cosmological designs, and inward, into equally dark and fatalistic spiritual interiors. The tales of "cosmic indifferentism" and the interior disintegration into madness characteristic of Lovecraft's mature period show him repudiating the patchwork of religious prescriptions once derived from Calvin—especially as these were appropriated by those cartographers of Protestant interiority, Mather, Edwards, and Emerson. In Lovecraft's fiction,

> we see the outcropping of that American Calvinism bred into his bloodstream, for he exploits all the close-reasoning logic and unyielding determinism of an Edwards but simply abandons the metaphysical superstructure which the Calvinist was always attempting to justify. What we are left with in Lovecraft is thus a full-fledged cosmic consciousness, without any overt religious dimension. . . . It is, in turn, the breaking of these natural laws of time and space that produces the sublime emotions of cosmic terror that characterizes his tales (St. Armand, *Roots of Horror*, pp. 31–32).

"At the Mountains of Madness," in particular, extends and inverts the ironies of Frost's poem, "Design," and like Frost, Lovecraft speculates about the horrific trap of an indifferent universe.[32] One of Lovecraft's last and most significant tales, it revises American cosmologies downward. In it Lovecraft reflects upon the grand master narrative of American mythology, that pathological confusion of exaltation and abasement reflected in a national program of racial dominion on the one hand, and abject submission to the Divine on the other.

"At the Mountains of Madness": Lovecraft's Perverse Eschatology

> Science, already oppressive with its shocking revelations, will perhaps be the ultimate exterminator of our human species—if separate species we be—for its reserve of unguessed horrors could never be borne by mortal brains if loosed upon the world.
>
> —LOVECRAFT, "ARTHUR JERMYN"

"At the Mountains of Madness" builds on a simple, even conventional, fictional premise that he may have borrowed from Poe. He allegorizes a journey into the distant lands of the South Pole as a maddening descent into horrifying enlightenment.[33] Of course, in 1931 when Lovecraft wrote the story, Antarctic explorations were no longer fictional, and so Lovecraft's fantasy captures a sense of reality that Poe misses. Lovecraft's archeological expedition to the South Pole has as its background histories and records of various recent actual expeditions. Lovecraft's tale thus begins within the boundaries of the quotidian actual. The narrator reports that the Miskatonic University expedition was to be a geological survey of "regions explored in varying degree by Shackleton, Amundsen, Scott, and Byrd" (*Mountains*, pp. 4–5). But after this conventional beginning, both narrative and expedition veer off into unknowns, as the "strange and dogged insistence" (p. 11) of Lake, the group's biologist, turns up what seem at first to be a kind of unfamiliar ancient fossil. It soon becomes apparent that the fossils are more significant than they first appear. Lake organizes a sub-expedition for further investigation and makes some astonishing discoveries. What seem to be fossils are actually footprints of incredibly ancient creatures, some complete specimens of which Lake finds under ice, buried in a way that indicates more than chance at work. Lake's excited wireless reports say the discovery "will mean to biology what Einstein has meant to mathematics and physics" (p. 19). In further radio reports, Lake continues his enthusiastic reportage; his discovery "is transcendent" and he exults that the hitherto unexplored mountain range stretching across the Polar horizon will "surpass anything in imagination. . . . Everest out of the running" (p. 14).

Lake's sub-expedition sets out for a closer inspection of the mountains in the "aeon-dead world of the ultimate south" (p. 10), and they lose radio contact with the main base of the expedition. The narrator—named Dyer—observes that he and the main base believed violent windstorms had broken off communications. Later, however, they discover that Lake's camp has been thoroughly destroyed—again, in such a fashion to suggest that the destruction may not have been attributable to "natural" forces, after all. Dyer explains that after surveying the destroyed camp, he and a student assistant (Danforth) travel on ahead to view the illusory citylike battlements encrusting the massive mountain range. There they find "a Cyclopean city of no architecture known to man or to human imagination, . . . embodying monstrous perversions of geometrical laws and attaining the most grotesque extremes of sinister bizarrerie" (p. 30). Appalling revelation builds upon revelation. After exploring the "ruins," Dyer concludes these sophisticated ancients predate the human race by millions of years. Interpreting the bas-relief sculptures along the city's walls, Dyer concludes these ancient beings were responsible for creating a "shambling primitive mammal, used sometimes for food and sometimes as an amusing buffoon by the land dwellers, whose vaguely simian and human foreshadowings were unmistakable" (p. 65). S. T. Joshi comments that Dyer's statement "is probably one of the most fiercely cynical and misanthropic utterances ever made: the degradation of humanity can go no further" (*Weird Tale*, p. 197). Still, more shocks await. With the theocentric story of creation thus shattered out of hand, a further revelation drives Danforth into madness and commits the narrator to a policy of resolute silence.

"At the Mountains of Madness" is written in the form of a third-person retrospective, a form often used by Lovecraft and one already familiar to us. Lovecraft learned the confessional diary mode from Poe, who taught him the possibilities for terror in the self-haunting of the "obsessing I." Indeed, in Lovecraft's hands, spiritual autobiography becomes the soul's hysteria; the customary intimacies of the form become, like his universe, something wilder, more transpersonal, while remaining at the same time intimately confessional, since the final pathology of the religious imagination is to focus it, obsessively, upon itself. So Dyer's carefully scientific discussion of the expedition and its awe-ful discoveries is only part of the puzzle posed by his narrative. Says Dyer, "In my case, ingrained scientific habit may have helped; for above all my bewilderment and sense of menace there burned a dominant curiosity to fathom more of this age-old secret . . ." (*Mountains*, p. 47). Accordingly Dyer catalogues equipment, logs dates and sites as dispassionately as he describes the remarkable fossils. But as so often in Poe, the narrator's attempts to speak the self truthfully lead only into a maelstrom of ever-ambiguous interiority and self-defeat. Dyer's studied calm is in direct contrast to his obvious discomfort, his inability to speak what he must or to say what he knows. He knows in fact that what he says will not be heard. The first six lines of the narrative chart Dyer's fears and negatives: "I am forced into speech . . ."; "It is altogether against my will . . ."; ". . . I am the more reluctant because my warning may be in vain" (*Mountains*, p. 3).

Thus, despite Dyer's subsequent specificity and dry recitation of equipment, maps, and dates, the overall effect of his narrative is a chronicle of evasion and deflection; the varieties of silence he invokes, quite literally, in order to unspeak, or at least diminish, the force of the revelations he fears to make. This text, like a Frost poem, excludes the wrong ones. The narrator's descent into silence, like Danforth's subsequent lapse into madness, is the price both pay for the revelations they find at the mountains of ice and madness. The civilization that once built the Elder City is not dead at all. After all these years it still guards its ancient gates against intruders. What Danforth sees is apparently so horrifying that Dyer will only hint at it in the text; the reader has only his confession that Danforth *has* seen something, though *what* he has seen Danforth will not say. The irony, of course, is that Dyer must speak now to prevent the organizing of a follow-up archeological dig, the Starkweather-Moore Expedition, whose purpose is a "wholesale boring and melting of the ancient ice-cap" (p. 3). The horrible details of alien beings still living on this planet that Dyer had previously silenced, he must now speak *precisely* in order to prevent an expedition that will cause, in the end, "unnameable and perhaps immensurable evils" (p. 40) to the human race.

Early in the narrative Dyer recalls how Danforth, a "great reader of bizarre material" (*Mountains*, p. 8), intrigued by the volcanic texture of the landscape, cites Poe's reference to polar volcanic activity in "The Narrative of Arthur Gordon Pym." Dyer remarks that he found Danforth's reference to Poe's tale "disturbing and enigmatical" (p. 8), although he doesn't say why. Lovecraft's allusion to Poe is curious, especially so early in the text before the reader has any notion of the secrets this "aeon-dead world" will reveal. However, the name of the graduate assistant suggests a reason for his presence.[34] In a 1670 Election Day sermon, Samuel Danforth was the first to describe the Puritan settlement in New England as an "errand into the Wilderness."[35] Danforth's allusion to Poe may suggest that the three of them—Lovecraft, Poe, *and* Danforth—are similarly engaged in imaginative cosmological ventures, advancing "into regions never trodden by human foot or penetrated by human imagination" (p. 12). Dyer's retrospective narrative, then, is also Lovecraft's journey back along mismemory lane into the wilderness of American cosmologies, almost a century after Poe's *Eureka* (1848) and two centuries after the colonial "errand."[36]

"At the Mountains of Madness" is a narrative of history lived as Original Sin and Revelation: where beginnings are endings, and where divinity uncovered is recovered in time—but as doom, an ultimate secret that is as much awful as awe-ful. Religious textuality suffuses the narrator's tale. Dyer's covert acknowledgement of "ancient mythic Scriptures" such as the fabulous *Necronomicon* further adds to the religious dimension of this journey back to the source. This journey to the Pole, back to unwelcome knowledge and origins, is quite definitely also an end, a genesis, and a revelation, since the unlocking of the seals at the South Pole precipitates a shattering of worlds. And so the ironies abound. By rewriting cultural mythology as history, Lovecraft revises a biblically based myth of history, just as the Book of Revelation (Apocalypse) essentially rewrites Genesis. Conservative Christianity, trying to diffuse the crisis of faith prompted by Darwinian ideas, sanitized theories of evolution by specifying a moment of "soul-creation" in an otherwise evolutionary, "designed" universe. But Lovecraft subverts both Darwinian and theological creationism. In the final paragraphs of the story, Danforth and Dyer find themselves pursued from the vast depths of the city by something which begs description. Lovecraft's text here implicitly parallels the story of the expulsion from the garden, where the appearance of the angel guarding the Eastward Gate signifies that first great converting moment when, in a twinkling, all—history, theology, the great texture of all human narrative—is changed irrevocably.

The archeological investigation of the "utterly tenantless world of aeon-long death" (*Mountains*, p. 13), begun by Miskatonic University, then, offers a revision of successive epistemologies. It reverses geographic, racial (and thus national) narratives; finally, it overturns conventional theological and cosmological myths. The journey southward parallels, in addition, a series of psychological removes. The "ultimate south" exists in opposition to the North Pole, and thus, by implication, is the absolute point of negation and disorder. What the expedition learns there about the beginning of the human race means a complete revision of the imagination; the expedition in effect travels into areas never "penetrated by human imagination" (p. 12). The knowledge gained by this journey is costly—death to many in the expedition, madness to one; mute witness on the other, as the revelation of the human race's first moments provokes a moment of intense, almost mystical, clarity and humility. The vision in the templelike city of the Old Ones is shattering, annihilating, self-emptying—almost conventionally religious. Yet Lovecraft's horrific moment is a revelation not so much about the Old Ones, but about the accidental, even ephemeral, fact of human presence, and so wonder and horror are equally mixed. The moment is taut with a religious energy all the more intense because, as Dyer explicitly suggests, it is completely beyond the "accustomed conception of external Nature and Nature's laws" (p. 28). Recalling the tragedy of the Lake Expedition and subsequent events, Dyer acknowledges "There came a point . . . when our sensations could not be conveyed in any words the press would understand; and a later point when we had to adopt an actual rule of strict censorship" (p. 28). That imagination, Dyer acknowledges, is partly private and public, constructed within the constraints of language, responsible, in the end, not to private but to public needs. His silence must now become speech for the public weal. Winthrop had said the same thing, remember: "not only conscience but mere civil policy doth bind us" (Heimert, *The Puritans*, p. 89). Some things couldn't be *said*; some things would not be *heard.*

And so, in an attempt to efface the past, Dyer's text itself is an ironic sort of exposition—its words spoken in the interests of silence. The expedition's originally enthusiastic radio reports, distributed through the "*Arkham Advertiser* and Associated Press" (*Mountains*, p. 5), become less and less "saleable" to the public. Why? Because the expedition faced a "hideously amplified world of lurking horrors which nothing can erase from our emotions, and which we would refrain from sharing with mankind in general if we could" (p. 28). Dyer's position regarding both the expedition and the archeological site is finally analogous to the creature who determinedly pursues him and Danforth out of the Elder City. The two of them—Creature and Dyer—stand guard at the gate of knowledge, agents of silence, witnesses to prevent disclosure. Though he has refrained from speaking what he knows, he now must speak "the tremendous significance lies in what we dared not tell—what I would not tell now but for the need of warning others off from nameless terrors" (p. 31). The point, of course, is that the terrors have names; it is Dyer who will not name them.

The final revelatory moment of "Mountains" is horrifying, yet it is also potent with the *mysterium tremendum,* the "utter, objective embodiment of the fantastic novelist's 'thing that should not be' " (*Mountains*, p. 101). The moment's clarifying power is its ability to shatter grammar and all meaning. It is, indeed as Lake had radioed, of "highest . . . —transcendent—importance" (p. 20), since it makes and unmakes worlds. In Lovecraft's metaphysics of the terrible, the final revelation is a recognition of what happens when "we cross the line to the boundless and hideous unknown—the shadow-haunted *Outside*" where "we must remember to leave our humanity and terrestrialism at the threshold (*Selected Letters*, II, p. 150). The absence of human order—or *worse*, its *necessary* submission to an outside order—can only be revealed, and perceived, as inimical, since the *forms* of human intelligence reflect its need for teleological and grammatical order. The cosmos, as Lovecraft pictures it, is a "void," a source of "clutching ontological terror" (Joshi, *Weird Tale*, p. 182).

In "At the Mountains of Madness," a hierarchy of metaphysical assumptions slips into the opaqueness of sheer, *embodied* nihilism. Human technologies of knowing are successively undercut, while one anthropocentric certainty after another is overturned, until in the end even the last must give way. The alien creatures accidentally revived from dormancy by Lake's expedition are, Dyer admits, alien *only* when viewed from a human perspective. In many ways they are as scientific, as curious—indeed, as rational and as "humane"—as the human race. Dyer readily acknowledges that despite their appearance, the long-lived creatures at the Pole, who had endured and struggled for civilization for all these years, "were the men of another age and another order of being" (*Mountains*, p. 95): "Radiates, vegetables, monstrosities, star-spawn—whatever they had been, they were men!" (p. 96). Dyer's abstracting, allegorizing—and disruptive—intelligence seeks conventionally to anchor human life against a metaphysics of authority, one which includes authority over representation, history, the imagination. Yet revelation is always dark; here in the wilderness, the Pole refuses resolutely to be read with any certainty, positioned as it is against the indifferent processes and random couplings of a soulless, material universe. In Lovecraft's postlapsarian universe, "common human laws and interests and emotions have no validity or significance in the vast cosmos-at-large" (*Selected Letters*, II, p. 150). Knowledge is both judgment and expiation, yet there has been in fact no lapse, no sin. Cosmic "indifferentism," historical grotesquery, and personal blindness are, in the nature of things, the final unrevealable secret that nonetheless must be told. No wonder Dyer finds himself, angellike, standing guard: returning to the garden—emblematic of any version of the historical quest—is a mistake.

Conclusion

Were the entire corpus of American letters burned away, leaving only Mather, Hawthorne, and Lovecraft, a clear sense of the society's imaginative structure—its "overtones of the soul"—would be easy to construct. And looming large behind these three, authorizing them, so to speak, in William Channing's phrase, is that "complex and contradictory creature" worshiped by the Calvinists.[37] Traditional discussions of the Divine never seemed to know which to emphasize most—God's various perfections (focused, of course, in his powerful *all-mightiness*) or God's timeless and thus unchanging love. Interpreters of John Calvin underscored the inscrutability and distance of the Divine while, practically speaking, severely constraining His love. It would be Edwards's enduring ironic fame that he restored terror to the deity—not for reasons of his power—but precisely in the support of love. Lovecraft, whose fiction never mentions love, needed no such excuse to exercise terror. Lovecraft was a programmatic materialist who believed that "every event in the cosmos is caused by the action of antecedent and circumjacent forces, so that whatever we do is unconsciously the inevitable product of Nature" (*Selected Letters*, I, p. 132). Lovecraft gradually modified this position, moving toward a form of Einsteinian uncertainty, while never abandoning his belief that power was the central, motive force of the universe. And the universe known by human beings is, in Lovecraft's vision, only an infinitesimal glimpse of its loveless totality. Ironically, then, Lovecraft reinstates classic religious humility, since in his exploded cosmology, *that* one can know so little is a final and dark kindness. The first lines of "The Call of Cthulhu" are worth quoting:

> The most merciful thing in the world ... is the inability of the human mind to correlate all its contents. We live on a placid island of ignorance in the midst of black seas of infinity, and it was not meant that we should voyage far. The sciences, each straining in its own direction, have hitherto harmed us little; but some day the piecing together of dissociated knowledge will open up such terrifying vistas of reality, and of our frightful position therein, that we shall either go mad from the revelation or flee from the deadly

light into the peace and safety of a new dark age (*The Best of Lovecraft*, p. 76).

Lovecraft, then, achieves his effects by the doubleness of his vision: questions of origin and the authority of knowledge, thoroughly material and textual, beg to be answered in another discourse altogether. Lovecraft's argument is as much Emerson's and Channing's as it was Poe's, Twain's, or even Darwin's. At stake was not so much the origins of species, but its authorizations, endings, and purpose—not so much physics and biology as metaphysics and theology. Directly central to theological and fantasy formulations alike is an acute metaphysical dis-ease, a point articulated by Emerson in *Nature*: chiefly what relation, if any, exists between the Self and the universe. Is solipsism the new Holy? Is the Self the new transcendent? What should be the relationship between oneself and what one knows—and thus, between oneself and one's history? While Lovecraft seems completely to disavow the theocentric/anthropocentric universe bequeathed him by a sentimentalized religious tradition, in actuality he merely turns it inside out. Like the crafty Minister D— in Poe's "The Purloined Letter," Lovecraft deflects attention away from his theological borrowings by making them completely apparent. As a consequence Lovecraft's epistemological revision of the supernatural reinstitutes the absolutism of the Calvinist cosmology. He refigures its curious blend of orthodoxy and blasphemy, of ecstacy and pain, loyalty and apostasy; nonetheless, he leaves intact the ever-fluctuating boundary joining the madness of fantasy and the fantasies of theology.

Like Mather and Edwards before him, Lovecraft entangles theological and fantastic discourses of "the end," rewriting the one in the terms of the other. Indeed, Dyer's final vision of horror in the city of the Old Ones is a pastiche of the Holy—"the original, the eternal, the undying" (p. 106). From this perspective, then, "At the Mountains of Madness" is an essential document in an ongoing cultural critique of religion. As an apocalyptic tale, "At the Mountains of Madness" offers a reading of history not as conversion (Edwards), but as judgment and the failure of conversion. Lovecraft's obsession with the shape of final things (eschatology), and by implication, its *theological* pressure upon the political imagination, connects Lovecraft to a wider tradition of American apocalyptic readings. This tradition argues "both a rejection and a signal exploration of American ideologies of the self, of nature, of God and the supernatural, and of the community" (Robinson, *American Apocalypses*, pp. xi-xii). From another perspective, the spirit of American apocalyptic is an attempt to read, and to expiate, the failure of spiritual identity. The apocalyptic mode in American culture represents the shadow of the spiritual, or at least idealized, world: apostasy, metaphysical disarray and fragmentation, decadence.[38]

It should be clear that Lovecraft's theologizing Gothic is an attempt, at one level, to resist the pressure of an idealizing culture.[39] Punter explains that it is the "function of ideology" to "naturalize the presented world," making its "cardinal features" seem to be "natural, eternal, unchangeable" (*Literature of Terror*, p. 419). Lovecraft's Gothic tales then become part of a process by which the Gothic writes the "negative" of culture, and by that very process, saving the repressed and disallowed at the very limits of culture. Pulp fiction, of course, represents both a cultural judgment and aesthetic boundary; its repudiated texts form a "borderland" (*Literature of Terror*, p. 417) reflecting a culture's compulsive need to police its spiritual and civic imaginations. One example of this trend can suffice for many. Writing about Lovecraft for the *New Yorker*, Edmund Wilson titled his essay, "Tales of the Marvelous and Ridiculous." Wilson's comments are uniformly dismissive, even censorious. He remarks that Lovecraft's "creatures would look very well on the covers of the pulp magazines, "but they do not make good adult reading" (Wilson, p. 47).[40] The critic says that the "only real horror" in Lovecraft is "the horror of bad taste and bad art"; and that Lovecraft's poetry is, "like his fiction, quite second-rate" (Wilson, pp. 47–48).[41] Wilson's shifting aesthetic/moralistic metaphors give him away. Another critic sums up the critical response to Lovecraft in general, condemning his weird tales because, in his opinion, "The purpose of shocking—of frightening or horrifying—is in literature a meretricious one."[42]

One wonders, indeed, how Jonathan Edwards would have responded to this charge, believing as he did that terror had its salutary, even reasonable, uses. But then, perhaps Edwards might not have minded being labeled meretricious. He was writing theology, not literature, right? In my next chapter I will examine how the theological anxiety representative of Edwards and the early American metaphysical tradition will not rest in peace; it returns as pulp horror, beginning as we have seen with H. P. Lovecraft, whose influence can then be traced to the crypto-religious horrors of William Blatty and Stephen King.

NOTES

1. *The Poetry of Stephen Crane*, Daniel G. Hoffman, ed. (New York: Columbia University Press, 1957), p. 93.
2. One wonders whether Lovecraft knew his Dostoyevski. In *The Idiot*, Ippolyt offers a view of God that contrasts Myshkin's romantic notions of the Christ. Referring to Holbein's painting of the "Dead Christ," Ippolyt argues for the evilness of God: "But at times I did imagine that I saw, in a sort of strange and impossible form, that infinite power, that dark, deaf-and dumb creature. I remember that someone seemed to lead me by the hand, with a lighted candle, and show me some huge and horrible tarantula, assuring me that that was the dark, deaf-and dumb, and all-powerful creature, and laughing at my indignation" (III, p. 5–6). Nietzsche picks up the image of God as spider in *The Anti-Christ* (p. 18).
3. Robert F. Geary, in *The Supernatural in Gothic Fiction: Horror, Belief, and Literary Change, op. cit.*, uses this expression regarding Lewis's *The Monk*, p. 94.
4. In a 1935 letter, Frost comments on his earlier reading and notes he "almost learned all of Poe by heart" (Thompson, 1964, p. 500). Thompson also cites Frost's abiding interest in Poe, noting that in 1936 Frost acknowledged that Poe's "Tales" was one of his "top ten" favorite texts (Thompson, *The Early Years, 1874–1915* [New York: Holt, 1966], p. 549, note 4). While this is not the place to discuss Frost's own derivative Gothicism at length, I can at least cite a few examples. See his poems "Once by the Pacific" or "Bereft"—these last two poems positioned on opposite pages to heighten the effect. In "Once by the Pacific," God makes his ultimate will known in a most unpacific way: "Someone had better be prepared for rage. / There would be more than ocean-water broken / Before God's last *Put out the Light was spoken*" (p. 250). The image of God, of course, says more about the speaker's need for the frisson of melodrama than God's need for vengeance. For a discussion of Frost's domestic Gothic mode, see Ingebretsen, "Robert Frost's 'Home Burial' as Gothic Drama," *Robert Frost Review*, Summer, 1993. Brian W. Aldiss, speaking about Poe, could also be addressing Frost: "His are the domestic horrors, the glimpses of little lives riddled with fears of life and sex. . . ." *Trillion Year Spree: The History of Science Fiction* (New York: Avon, 1973), p. 58.

Lovecraft, too, discovered Poe at an early age, and much of his earlier work remained derivatively Poe-esque. See S. T. Joshi, *H. P. Lovecraft* (Mercer Island, WA: Starmont House, 1982), p. 8ff.

5. Lionel Trilling, "A Cultural Episode," in *Robert Frost: A Collection of Critical Essays,* James M. Cox, ed. (Englewood Cliffs, NJ: Prentice-Hall, Inc., 1962), p. 157.

6. In this same address Frost discusses his religious background and remarks about his mother—"fresh a Presbyterian from Scotland": "The smart thing when she was young was to be reading Emerson and Poe. . . ." A combination that Frost, perhaps unwittingly, continued. See "On Emerson" in Hyde Cox and Edward Connery Lathem, *Selected Prose of Robert Frost* (New York: Collier Books, Macmillan, 1977), p. 112.

7. See "The Faith of Robert Frost," Victor E. Reichert, in *Frost: Centennial Essays, op. cit,* p. 421.

8. Victor E. Reichert, "The Faith of Robert Frost," *Frost: Centennial Essays* (Jackson: University Press of Mississippi, 1974), p. 421.

9. See Alan D. Hodder, *Emerson's Rhetoric of Revelation: Nature, the Reader, and the Apocalypse Within* (Philadelphia: University of Pennsylvania Press, 1989). For more background on Emerson's apocalypticism, see Barbara L. Packer, *Emerson's Fall: A New Interpretation of the Major Essays* (New York: Continuum, 1982) and Joel Porte, *Representative Man: Ralph Waldo Emerson in His Time* (New York: Oxford University Press, 1979), esp. pp. 64–86.

10. "Design," in *The Poetry of Robert Frost,* Edward Connery Lathem, ed. (New York: Holt, Rinehart, and Winston, 1969), p. 302. Other citations to Frost's poetry will be to this edition. References to other editions of Frost's poetry will be noted in the text.

11. From a letter to Louis Untermeyer (1 January 1917), cited by Lawrance Thompson, *Robert Frost: The Years of Triumph, 1915–1938* (New York: Holt, Rinehart and Winston, 1970), p. 300.

12. Frost wrote this poem after a troubling decade or two in which he wrestled with his own ideas as well as struggled with death at home and failure in his writing life. See Lawrance Thompson, *The Early Years: 1874–1915, op. cit.*

13. Hayden Carruth, "The New England Tradition," in *Regional Perspectives: An Examination of America's Literary Heritage,* John Gordon Burke, ed. (Chicago: American Library Association, 1973), pp. 34–35.

14. Rexford Stamper, "Robert Frost: An Assessment of Criticism, Realism, and Modernity," in *Frost: Centennial Essays, op. cit.,* p. 61.

15. "A Letter to *The Amherst Student,*" in *Robert Frost: Selected Poetry and Prose,* Edward Connery Lathem and Lawrance Thompson, eds. (New York: Henry Holt, 1972), p. 344.

16. Friends of the poet recall that Frost's favorite "hobby" was house and property hunting.

17. Edwards, too, belongs in this discussion; he, too, liked walking in woods, and even had visionary moments in them: "a flood of tears and weeping aloud. I felt withal, an ardency of soul to be, what I know not otherwise how to express, emptied and annihilated" ("Personal Narrative," Levin, p. 36).

18. #274, *Final Harvest: Emily Dickinson's Poems*, Thomas H. Johnson, ed. (Boston: Little, Brown, 1961), p. 168. In "Other 'Desert Places': Frost and Hawthorne," Edward Stone traces the sentiments in Frost's poem to his reading in Hawthorne, which makes perfect sense in terms I am describing here. See also the companion essay by J. Donald Crowley, "Hawthorne and Frost: The Making of a Poem" (pp. 288–309); both essays can be found in *Frost: Centennial Essays, op. cit.*

19. Holmes's satire on Jonathan Edwards's "Freedom of the Will" was published in 1858, the text's centenary year.

20. In *The Best of H. P. Lovecraft: Bloodcurdling Tales of Horror and the Macabre*, introduction by Robert Bloch (New York: Del Rey, Ballantine Books, 1963).

21. Fritz Leiber, "A Literary Copernicus," in S. T. Joshi, *H. P. Lovecraft: Four Decades of Criticism* (Athens: Ohio University Press, 1981), p. 51.

22. Lovecraft, *Supernatural Horror in Literature* (New York: Dover Publications, 1973). For Lovecraft and Hawthorne, see Peter Cannon, "H. P. Lovecraft in Hawthornian Perspective," *H. P. Lovecraft in Hawthornian Perspective*, in *Four Decades of Criticism*, pp. 161–65. In that same volume, S. T. Joshi explores Lovecraft's connections to Hawthorne in context of Lovecraft's "New England" tales (pp. 25ff). Also in the same volume, George T. Wetzel, "The Cthulhu Mythos: A Study," explores the connections between Lovecraft's "The Outsider" and a passage of Hawthorne's "The Journal of a Solitary Man" (pp. 86–87, also note no. 14).

23. Neil Barron, *Horror Literature: A Reader's Guide* (New York: Garland Publishing, Inc., 1990). Lovecraft never named his stories the Cthulhu Mythos; that name was the product of Lovecraft's "disciple and correspondent, August Derleth." See Dirk W. Mosig, "H. P. Lovecraft: Myth-Maker" in *H. P. Lovecraft: Four Decades of Criticism*, for Derleth's rewriting of Lovecraft's mythology—which adapt it, says Mosig, to Derleth's Catholic heritage. Derleth, he claims, constructs a "anthropocentred universe" out of Lovecraft's "incomprehensible Reality" (p. 108).

24. See *Institutes of the Christian Religion*, John T. McNeill, ed. (Philadelphia: The Westminster Press, 1960), p. 68, 70.

25. Emerson employed fantasy incidentally as a way to contain the Holy in language. Lovecraft, to the contrary, purposely invokes the Holy in pursuit of fantasy. One example will suffice to show the odd synchronicities at work here. Remember Emerson's overheated *metaphor* ("transparent eyeball") in *Nature?* In Lovecraft's "The Whisperer in Darkness," a similar metaphor becomes *actual*, as Vermontian Mr. Akeley, held captive by a race of cosmos-roving aliens (where have we seen *this* scenario before?) is transformed into a disembodied, cosmic consciousness, contained in a sort of canister for easy transport. No doubt about it, Emerson's metaphor is heresy, and one can hear Calvin issuing edicts for Emerson's silencing the way he silenced Michael Servetus, whose mistake was disagreeing with Calvin's theological good sense. Calvin arranged to have Servetus executed; one thinks Emerson would have fared poorly at his hands as well. In his mystical transports, Emerson may often seem to teeter on the edge—either of madness or bad

taste, one doesn't always know which—as, for example, when he invokes the "occult relation" between man and the vegetable. Lovecraft sees the edge but brashly plummets over anyway. In the concluding pages of "At the Mountains of Madness," for example, a horror is revealed that quite literally is unspeakable. Is it any accident that what the narrator sees, and cannot express, is a creature right out of Emerson's worst fantasy—part vegetable, part human, one transgressing the line between the vegetable and the humanoid? One wonders what Emerson would think about *that* occult relation.

26. The expression is from the preface to Poe's *Tales of the Grotesque and Arabesque*, 1840.

27. Compare Lovecraft here to Peter Brooks's model of desacralization (a collapse of epistemological structure) as it evidences itself in the Gothic novel: "What has in fact been left after the desacralization of the world is not its rationalization—man's capacity to understand and to manage everything in terms of a rational epistemology, and a humanist ethics—but rather a terrifying and essentially uncontrollable network of violent and primitive forces and taboos which are summoned into play by the dialectics of man's desire" (p. 262). See "Virtue and Terror: *The Monk*," *ELH*, vol. 40, no. 2, Summer 1977: 249–63.

28. See Lovecraft's 1927 letter to Austin Dwyer concerning his reading of the "ancestral copy" of Mather's *Magnalia Christi Americana* (*Selected Letters*, II: 139). He mentions Mather again in a 1931 letter to August Derleth (*Selected Letters*, III: 407).

29. Interestingly, "The Outsider" sounds like a retelling of Poe's "Masque of the Red Death" from Death's point of view.

30. Lovecraft turns to the "American weird tradition" for much of his best work. In a 1927 letter, Lovecraft recalled that "The Unnameable" was based on a paragraph of Cotton Mather's *Magnalia Christi Americana* (*Selected Letters*, II: 139). Likewise, "The Outsider" probably owes its genesis to a passage in Hawthorne's *Commonplace Book*. Most of his better tales are situated in and around the Massachusetts environs, and some of them, like "Dreams of the Witch House" and "The Dunwich Horror," explicitly play upon the memories of Salem. Apparently the "overtones of the soul" Lovecraft most prized were local rather than imported. The arcana of "witch-blood, Satan-worship, and strange forest presences" (*The Best of Lovecraft*, p. 100) form the core to many of Lovecraft's stories.

31. See Lovecraft's 1922 letter to Frank Belknap Long in which he writes, "I never *try* to write a story, but wait till a story *has* to be written. It was thus with *Nyarlathotep* and *Randalph Carter*, which I *dreamed*. When I set to work deliberately to fashion a tale, the result is cheap and flat" (*Selected Letters*, 1: 166).

32. Tales like "The Outsider," on the other hand, move inward in the mode of spiritual autobiography, where lurks yet another annihilating fate—the Revelation of self-illusion. In both cases at issue is the intimate devastation, the cost of "the maddening revelation," the doom that, nonetheless, must be

survived. Knowledge must be expiated, whether it brings the collapse of human designs on the universe, its narcissistic theologies and cosmologies; or human designs upon the self, its self-absorbed, sin-seeking autobiographies, and historical narratives.

33. Howard Phillips Lovecraft, *At the Mountains of Madness and Other Novels* (Sauk City, WI: Arkham House, 1964).

34. For a discussion of Poe's text see Jules Zanger's "Poe's Endless Voyage": *The Narrative of Arthur Gordon Pym*, *Papers on Language & Literature*, vol. 22, Summer 1986: 276–83.

35. Danforth was the second, actually. As A. W. Plumstead points out in his introduction to an edition of Danforth's sermon, "The phrase 'errand into the wilderness' first occurs in [Jonathan] Mitchel's sermon in 1667; three years later, Danforth knew a good title when he saw it." *The Wall and the Garden*, *op. cit.*, p. 48.

36. Poe's *Eureka* "begins with the proposition that existence implies ultimate annihilation—not only of the individual, but of all things, in a pointlessly pulsating cosmos which endlessly creates and destroys itself" (Thompson, *Poe*, p. 5). St. Armand writes that "Lovecraft was no doubt inspired by the cosmic masterwork of his American model, Poe, whose *Eureka* envisions a universe 'sinking into unity, . . . into that Nothingness which, to all Finite Perception unity must be' " (p. 42). The linkage of the three writers (there are many others, including Winthrop, Wigglesworth; Frost in the twentieth century) shows how profoundly *entangled* eschatology and imagination are, further evidence (if one wanted or needed) of the indivisible quality of religious and aesthetic discourse throughout the American canon.

37. Dismissing the "mysterious doctrines" his religious predecessors had "ingeniously" derived from Scripture, Channing says, "we do not blame them for reasoning so abundantly, but for violating the fundamental rules of reasoning, for sacrificing the plain to the obscure" (Schurr, *Rappaccini's Children*, p. 37).

38. Nor was Lovecraft alone in his fear of the "decline of the West" (Joshi, *Weird Tale*, pp. 168ff). We have already considered Mather's *The Wonders of the Invisible World*, called by Bercovitch a "preview of Armageddon" (*The American Jeremiad*, p. 54). Other documents in the tradition include Edwards's apocalyptic reading of American history as a "metaphor of conversion," left incomplete at his death; Poe's cosmological poem, *Eureka* (1848); Twain's "The Great Dark"; Henry Adams's *The Education* (1907); West's "The Day of the Locust" (1933); even Frost's wry little confection, "Fire and Ice" (1920).

39. See Paul Buhle, "Dystopia as Utopia: Howard Phillips Lovecraft and the Unknown Content of American Horror Literature," in *Four Decades of Criticism*, pp. 196–210.

40. Edmund Wilson, "Tales of the Marvelous and the Ridiculous," reprinted in Joshi, *Four Decades of Criticism*, pp. 46–49. Wilson did have his moments, as when he characterizes Lovecraft's "Old Ones" in the forbidden city ("The Shadow Out of Time") as "the invisible whistling octopus."

41. See Will Murray, "Lovecraft and the Pulp Magazine Tradition," in *An Epicure in the Terrible: A Centennial Anthology of Essays in Honor of H. P. Lovecraft*, David E. Schultz and S. T. Joshi, eds. (Rutherford, NJ: Fairleigh Dickinson University Press, 1991), pp. 101–31.

42. Cited in "Lovecraft Criticism: A Study," by S. T. Joshi, *Four Decades of Criticism*, p. 22.

CHAPTER FIVE

"It Came from Beyond": The Sacred and the Scary

Remember death; think much of death; think how it will be on a death bed.
—"COMMONPLACE BOOK OF JOSEPH GREEN," 1696[1]

The unseen, unthought-of ways and means of persons going suddenly out of the world are unnameable and inconceivable.
—EDWARDS, *WORKS*, P. 453

Do not walk, run to your nearest public library . . . and find out what your elders don't want you to know because that's what you need to know.
—STEPHEN KING ON CENSORSHIP[2]

We fall from womb to tomb, from one blackness and toward another, remembering little of the one and knowing nothing of the other . . . except through faith.
—STEPHEN KING, *DANSE MACABRE*, P. 380

———————— ▓ ————————

Introduction

> . . . the reader would do well to remember that it is [Lovecraft's]
> shadow, so long and gaunt, and his eyes, so dark and puritanical,
> which overlie almost all of the important horror fiction that has come
> since. It is his eyes I remember best . . . black eyes which seem to look
> inward as well as outward.
>
> —STEPHEN KING, DANSE MACABRE, P. 102

The use of terror was, Edwards knew, a "reasonable thing"—and
its delights are apparently ever fresh in the telling, no matter how
poorly done. Stephen King learned his trade from Lovecraft, and
both traffic in antique Americana, a kind of spiritual kitsch.[3] The
culture's closets of horribilia, their tales suggest, are a dark litany of
patterns visible during daylight hours. In its political and cultic
fantasies a habit of the Word still plays out in moral allegories of
scrutiny, judgment, and expiation; a nationalistic myth of chosenness reads a theological heritage of abasement and mystifies it as
spiritual exaltation.[4] Despite their different interests and fixations,
the pleasure of pain—especially the excruciations of metaphysical
distress—is their subject. King, in fact, makes it a very profitable
business.

Lovecraft's terrors, as we have seen, are instructively familiar.
There may be a great deal of Poe in him, but a Poe, who had, in a
manner of speaking, grown up on a diet of Jonathan Edwards: a
Poe turned fallen-away preacher; one who got religion, and then
abandoned it, cursing its dark secrets and empty revelations. Lovecraft's constant meditations upon guilt, history, and the doubting,
inconsequential self are familiar because we have heard them all
before. We have caught their echoes and obsessions earlier in the
discourse of awful, hidden things—the discourses on witches and
spirits in Mather and Hawthorne, the telling of the Divine in
Edwards. As we have seen, Lovecraft situates a theological rhetoric
of sin and expiation against another ultimate horizon, that of the
endlessly fictive human memory in a literally godless universe.
Lovecraft's universe is populated with beings who are neither
benign nor indifferent to man. And therein lies the terror. Not

surprisingly, Lovecraft catches an Edwardsean tone almost perfectly. When the gods go the half-gods arrive, as Emerson reminds us, and Lovecraft was ready for the transition, displaying theological "content" without a trace of "piety."[5]

A major comfort of the Christian tradition is the terror it generates and presupposes, and the way those terrors familiarly return in a variety of contexts. Even our language gives the game away—consider how words like "grotesque," "awful," "disgraceful," "dreadful" (and others) derive from religious discourse. In this chapter I wish to elaborate upon a horrific possibility lurking directly at the heart of the Christic imagination. I speak here of "possession" in a sense somewhat different from Winthrop's conception of it—the threat of intrusion, invasion, and violation that invariably signals the approach of the transcendent. What happens when the Divine intersects the world's mundane order? When gods, powers, and principalities slouch from Bethlehem among us? When outer spaces come calling? Metaphysical dispossessions will be key in this chapter: from the inscrutable outer spaces of Lovecraft and Frost I turn to entrapments and shrinking inner spaces much nearer home. Spiritual dispossession, once a metaphor expressing a loss of God, now plays out in a rhythm of demonic domination. Narratives of captivity become narratives of invasion and violation.

Manifestations of the Divine inevitably reflect upon history, upon its writers and its *writtenness*—although they do so obscurely, in Saint Paul's phrase, through a glass darkly. It was, after all, the Word that was made flesh, sacred writ tells us. Consequently those moments of epiphany in which the Divine manifests its presence usually provoke distress and fear, prompting quick reactions from the communities involved. The Reformation had spent long years and much blood hoping to accomplish in general what Cotton Mather attempted to do in Salem—that is, to divide and separate visible from invisible worlds; to map Heaven, in a manner of speaking, and thereby to map a human world and to set a firm boundary between the two kingdoms. A thinker ahead of his time with regard to many scientific issues, Mather could also be called one of the first post-Christian theologians. Although he may not have been aware of it at the time, he attempted to make sense of Christian theology by reshaping it as history, as polemic, as moralism, as fantasy—as anything, that is, but theology, where it would always be the slightly perverse tale of an ineffable, unspeakable, endlessly disruptive God.

The eruption of the timeless Divine into mundane time is rarely convenient to earthly political systems. For instance, as authoritative a source as the New Testament confirms this point. Describing the birth of Jesus, Matthew the Evangelist notes matter-of-factly that "At this news King Herod became greatly disturbed, and with him all of Jerusalem" (New American, Matt. 2:3). Maps of Heaven do indeed regulate maps of the earth and the regions below it. We have seen how early in New England history these maps intersected and in effect redrew each other; in Salem, remember, trafficking with the Divine became a matter for the display of civil law. Indeed, the issue at Salem was actually civic power—its placement and dispensation. The witch trials implicitly aimed to establish a ritual by which civic power could be maintained, authorized, and justified.

Thus the Divine's intrusion into human society tests worldly grammars and undermines their authorities. Its manifestation by implicit contrast sets the outer limits of a culture, mandating what a society can hope while at the same time clarifying what it must fear. In popular Christian iconography, God's hidden face is to be revealed in time as history's judge and final moment of self-reflection. It should not be a surprise, then, that fears of the disruptive transcendent underlie so many fantasies of how the world ends, since *any* encounter with the Divine is likely to be world-shattering.[6] Reflect again on the narratives of Jesus' birth. One thing to be noticed is how the Infancy Narratives in their own right can be read as fantasy tales, texts of anxiety describing the ending of one political order and the beginning of a new. Matthew and Luke speak directly to the impact of Jesus's birth on the civic world of the time, two of which are specified in particular: kingly carnage and civil disruption. Threatened by the prophecies and the possibility of an unwanted heir, Herod slays all male children under two years of age. In desperation, Joseph is roused by a messenger from God and told he must take Mary and the child and "flee to Egypt." Incidentally, another point to be observed here is how this simple tale might be called proto-Gothic: the true heir, noble though seemingly low born, seeks sanctuary in a foreign land, and only after years in exile emerges from silence to claim his rightful kingdom.

For a moment, set aside the political tensions evident in Matthew's account, and recall that philosophically the *idea* of Christianity *in general* depends upon a mixing and fusing of domains, avowedly a sort of miscegenation, that—were it found in any Gothic text—would be read as disgusting, horrible, unspeakable. Gods and virgins, indeed. But this is Scripture, and so, wrapped as it is in a rhetoric of the Sacred, the reader ignores the horrible possibility. Indeed, much of the overt horror of the Scriptures is routinely "not seen" for what it is. For instance, in Mark's account of Jesus and the Gerasene demoniac, the evangelist notes that the people align Jesus with the possessed man he cures; in their horror at his show of power, they ask him to leave their town. Again, one can argue that the Infancy Narratives proper to Matthew and Luke—the stories of the manger, the animals, the angels, and shepherds—serve to sentimentalize, and thus diminish, the power of the awe-ful. The cloying contemporary fetishization of the Baby Jesus and his spectacular marketing at Christmas only further domesticates the potentially dread-ful story of the Incarnation. Yet the deflection barely disguises the grim terror that has been historically associated with the event. Yeats therefore catches a more appropriate if less conventional tone in *his* meditation upon it. In "The Magi" (1914), one of the kings muses upon "the uncontrollable mystery on the bestial floor" (p. 49). Or again, as the same author asks in "The Second Coming" (1920): "what rough beast, its hour come round at last, / Slouches towards Bethlehem to be born?" (p. 91).[7] And even T. S. Eliot, of course, ever rewriting the sacred Scriptures for his own arcane purposes, has *his* king problematize the event, denying the birth in favor of death: "There was a Birth, certainly, / We had evidence and no doubt. I had seen birth and death, / But had thought they were different; this Birth was / Hard and bitter agony for us, like Death, our death" ("Journey of the Magi" [1927]).[8]

It may be that to human ways of knowing the Divine must inevitably appear demonic and transgressive, its revelations fearsome, always shrouded in mystery and terror: *pietas*. The earliest stories of the Divine at play with its mortal favorites confirms Saint Theresa's trenchant observation—no wonder God has so few friends, considering the way he treats them. Jacob, Abraham, Moses, David: they each knew what the subsequent tradition of mysticism confirmed, that one cannot look upon God's face and remain the same. At the very least, such an encounter transforms, changes, perhaps radically undoes the human. This insight accounts for the gradual slippage of the Divine into the demonic, as *pietas* gradually becomes *tremens*, and eventually, unconcealed horror.[9] When does longed-for conversion become unwanted metamorphosis? Where is the line between self-possession and other-possession? William Blatty's *The Exorcist*, for example, may advertise itself as a theological text about the transcendent divine; nonetheless, in the cinematic remake of the novel, God is rarely mentioned except as ritual curse and the film is clearly more interested in the demonic's lurid display of power. However, even this observation must be qualified, since the demonic presence in the film seems of less interest than the vulgarities he occasions and the spectacular transgressions and captivities he makes possible. Indeed, the title of Blatty's text reflects its concern not with the Divine, nor even with the demonic, but with the agencies of power who ritually control these forces—both good and evil—and who render them benevolent. Mather would understand.

Like *The Exorcist*, to which we shall turn in a moment, Lovecraft's "The Dunwich Horror" displays the inevitable confusion of roles and domains that must follow such a metaphysical transgression. Do spirits have genders, for instance? Is the demon in Blatty's text male or female? "The Dunwich Horror" suggests that gods-made-flesh somehow connive in the frailties of the communities they inhabit—an even more unsettling way to think about the spiritual consequences of the Incarnation. In particular, Lovecraft's tale asks us to consider more plainly the spiritual confusion and collapsing epistemological boundaries that undergird Christian mythos. As a background for the discussion, I wish to cite Stephen King's suggestion that the "crazed and blasphemous results of liaisons between gods and human women" is a Lovecraftian idea.[10] This, of course, is not quite the case. Obsessed as he was by peculiarities of breeding, mixing, and defilement, Lovecraft took especial delight in "half-breed, degenerate aberrations" (*Danse Macabre*, p. 103), and he used the idea often in numerous tales. However, liaisons between gods and humans are certainly not new to him—but we will take up that point later.

"The Dunwich Horror": The Uncontrollable Mystery

> *. . . icky things infecting, invading, and wasting the whole landscape of America.*
> —MARSHALL BLONSKY, P. 340

Lovecraft's variations on the theme of the Unholy signals the extent to which he interiorized the theo-social formulas he ostensibly denied. I am tracing a similar process in the culture at large— an attempt *in practice* to diffuse or dissipate a problematic religious heritage while reaffirming it as *myth*—or, in this case, of course, as *horror*. "The Dunwich Horror" is an example, I think, of how a private fear reflects public obsession. It demonstrates what Michael Levenson observes in another context: "In learning how a community chooses its freaks and invents its deviants we construct a photographic negative of its social life."[11]

Briefly, the narrative recounts the events surrounding the attempted invasion of earth by creatures from another cosmos, perhaps even another dimension. George T. Wetzel explains Lovecraft's "Cthulhu Mythos" as the "struggle of supernatural entities to regain their mastery over the world and Man from which they were once ousted" (p. 79).[12] "The Dunwich Horror" relates the birth and mysterious life of Wilbur Whateley. He and his invisible twin brother are later revealed to be an "advance guard" for these creatures from another dimension. Fast-growing and precocious, Wilbur's unmarried mother is "a somewhat deformed, unattractive albino woman" (*The Best of Lovecraft*, p. 103) named Lavinia, who is herself a member of the "decadent" branch of the Whateleys. Further, this obvious evidence of biological impropriety (hence immorality, since Lavinia is unmarried) compounds the suspected metaphysical malfeasance already evident in the family line; Lavinia's "aged and half-insane" father, Old Wizard Whateley, prompts "the most frightful tales of wizardry" (p. 103). But *Wilbur's* father, on the other hand, is unknown, although the boy's extraordinary physical development and early mental acuity indicate that there is something odd, at the very least, about Lavinia's mate. For instance, at age three Wilbur deciphers and reads the dread *Necronomicon*, Lovecraft's unspeakably demonic text. So an ironic parallel becomes explicit as a familiar shadow crosses the text. Born of the hardly virginal Lavinia, Wilbur is fatherless; spiritually adept at a very young age, he is early about doing the work of his unknown father. Lavinia's son, in short, is a dark conceit of the Incarnation. Like Jesus, he is a god among us, monstrously conforming to our flesh. The people who have lived in darkness have lived to see a greater dark.

Yet for all Lovecraft's cosmicism, as I observed earlier his horribles are deeply rooted in the body's demonic potential. The body is Lovecraft's favorite source of outrage—its generations and degenerations, and the way these affect identity, its duplicities and perplexing fluidity. The human form's disconcerting talent for losing focus, changing shape, or for transgressing the boundaries of the humane is, in short, Lovecraft's definition of the *monstrum.* Wilbur, for example, the product of a metaphysical as well as biological misalliance, exhibits deficiencies in both biological and spiritual realms; in him precocity of intellect is set off against genetic decadence. The horror of Dunwich, then, to be blunt, is less Wilbur than his problematic issue and generation: his origin, its mechanics, and its consequences. As the issue (in a number of senses) of unknown gods and a mortal woman, Wilbur Whateley embodies the deeply discountenanced horror of the flesh central to the abstracting, spiritualizing Christian imagination.[13]

Despite his mix and jumble of contraries, Wilbur is fairly typical of the population, since according to the narrator, downward distortions of the norm in all phases of life are *customary* in Dunwich. For example, familial isolation in the Whateleys (extreme racial separation, ostensibly for racial purity) makes incest and inbred relationships conventional. Further, these particular abnormalities generate a complete social system of "wholesale regional decadence" (*The Best of Lovecraft*, p. 107). Town annals "reek of overt viciousness and of half-hidden murders, incests, and deeds of almost unnameable violence and perversity" (p. 101). All in all, a general collapse of racial and social boundaries—and thus of aesthetic and moral ones as well—typifies normal life in Dunwich. The Whateley family has lived in Dunwich for generations, and its reputation for peculiarity was already established back when "talk of witch-blood, Satan-worship, and strange forest presences was not laughed at . . . " (p. 101). Tourists avoid Dunwich, the narrator says, because its "sordid populace" are "repellently decadent" (p. 101). Contagion is the unspoken fear, as disorder reflects its potential to spread, which in turn accounts for the narrator's Matheresque sense of urgency: the evil must be discovered and contained; it must be narrated, while at the same time speech about it must be curtailed.

Lovecraft's pulp tale of decadence is thus oddly—and interestingly—reminiscent of Faulkner's more canonical Yoknapatawha County chronicles, outlining a grammar of inappropriate fusings, degenerations, misalliances, and misgenerations. The narrator returns constantly to the theme of failed purity, which in his view suggests how a wide variety of civic and spiritual discourses verge on collapse. In this respect Dunwich is almost a parotic example of nationalistic nineteenth-century Protestantism. The narrator confirms the pious, ideological cliché (cleanliness is next to godliness) by reinforcing its opposite; he asserts, implicitly, that the demonic and the unclean are near and neighborly.[14] Accordingly, in this jumbled mix of aesthetic, moralistic, and legal discourses, the physically unclean or racially impure becomes, by definition, the morally impious. Lovecraft's alignment of the conventional, the speakable, and the pious results in a parallel alignment of the unconventional, the unspeakable, and the impious. Dunwich, like Lavinia's home— and like Lavinia herself, Armitage implies—is a place, where "all standards of order and cleanliness had long since disappeared" (*The Best of Lovecraft*, p. 103). The resulting indiscriminate mixing of blood, race, and the consequent collapse of the moral order, however, signifies something rather more troubling than the failure of aesthetics or morals in the human community. The narrator equates the collapse of earthly grammars with the collapse of boundaries at the cosmological level, suggesting a profound spiritual dissembling at work in the universe.[15] So, while the weakening of the body politic begins with the physical, it is not limited to that dimension. Further, with things as morally degraded as they are in Dunwich, it comes as no surprise, says the narrator, that the "intruding horror" from "blasphemous outer spheres" (p. 112) should choose Dunwich as the site of its predations—a metaphysical violation that provokes a "state of really acute spiritual fear" (p. 113).

Lovecraft's personal "racialism," then, finds a convenient public ally in the theo-national myth of "chosenness" in which exists an alignment as old as Genesis—a conflation of the discourse of the *holy* and the *lawful*, which establishes, by implication, its opposite: the horrific and the unlawful. In Lovecraft's fiction, the "unnameable" never remains merely a divine honorific for long. It becomes very quickly mixed up with questions of the social unspeakable, with matters of laws, limits, conventions. Dunwich, then, offers a sort of latter-day "city upon a hill" whose secrets and secretive ways play out the moral entropy implicit in John Winthrop's vision of dispossession. In Dunwich, transgression and deceit, scrutiny and dissemblance—rather than charity and love—are structured into the social order. Its endemic, almost "natural" decadence thus becomes emblematic of postlapsarian humanity. Indeed, this is Lovecraft's point, apparently, as he details with especial relish the "shipwrack" endlessly anticipated, endlessly sought, as the unregenerate "prosecute [their] carnal intentions" (Winthrop, cited in Heimert, p. 90). In this respect the blasphemous Wilbur, a godlike creature taken flesh in Dunwich, replicates the decadence of the human scene.

The narrative energy of "The Dunwich Horror" centers not upon the monster but upon the agent of its "binding" (The tale resembles *The Exorcist* in this respect.) Armitage, librarian at Miskatonic University at Arkham, has multiple degrees and speaks many languages. As town librarian he is keeper of books and ward of knowledge, the "dis-coverer" of the sign and the center of privileged power. As his name implies, he "arms" the heritage, protects it. As the apex of literacy, in this social order of the Word, Armitage assumes responsibility for thwarting the horror—although just exactly *what* the horror is he seems to keep vague. Part of thwarting it involves *not* speaking it; or, at any rate, misspeaking or speaking it by deflection. Armitage rarely specifies the nature of the horror, and the ambiguous term at different times easily describes the decadent people and the town, Wilbur, or his invisible twin—or perhaps all of the above. Shut out from the actual events themselves, the community can read about them in the narrative that Armitage alone writes/tells. Since he carefully controls how the "facts" will be disseminated and to whom, Armitage thereby keeps himself at the center of linguistic power. Armitage seeks essentially the same end as Mather in *The Wonders of the Invisible World*, since Armitage likewise uses his position as teller to parlay narrative power into social power. He exchanges bodily possession by the demonic with textual possession-by-the-community. It is evident from his struggle to contain Dunwich's ambiguities in the closed system of narrative that from Armitage's embattled position as *teller*, perhaps even *sage*, the story takes on the trappings of an epic of civilization; it is clear that the threat the alien poses is a moral one, directed at the community's *soul*— although evidenced in the chaos of the body politic and symbolized in the body of Wilbur.

Lovecraft's tale anticipates Stephen King's technique in *'Salem's Lot*, in which a pluri-textual narrative generates a network of unknowns and unspokens, secrets and taboos. By withholding facts Armitage colludes with the intruding horror. Indeed, information *about* the events seems more threatening than the facts of the case themselves, so carefully are the facts controlled. Armitage declares with a note of self-justification that police *were not* notified, and that "abnormal details were duly kept from press and public" (p. 116). In effect Armitage "re-covers" revelations by keeping them hidden, not only from Wilbur (to whom, as librarian, he had refused to give the *Necronomicon*), but from the town—and even from himself, as evidenced by his reluctance to speak about the horror in specific detail. Thus he creates a parallel discourse of *dis*-revelation, one working *in concert* with the status quo. In this way a rite of secrecy— the articulation of secrets and hidden transgressions—offsets the ritual of discovery and release, both of which are conducted by Henry Armitage, the ritualist. Indeed, it seems part of Lovecraft's point that in Dunwich the simultaneous speaking and unspeaking of the town's taboo is an important communal ritual, not unlike the "thrill" of blasphemy. Thus, while seeming to distance himself from what the "people concluded" or "noticed" (p. 105) Armitage ingenuously keeps ever central to the reader—as to the community at large—not only what the Whateley family do and where they go, but, importantly, what the town *thinks* of their activities.

Although socially ostracized and silenced, the affairs of the Whateleys (clearly in all senses of that word) seem to be *the* events in town. Even the telephone provides access to the communalizing, unifying activity: "Everybody was a-listenin', an' we could hear lots o' folks on the wire a-gaspin' " (p. 127). A similar scene occurs in *'Salem's Lot*. As Straker observes, "The townspeople always talk. They are no different from the magpies on the telephone wires" (p. 56). Straker, the vampire's mortal companion and general *factotum*, deftly leaves unsaid here the element common to his avaricious birds and the human community: both are carnivorous;

both, specifically, are eaters of dead flesh, carrion. Gossip is the town fare, its feed. By "speaking" the transgression openly, it can, simultaneously, be reaffirmed as taboo, and thus prohibited. In addition, the desire to view the "apparel of the soul" (Robert Frost's phrase) in effect exchanges a system of intrusion and violation for personal intimacy. In Mather's Salem and in Lovecraft's Dunwich, the textifying of the individual, and the resulting "display" of the person, is erotic and voyeuristic. Words go where bodies cannot or will not. The narrative of possession by which the community comes to "own" the case becomes only another variation of the perversion of intimacy, and is itself another sort of possession.

This exchange of intrusion for intimacy—what I am calling voyeurism—reinstates the unspoken power of the group, and authorizes its intrusions under the ostensibly benevolent rhetoric of community. In turn, this discourse of the body politic creates and reaffirms the sanctimonious effects of social management. Gossip becomes an act of communion as well as a civic strategy: a dismembering and a consumption that unites people as an undifferentiated crowd—a potential army waiting to be mobilized by the right rhetorical suasion. Thus the network of silences and evasions seems mostly an excuse for the citizenry to engage in a voyeuristic stripping, as it were, a baring of the inside. This public rendering of the soul is tantamount to a public accounting. Armitage writes the private soul and in so doing normalizes the abnormal—or at least, shows how useful the perverse can be useful for purposes of management and spectacle.

In Dunwich there are secrets within secrets, secrets becoming secrets, yet all the secrets seem surprisingly *public*. As Eve Kosofsky Sedgwick would define it, Dunwich society is one of the "open secret."[16] Wilbur may be the most obvious of the secrets involved, but even he defies even the most rudimentary analysis. Clothed, Wilbur is a closed secret, a grotesque confusion of species and biological taboos. After he is killed by the library watchdog (where he has broken in trying to read the *Necronomicon*) his secret racial and metaphysical confusion is horribly revealed. But this discovery only further complicates the Whateley affair, since Wilbur's physical dissolution into a puddle of "a sticky whitish mass" and a "monstrous odor" (*The Best of Lovecraft*, p. 116) only raises more questions. The narrator observes that the rapidly dissolving remains on the library floor did not have a skull or skeleton, "at least, in any true or stable sense" (*The Best of Lovecraft*, p. 116). Thus Wilbur's biological decenteredness mimics Dunwich's instability; its social center is as fluid and shifting as its network of chatter and gossip and silences. After Wilbur dissolves in a puddle, and after subsequent events reveal the presence of his hitherto unknown brother, the town rapidly organizes its defenses.[17]

Armitage has decoded relevant parts of Wilbur's journal and the *Necronomicon*; and following the directions contained in those texts he concocts a powder to render Wilbur's brother visible. Whispering incantations and sprinkling his powder, Armitage intends, therefore, in a literal fashion to control, even manipulate, the horror's manifestations. He will render the absent present; he will discover the secret. Yet it is not to be overlooked here that Armitage's less-than-scientific methods are practically indistinguishable from Whateley's. Indeed, Armitage is the magus, the good wizard who challenges Old Whateley's black magic; in essence Armitage's powers derive from the same arcane source, a point which underscores the social reality at work: it is the "licensing" of the magic, and not the magic itself, that is at issue; white or black depends upon the system of authorization it invokes. Remember Salem in this regard. In the tradition of Samuel Parris or Cotton Mather, Armitage takes it upon himself to traffic in divinity, whatever its guise. Even though Armitage can only partially "divine" the revelation, his ministerial task is to "read" and thus control the "uncontrollable mystery" that lies dead on the library floor, and which still is capable of threatening the town.

Assuredly, however, Armitage's linguistic power—the magic of "spelling" and the "enchantments" of language—is greater than his silly powders and incantations. As custodian of the town's tales he has power to define and articulate the domain of the "Outside." Thus he sets the ideological fence by which society guards its vulnerabilities. The lesson of "The Dunwich Horror" is clear. A community needs the outlandish, the barbarian, even the "intruding horror," in order to help it shape and define itself. As librarian and priest of the Word, Armitage is given control over community interpretation; he must write the sacred tales by which the community understands itself. Thus Armitage is charged with reading the body politic as moral allegory. He tells the civic narrative as an authoritative parable informed by divine, or at least transcendent, purpose; and he safely frames the "horrible" by allegorizing it "meaningfully." In his preachment the visitation is no longer merely an "event"; it has become a "sign" which Armitage construes as an "example" (*exemplum*) and as *monstrum*. In good preacherly fashion Armitage moralizes the events as a form of apocalypse. Behind the materialization of the "monstrous blasphemy" (*The Best of Lovecraft*, p. 115) in Dunwich, he says, lies an even greater horror: "some plan for the extirpation of the entire human race and all animal and vegetable life from the earth by some terrible elder race of beings from another dimension" (p. 123). Then in a strategy familiar to the often deceptive closure of Gothic texts, Armitage robs the Whateley incident of its horrific qualities by recasting it as didactic lesson: "We have no business calling in such things from outside, and only very wicked people and very wicked cults ever try to. . . . I'm going to burn his accursed diary, and if you men are wise you'll dynamite that altar-stone up there, and pull down all the rings of standing stones on the other hills" (p. 133). Apparently the Sacred can only be reconfirmed by what amounts to a parallel act of blasphemy. The Unspeakable must remain unspoken, just as the ineffable must be made unspeakable, by legal imperative if not by linguistic definition.

For all practical purposes Dunwich's "normal" transgressive decadence makes it invisible—perhaps dismissable—on the maps of human aesthetics or morality. In the introduction to the tale the narrator speaks only in abstract, oblique terms of the "recent horror" (*The Best of Lovecraft*, p. 101). And if Dunwich was a town of unspeakables long before Wilbur's birth, in the revelatory epiphany of his aftermath the town becomes even more so—an unmarked, unspoken place, silenced by shame, effaced from maps and language, erased even from the imagination: "since a certain season of horror all the signboards pointing toward it have been taken down" (p. 101). So the text ends where the mythical narrative of Dunwich begins: the price for trafficking with "*outsidedness*" (p. 133) is annihilation. All signs of the intrusion, imaginative and geographic, must be erased. Dunwich's literal erasement from human maps is the price it must pay for cosmic dalliance. In Dunwich we witness the final dispossession of the spiritual inheritance promised by Genesis, an undercutting of its rhetoric of triumphant colonialism. Dunwich becomes the new city upon a hill, a site of degradations and silence. The Word, spoken in the beginning, is now mute, its secrets unspeakable.

Thus inevitably, Dunwich recapitulates the history of New England's theocracy: the Sacred recedes even as it is being contained. After Armitage finally translates Wilbur's journal, he penetrates to another secret—and the *real* horror (or so it initially seems), because it becomes apparent that to the keeping of secrets there will be no end. Wilbur's twin brother is invisible because he takes after his other-worldly father rather than after Lavinia, his mother. Yet even in the dissolution of *this* creature, secrets remain. So, in the end, while some limited disclosure might be possible, *closure* will not be possible. Armitage muses, but "what thing—what cursed shapeless influence on or off this three-dimensional earth—was Wilbur Whateley's father?" (*The Best of Lovecraft*, p. 103) The father may always be unknown, always inscrutable, and thus all the more terrifying to our xenophobic eye: "What Roodmas horror fastened itself on the world in half-human flesh and blood?" (p. 113).

It should be noted here that Lovecraft's tale hints at a far more ancient text, since even the sacred Book of Genesis registers a fear of extramortal visitations. It is something of a cliché to associate the policing of *human* sexuality with a narrow-minded Christian civic ethic; nonetheless that same tradition acknowledges that even the gods are perverse, and that *their* comings and goings must be carefully scrutinized and monitored. Genesis 6:3, for example, assumes matter-of-factly that "sons of heaven" desire, "find beautiful," and "took for their wives" "daughters of men" (Gen. 6:2). So what Armitage does not need to tell us, because as readers we should see the parallels ourselves, is that the Dunwich horror is in fact very familiar; and Lovecraft's tale in effect merely retells from another perspective the opening chapters of Genesis. In addition, Lovecraft looks again at the horrific possibilities screened out of Matthew's Gospel by centuries of fervent piety. Tales within tales, horrors within the Sacred—or is it the other way around?

Tales Within Tales

The usual Walls *of defence about mankind have such a Gap made in them, that the very* Devils *are broke in upon us.*
—MATHER, *WONDERS*, P. 80

Like the Elder City of "The Mountains of Madness" or the symbolically complex Jerusalem of Matthew's account, Dunwich presents
a crossing of multiple unreadabilities; it offers a plurality of over-
abundant, allegorical possibilities. As Armitage alone cannot
translate Wilbur's multilingual diary, neither can social grammars
contain the event's "discrepancies, duplications, and ambiguities"
(p. 111). And the apocalypse in Dunwich that cannot be contained, of course, is that all socially normative boundaries, separations, and hierarchies have collapsed. So Dunwich is not unlike
Salem in this respect. The body politic, uncovered and exposed, is
discovered to be like Wilbur—amorphous, dissolving without dis-
cernible structure or support. And the implicit connection that is
made in a fictional text becomes, in a real society, habitual: what is
human *must* be policed, managed, arranged, and codified, tex-
tified, narrated. Conversely, which cannot be managed (the human body, sexuality, God's spirit) implicitly assumes the status, or
maybe a role, of being *not human*, perhaps demonic.

Armitage's efforts at controlling metaphysical intrusion also
draw attention to his self-appointed task of civic policement. Indeed, historically these projects have always been twinned and
entangled. Just as sprinkling the intruding creature with magic
powders made it more accessible to Armitage, in much the same
way speaking the Divine in language, or controlling the way in
which it could be spoken, has been a theological strategy long
employed to render the Divine compliant to human grammars.
Because if the Word is made flesh, these questions remain to be
answered: How is the Divine to be controlled, and in what manner is
Revelation to be licensed or dispensed? Who are its agents? Dostoyevski's Grand Inquisitor would certainly be sympathetic. While
according to strict Calvinists the unapproachable and illimitable sovereignty of God could not in any way be contained, none-

theless, rendered as discourse the Divine *could* be slyly kept under
linguistic wraps, as it were, massaged and manipulated through
the systems of speech and law. Its comings and goings could thus
be monitored through grammar. That is why theologians like
Jonathan Edwards resisted the language of Covenant, and further,
why Edwards in particular distrusted language. Presumably, the
Covenant implied a control over God that was incompatible with
his sovereignty. No wonder, then, that language of the demonic is
so often used to describe the Divine, an impractical and *always*
impolitic intruder from a world elsewhere. The language of the
horrific enables theologians, linguists, *and* horror writers to jointly
teach the Divine to behave—at least, that is, while it is a guest on
our turf.

And the Divine, it seems, *likes* our turf. Permit me to return for a
moment to an earlier point, namely that a Christian metaphysics
posits just such an extraterrestrial disruption, a visitation from
beyond that profoundly affects all experience and systems of value.
Christian doctrine *depends* upon making the transcendent at home
in our world. This particular manifestation we call the Incarnation.[18] Indeed, the story of Jesus, when viewed from Lovecraft's
point of view, could well be simply another case of an "intruding
horror" (*The Best of Lovecraft*, p. 112) from the "blasphemous outer
spheres" (p. 112). The idea of "blasphemous liaisons," then, is
certainly not new to Lovecraft.[19] Having discussed Lovecraft's tale
of such a union, it is time briefly to explore this point. The phrase
"blasphemous liaisons" itself implicitly suggests that some, or at
least *one*, such affair is *not* blasphemous. To borrow an expression
from Anselm, this liaison we call the Holy. A fascination with
spiritual miscegenation (like the fear and xenophobia associated
with its racial counterpart, for which it serves as a metynomic
substitution) is part of western cultural mythologies from Genesis
to *The Odyssey*. As the early reference in Genesis reminds us, apparently the Word *made* flesh before it *was* made flesh—is this not in
fact the central icon of Christianity described in Scripture? However, in popular visual renderings of the birth of Jesus, the troubling suggestion of sexual misalliance is softened by figuring "the
Holy Ghost" as a dove. (The text merely says that Mary was "over-
shadowed by the Most High.") This is a deft way to speak the
unspeakable, although Saint Thomas Aquinas, for one, was not
fooled; hundreds of years before its final dogmatization he argued

against the doctrine of the Immaculate Conception on the grounds that the Holy Spirit would never have anything to do with anything so dirty as sex.[20]

So the sacred tales have tales within tales, and some suggestively scary. Sacred Writ, at least in the examples here of Genesis and the conception of Jesus (other passages could be adduced) seems not unlike Yeats's "Leda and the Swan" (1924):

> *Being so caught up,*
> *So mastered by the brute blood of the air,*
> *Did she put on his knowledge with his power*
> *Before the indifferent beak could let her drop?*
>
> (*YEATS*, p. 115)

There's the theme again. A different "take" upon the story of gods and men (the randy Yahweh and the dirty old Zeus?), but one with terrible implications nonetheless. No wonder angels in Scripture need always to say, "Be not afraid"; no wonder, at Christmastime, the machinery of consumer joy turns these awe-some creatures into tiny, cherubic *putti* flitting nakedly about. We'd be fools not to be scared out of our wits, as indeed we are when we shift our focus, and see the Christmas story from a *completely* different perspective, as of course is the case with possession narratives. In some respects the Incarnation is the ultimate captivity narrative, as the maid Miriam, in the hands of a hungry God, writes the text of a most awe-ful providence. Here, in a most rudimentary form, we have yet another captivity narrative, a tale of overpowering and eroticized possession. Like Lavinia, Miriam the Jewish maiden is offered a most inhuman (or at least *extra*human) grace.

And let us not forget the basic plot to Blatty's novel *The Exorcist*, for example. When you think about it, Matthew's and Blatty's narratives are not unalike, although Blatty's horripilatory tale restores the violation, bondage, and spiritual dread that piety— itself a form of fear—has carefully drained from the original story. In effect all of these narratives tell how a discourse of divinity— one that presumptively *authorizes* social order—also transgresses it. Gods have become men and dwelt among us, upsetting social order in Bethlehem and in Georgetown as well. This revelation is intolerable, of course, and so it is wrapped in the forbidding language of the sacral and the taboo. Such an idea of divine predation must be rendered politically unspeakable, as it is grammatically ineffable. As Blatty's *The Exorcist* shows us, such an idea is unhearable, unimaginable except at the limit of human perversity—and then, only as horrible.

Finally, the topic of such mortal/immortal issues has significant cultural and linguistic implications for us, since, as Holy Writ solemnly, even perversely, proclaims, the "*Word* was made flesh." And there you have it, another inappropriate fusion, a misalliance/miscegenation at the heart of language. Perhaps Edwards was correct, who thought our language guilty of perversity, being partly fathered by the ineffable, and, like Wilbur's half brother, partly containing it.[21] And no wonder that congress between gods and mortals—*the* subject, even plot, of the history of mystical eroticism—is also part of the *horribilia* so oddly comforting to the mythography of this culture. Friedkin's film version of *The Exorcist*, to which we turn, clarifies again the obscured, sometimes willfully effaced, link between spiritual hopes and horrors, since staring unblinking into the face of the demon is a way, indirectly, of facing the Divine. Georgetown of *The Exorcist*—like Salem or Dunwich, or even Bethlehem—is a place where the Divine/demonic contests the human for space; a site where the human begins to lose its normative, socialized shape, and where the often-contested line between mortal and Other fails. When this happens, all bets of normalcy are off: the horror tale, says King, "scream[s] at the top of its lungs: 'Aren't you afraid that your normality is in itself a lie? That there is no such thing as normality?' " (Blonsky, p. 361).

Possessions and Dispossessions: *The Exorcist* and *'Salem's Lot*

> This *man can scare the death out of you. . . . There must be some* meaning *in that.*[22]
> —DON HERRON ON STEPHEN KING

Indeed, during the late sixties and early seventies one *could* say there was no such thing as normality in the United States, or at least that the very notion of the normal had come under heavy criticism. During these years the Vietnam conflict and various movements of civic unrest had organized social sensibilities in a way not previously imaginable, and the effects of those multiple conflicts—of worlds, cultures, epistemologies of belief—lacerated the nation. Two best-selling American horror fictions of the time reflect these problematic intersections, portraying as they do embattled humanity facing metaphysical invasions. In this concluding section I wish to show how two persistent themes—metaphysical intrusion and spiritual miscegenation—play out in Friedkin's cinematic remake of William Blatty's *The Exorcist* and in Stephen King's *'Salem's Lot.*

In *The Exorcist,* accredited as "the inaugural work" (Carroll, p. 102) of contemporary horror fiction, the demon comes from an exoticized Middle East; in Stephen King's *'Salem's Lot* the demon—fresh out of old-world fiction of an imperialistic nation and era (*Dracula*)—invades the slightly exotic, backwoods towns of Massachusetts. In each case culture ceaselessly speaks its unspeakables, even haltingly, fragmentedly, madly. Just as a cultural unconscious—fears of invasion, of being overpowered, annihilated, dispossessed—made itself visible at Salem, so similar fears are registered in this pair of novels. Both texts reflect a metaphysics of Revelation, in which theological revelation, debased, becomes a search for secrets fueling an industry of gossip. The secret runs both ways; the demon "knows" the people he confronts because he "reveals" their secrets, and they in turn must do likewise. In each instance the demonic succeeds in "deconstructing" society because somehow it can read the civic text for its secret. Likewise, the demon must be "revealed" as himself and not as something else. He must be seen as the authentic sign of the Divine Order intruding into the human order, and not merely dismissed as psychological aberration or a young girl's bid for attention.

I will start off by saying that in general, Blatty's *The Exorcist* aimed at one polemical point and connived, probably inadvertently, in another. The first has to do with the moral epistemology of possessions; that is, how one reads their theological significance in a human life. The second point is much simpler, but historically related to the first point: terror is captivating and nothing terrifies like God. Blatty's text, intended no doubt as a moral examination of evil, one that intends a conservative—and doctrinally correct—

explanation of evil, becomes a spectacle of quite a different sort. Blatty's novel depicts the lurid demonic possession of a young Georgetown girl, a fictionalization, he said, of an actual possession case involving a young boy. Friedkin's cinema adaptation of the novel opened on December 26, 1973. Response to the film can only be characterized as a firestorm of indignant moralizing mounted in protest of the graphic and gruesome film.[23] Not every one protested, however. Long lines of viewers stretched around city blocks, waiting patiently to be admitted to theaters, eager no doubt for a chance to see unspeakable acts on the wide screen, and to cheer on the priest/demon Karras as he punched hell out of a monster-faced, nightgowned girl. Nonetheless, while the plots remain essentially similar in both, Friedkin's *The Exorcist* is not really Blatty's novel. What is theological meditation in Blatty is technological *Grand Guignol* in Friedkin. Father Merrin, archaeologist-priest, returns to the United States after working on an archeological dig somewhere in the Middle East. There he had received premonitions of another combat with the demon Pazzuzu, whom he had apparently encountered once before. Meanwhile, in domestic Georgetown, twelve-year-old Regan MacNeil begins to behave strangely. Her at first merely idiosyncratic behavior steadily becomes more disruptive and vulgar, until eventually the diabolic manifestation represents itself in a hideous reconstruction of the girl's body and face. Psychological and social reasons are proffered ("Mrs. MacNeil, the problem with your daughter is not her bed, it's her brain").[24] Yet it becomes evident that the typical answers, medical and psychological, are to no avail. Regan's increasing grotesquery, filmed in clinical detail, can, it seems, only be accounted for by possession; so Merrin and a younger, more "mod" priest-psychologist, Damian Karras, are called in for the Rite of Exorcism. A struggle ensues in which Merrin dies of a heart attack. Karras, who until this point had seemed rather passive, now challenges the demon, who leaves the girl and enters Karras. Momentarily possessed himself, Karras turns upon the dis-possessed and now helpless Regan and begins to slug her. But Karras comes briefly to his senses, and in a gesture of heroism throws himself out the window, killing himself, and apparently vanquishing the demon as well.

Of course, neither Blatty's subject nor his treatment of it is new.

His ostensibly historical *The Exorcist* (1971) barely disguises its familial origins in the tradition of captivity narratives.[25] Behind Blatty (Jesuit-educated, and thus, to some, demonic himself) and his retelling of a historically based exorcism lies a vast array of captivity/possession narratives, vaguely theologized tales of human excess, many of them often darkly erotic. I considered in an earlier chapter Rowlandson's "Captivity" and Lovelace's *Ordeal*. Beneath the often lurid details of any of these documents one can perceive a carefully delineated and systematically repeated subtext or formula: boundaries of Self are violated by some powerful Other, usually of supernatural origin—or if not supernatural, the agent is supernaturalized through a rhetoric of demonization.[26] Release, when it comes, is occasioned by the "awful dispensation of the Lord" in "God's time" (Rowlandson, p. 266). The narrative of deliverance becomes analogous to a religious experience itself, a "succession of disclosures" (Caldwell, p. 8), although the important issue is neither the captor nor the captivity, but the ritualistic and formulaic narrative of release, "spoken in the presence of God, and to his glory" (Rowlandson, p. 264). One understands, then, how instinctively both novel and film focus attention elsewhere; they are not really about the demonic visitation at all.

So far from being a Johnny-come-lately thriller of a trashy genre, *The Exorcist* conforms in general outline to this well-established American theological formula. Even Stephen King obliquely connected the two genres, situating the film in the "humorless Thudding Tract School of horror" (*Danse Macabre*, p. 282). Regan, then, that latter-day Rowlandson, is probably *the* formulaic American heroine of all time: captive, hapless, and of course on display. We witness her downward and spectacular "conversion" with our own eyes. Regan, however, is perversely sexual in a way that the demure Rowlandson only hints at. In a manner not unlike the earliest colonial private witness text, Regan's drama in placid, conventional Georgetown is a self-described melodrama of expulsion and captivity, of bondage and freedom which traces its roots back to the Old Testament trials of Job. The forces of evil hold the good soul bound for a divinely mandated time; after suffering a preordained time, he or she is released at long and painful last through the providence of God. Thus one can trace *The Exorcist* without too much difficulty to a tradition of moral *exempla*.[27] In fact the film recasts a very old idea: spiritual autobiography in the Protestant mode, soul-ful entertainment become doleful admonishment, even minatory spectacle.[28] Yet the possibility for the conversion of *confession* into spectacle had existed as early as Winthrop and Hooker, and traces of it can be found later in the tradition, as well. Concluding his account of the 1672 possession of Elizabeth Knapp in Groton, Samuel Willard, the town pastor, observed, "She is a monument of divine severity, and the Lord grant that all that see or hear may fear and tremble" (Demos, p. 436). Presumptively all did; for sure they would continue to do so, even into the next generation.

As a cinematic representation, *The Exorcist* both remembers a theological past and quickly ritually forgets it. Perhaps the ephemerality of the media itself serves this purpose. What is being remembered here, and why? What is being forgotten? Regan recalls Rowlandson and the Indian captivities, of course, yet she also recalls the exploitative spectacles of righteousness later associated with Salem. From another, perhaps modern perspective, however, Regan is only one more sign in a semiotics that writes women as fantasy text. She continues a venerable tradition of uncontrollable women (their name is legion), witches and social disruptors from Anne Hutchinson through Hester Prynne and beyond. The image of Regan "writing" on her body seems in fact to look backward to Hester, Hawthorne's complex signifier of the ambiguities of *kultur* and law.[29]

The Exorcist instructively shows how narratives of Self and the Other, Divine *or* Demonic, continue to patrol imaginative boundaries. Friedkin's downward revision of Blatty's moralistic theology, his recreation of theology as spectacle, suggests an answer and a memory not dissimilar from Cotton Mather's conclusion at Salem. Confession tells all. We read the writings on the bodies; Regan's HELP written across her stomach is not unlike the complex grammar of the A inscribed on Hester Prynne, and later revealed, significantly enough, as the "ghastly miracle" (p. 180) upon Arthur Dimmesdale's chest. The Divine reveals. Satan entertains. Not new or noteworthy conclusions, in light of Cotton Mather's Salem narratives. Following upon this point, the fabulous success of Friedkin's film adaptation underscores the fact that a well-developed habit already pre-existed films of this genre, reflecting a hunger for the horrific encounter with the Sublime. Religious captivities were conventional enough to be parodied, and all the better if the encounter can be sexualized. But if, as David Punter remarks, Gothic texts "revisit scenes of cultural trauma" then watching Friedkin's film, or reading Mather—or Poe's "The Fall of the House of Usher" (to name a few of many possible texts)— gives one pause for thought.[30] *Why* is there a woman bound and buried in these texts? Poe, of course, is famous for remarking that "the death of a beautiful woman is, unquestionably, the most poetical topic in the world." Perhaps he had been reading too many captivity narratives. In any event, Poe's equation becomes all the more horrifying in light of its existential possibilities, and here I am thinking about a certain variety of low-pornographic "captivity" or "snuff" film."[31] Indeed, it might be appropriate at this point to reflect on why Blatty found it necessary to exchange the boy of the actual possession case for the fictional girl. Was it for purposes of theology or for purposes of the formula? Which ritual thinking need we apply?

But William Blatty's reading of a putatively historical exorcism also contains a much more important allegory—the scene, of course, is the Everyman's Paradise Lost: the cosmology of terrors and graces; the elaborate and arcane metaphysics, if you will, of popular Christianity. Regan's struggle retells the epic of the powerless Adam and Eve, as powers and principalities engage in combat for their souls.[32] Blatty's exorcism, then, presumes a metaphysical order that once would have been invoked to condemn a witch to death. And what the exorcism intends to admonish is, in effect, her familiarity with the Divine. Blatty, by invoking the demon, names it incarnate among us, as had Matthew before him. Thus Plymouth, Salem, and the quiet, pastoral streets of Georgetown can be the site wherein an entire cosmological system of metaphysical imperatives comes to earth. In this way an ultimately silly film like *The Exorcist* functions as a *rite*. It re-presents—makes present again—a familiar pattern of events by which to embody and to make *right* the relationship between the community and its transcendent possibilities.

What is really horrific, of course, is not so much the failure of a religious vision but its inversion, and the uses to which this religious system has been put, "woven into an entertainment fabric producing publics of consumers for sale to advertisers" (p. 175).[33] The "Protestant assumption of internalized conscience" proper to Calvinism (Sage, *Horror Fiction*, p. xv), rendered as national myth, turns in upon itself as parody: "Theology . . . has the capacity to swivel and face in another direction, to present itself in another aspect . . . " (*Horror Fiction*, p. xiv). What had historically constituted a struggle for interior perfection translates, as Susie Snell observes in *Carrie*, into an imperative "to conform" (*Carrie*, p. 46). In a word, the demonic captivity of *The Exorcist* remembers, reinstates, and reconfirms, a hierarchy of power originally theological in intent, and which is now construed to other ends—moralistic in Blatty, parodic and satiric in King, whose *'Salem's Lot* plays out similar themes of conformity, invasion, and possession.

'Salem's Lot

> *The town knew darkness.*
>
> —STEPHEN KING, *'SALEM'S LOT*

Recall my earlier observation that the center of energy in Blatty's text, as even the title suggests, is not upon the demon at all, but upon the technologies of dis-covery and control by which the demon is bound. King, similarly, finds the demonic presence finally less interesting than the place to be violated and transgressed—and less interesting than the efforts made by its people to make darkness visible, thereby thwarting the demonic intrusion. King's title, like Blatty's, tells the story. King's vampire tale is less about vampires than about the town that Barlow's invasion reveals as soulless; Barlow's appearance in the town is less a revelation of supernal evil than of mendacious human evil. This evil, uncovered and revealed, serves a judgment upon our houses and on the secrets of mortal vacuousness. In King's small town (called The Lot), the vampire is only the occasion by which the fantasy obliquely criticizes a failed political order.

The plot of King's novel is fairly straightforward, even derivative. In an act of "literary homage" (*Danse Macabre*, p. 37), King borrows a few essential scenes from Bram Stoker's *Dracula*, transporting the Carpathian vampire to the backwoods of New England. There, aided by his "familiar," the vampire (named Barlow) buys an old house, opens an antique shop, and settles down for a leisurely campaign of decimating a small, isolated town in Massachusetts. King said when he was writing the novel that he "knew instinctively" that he "was trying to find a way to get home . . . " (Beahm, *King Companion*, p. 265). Home, it seems, is where the haunt is.

Both Blatty's and King's narratives are fantasies about the symbolization of theological power; both roughly reimagine Reformation politics. On the one hand, *The Exorcist* centers on the powers and principalities of a hierarchical metaphysical order—priestcraft, as Mather would call it. Appropriately enough, the rite of exorcism reflects a high-catholic praxis, a metaphysics of tradition and centralized power. The secret is only known by the secret: only power defeats power. *The Exorcist* is not, finally, a tale about goodness and love, but rather about the agencies of metaphysical power by which a community is organized. Regan is an object of voyeurism and horror—*exemplum* and spectacle—rather than love. On the other hand, *'Salem's Lot* reflects a low-Protestant vision of theological democracy in which the individual stands alone in moral combat against unseen forces. Any power that will be displayed is organized communally; the secret revelation is dis-covered by concerted effort as Ben and Mark gradually establish a relationship of mutual love by means of which they defeat the enemy. The terms, of course, are very much in accord with Winthrop's prescription to "walk together" in order to thwart "dispossession."

In a retrospective essay on his novel, William Blatty suggests that he never intended *The Exorcist* to be read as horror fiction, at least primarily. Rather, it was to be a meditation upon the nature of good and evil and their entanglement in human complexity. In effect, Blatty's final point is *exemplum* and moral. On the other hand, King's energy is satiric rather than directly moralistic—as James E. Hicks observes, part of King's purpose is to critique "the American pastoral."[34] King signals his intentions quickly. *'Salem's Lot* begins early to divide into two plots, perhaps even two discourses. As a fantasy text more appropriate to the genre of *Weird Tales*, the narrative describes Barlow's blood-hungry invasion of the town. As a horror story, *'Salem's Lot* is fairly formulaic, with lots of burning red eyes in the dark, much scratching at windows and other staples of the shudder pulps.[35] King constructs Barlow in the mold of Stoker's classic vampire; he is not Anne Rice's new-age vampire—he doesn't throw tantrums like her Lestat nor is he intensely introspective, even whiny, like Louis, Lestat's vampire son and companion. Instead, Barlow is very much an "old-school" Byronic vampire, well-heeled and aristocratic, imperious and patriarchal. He is also well-toothed, hungry, and bored, with just a touch of old-world lilt in his speech. Yet King manages to make him slightly comic, and stereotypically American, at the same time; by day Barlow rests in a large, Hepplewhite sideboard, while in town Straker, his human "familiar," deals in antique furniture. Together they prey upon the tourist trade. One soul-dead vampire deserves another, King seems to imply.

As a "realistic" text, the novel sharply focuses on the other world of 'Salem's Lot, drawing a prosaic, occasionally mean-spirited characterization of life in small-town America, where "scandal is always simmering on the back burner" (p. 19). Beneath the razzle-dazzle Gothicism—the horrid images of vampirized infants crawling under trailers, and corpses (with hair in curlers) sitting jerkily upright on mortician's tables— 'Salem's Lot is an exploration in "village virus" (Sinclair Lewis proposed this early title for Main Street) not unlike others in the American tradition of self-study. For instance, Henry James's "The Jolly Corner," Wilder's Our Town, Sinclair Lewis's Main Street, Masters, Anderson, Twain's Huckleberry Finn come to mind—although perhaps Flannery O'Connor's smugrified, sentimentalized Christianity seems, oddly, most in sympathy with King's vision.[36] As a group, these loosely similar "coming home" narratives reflect with varying degrees of awareness the horror of home that undercuts American rhetoric of domesticity. In this context, one can recall Edith Wharton's charge that while "The great American novel must always be about Main Street, geographically, socially, and intellectually," nonetheless Main Street offered "so meager a material to the imagination."[37]

Throughout this study I have argued that the rhetoric of civic (civilized) America—including those contained in its horrific repudiations—provides a sort of choral counterpoint to its theological idealizations, chief of which is the singleness of the separate, ever-reliant Self—the god in ruins, in Emerson's happy phrase. King's 'Salem's Lot takes its cue from Mark Twain's Huckleberry Finn, in that while seemingly about other business, the novel nonetheless manages to identify Main Street America as a home of monsters and vampires.[38] Writing about Twain (among others)

Leslie Fiedler characterized the canon of American literature as a "literature of horror for boys" (*Love and Death*, p. 29).[39] Fiedler's remarks of course outraged the literary institution that had grown up precisely to defend this literary canon. So it's ironic that Huck, the cherished exemplar of the Emersonian self-reliant man, is concerned to "tell the truth, mostly"—which, doubtless few really wish to hear. King, like Twain, is to be credited for fusing the culture's major oppositional narratives, realism and fantasy. King tells the one in terms of the other, as Skal observes:

> By night, King told very different stories people didn't want to hear directly, but would devour if presented in the veiled images of vampires, werewolves, rabid dogs, demonic automobiles . . . and the omnipresent favorite, the walking, rotting dead (*The Monster Show*, p. 354).

King interweaves "a fictional town with enough prosaic reality" to offset, in King's own words, "the comic-book menace of a bunch of vampires" (cited in Winter, *Stephen King*, p. 37). By bringing together these traditionally opposed genres, King helps clarify what has been there all along, the "major political and social tensions shaping contemporary American life."[40] As Hicks observes, "For the villagers of *'Salem's Lot*, the vampire's kiss is almost a welcomed relief, since the wholesome façades of the American pastoral and small town America have collapsed under the weight of pervasive boredom and triumphant evil" (p. 77).

'Salem's Lot, a fantasy town, is dense with real politics and theological imperatives. It is like Dunwich—or Lewis's Main Street, or even Faulkner's Jefferson, or Updike's Eastwick—or, come to think of it, even like Jerusalem, in 6 B.C. In these places reality and its fantasies are interchangeable, ever dependent upon each other. Change the focus slightly and King's horror novel reintroduces the horrific, although the horrific as it routinely exists in the real and the probable. The horrific, says King, is not a dismissable fantasy. Beneath, or through, the shifting screen of shadowy fantasy, King glimpses the profound truth of real American horror: we ourselves invite the demonic. What we abject, repress, toss away, returns to consume us, dressed often in the decaying flesh of outworn idealism. King may lean heavier on the allegorical dimension than does Updike or Faulkner, but at his fictional best, King likewise presents a compendium of human misery and grotesquery, a closetful of ghosts repudiated because they are too real. Sometimes King's painstaking detail of grotesquery, and the paucity of the human imagination he represents, seems purposefully indulgent: "I will try to terrorize the reader. But if I find I cannot terrify him/her, I will try to horrify; and if I find I cannot horrify, I'll go for the gross-out. I'm not proud" (*Danse Macabre*, p. 37). Some incidents even border on the pornographic, in the way, as Fiedler observes, historically such texts would have been read.[41] Vivid images of child-beating, rape (female *and* male), spouse abuse, cross-generational sex—all can be found in the thick novel. There is even a scene in which Susan Norton's father ruminates over dinner about the "defloration" of his daughter. Ben, the potential deflowerer, is the man's dinner guest. Strange fare, it would seem, for a book about vampires. Or is it? And strangely successful, for buttoned-up Americans in the land of Jesse Helms, no?

Douglas Winter observes that King's use of the vampire contains "important metaphors for the seductiveness of evil and the dehumanizing pall of modern society" (*Stephen King*, p. 37). The aforementioned dinner table scene, for instance, offers a graphic shorthand for the family values rhetorized from pulpit and political stump. The hardly veiled metaphors of sexual violence throughout King's intertwined plots buttress a culture heavily in denial about what it really values. Still, if King uses pornographic discourse to critique aesthetic and political idealizations, he is part of a well-developed tradition. In *Speaking the Unspeakable: A Poetics of Obscenity*, Peter Michelson argues that D. H. Lawrence, Faulkner, Genet, and Burroughs—and I would add King—use an "aesthetics of obscenity" as a "*contemplation of the unspeakable*" that "counterpoints traditional aesthetic assumptions" (p. xi).[42] In King's small town, sexual violation and gossipy exposure are the normative forms of intimacy. In the ever-shrinking imaginative spaces of the small town, the telephone links a community of snoops who never have to leave home. Its people feed upon the rag ends and bits of stray life coming through telephone wires. Afraid of life, the people of *'Salem's Lot* almost willingly connive with Barlow's "evangelistic" charms. In characters like Dudley, the dump's watchman who shoots rats as indifferently as he mentally undresses little girls; or Larry Crockett, the rapacious, vampiric real estate agent; or Mabel Werts, the snoopy, vampiric telephone operator, who lives out her life on the telephone, King satirizes the single, separate Self consumed by its own xenophobic mediocrity. A lust for the superficial and fear of the extraordinary marks the new conformity. Indeed, 'Salem's Lot is a community in flight from its civic emptiness. Afraid of change, inevitably it changes into death, physically and spiritually.

After about a hundred pages of King's novel, an alert reader asks, how do the predatory and brutal intimacies offered by Barlow the vampire differ from the brutalities exchanged between husband and wife (Bonnie and Reggie Sawyer); between boyfriend and girlfriend (Susan Norton and Floyd Tibbets); between mother and the child she beats (Sandy and Randy McDougal); or, finally, the brutalities implicitly exchanged between author and reader? There is little difference. People feed upon each other routinely, for business (like Larry Crockett), and for perverse pleasures (like Dudley). The townspeople are vampiric in the most real of ways; where an "econo-erotic code" (Michelson's phrase) is in force, consumption is intimacy; and power, rather than love, shapes human relations in its own likeness. No wonder Barlow finds himself comfortably at home in what Straker calls, with thin irony, the "so-fine" town. For all practical purposes, Barlow is indistinguishable from the townspeople themselves, conforming as he does to expected and conventional patterns of depredation and exploitation. Thus Barlow is a shadowy presence in King's text, and rarely the center of narrative action. Understandably those pursuing him find him hard to identify; harder to separate out; the hardest of all to stake. He is one of their own.

'Salem's Lot, in sum, is not a pleasant book to read, although "the comic-book menace of a bunch of vampires" has little to do with the book's unpleasantness. King works up scenes and representations that under another cover would indeed risk being labeled pornographic. Indeed, America's pornography of choice, a choice carefully deflected from self-reflection, *is* violence, and perhaps sexism.[43] Michelson concurs: "Violence is graphically pervasive in our culture in a way that sex is not" (*Speaking the Unspeakable*, p. xi). For this reason it amazes me to find readers so enthralled (the etymology of the word is instructive) by the subplot of the vampire that they pay little if any attention to the other text. For example, King's construction of the masculine point of view, in such passages as the defloration scene cited above, rarely draws a reaction from women readers, and *never* draws a reaction from men, so indistinguishable is it from the normal, or perhaps routine, point of view of an American consumer. Perhaps King's horror tale prevents readers from seeing them as real, though I rather suspect that its ingenuous self-advertising as fantasy gives readers an excuse *not* to see what they will not face. For example, Reggie Sawyer's vicious male-rape of Corey, the telephone installer whom he finds in dalliance with his wife—and then the subsequent brutalizing rape of his wife—is *just* a diversion, after all. It is of no real interest to the homophobic culture that ingenuously markets the male body as spectacle and which lauds womanhood and the home. Middle America, as described by King, suffers a fate like Dunwich in that apparently the town exists on no map its citizens would recognize. Yet when all is said and done, the terrain is very familiar. King commented that in writing *The Stand* he felt like he was "tap dancing on the country's grave" (Whissen, *Classic Cult*, p. 228). Nonetheless, a more appropriate metaphor for *'Salem's Lot* I cannot imagine.

Paul Buhle observes that the "sense of horror [is] organic to the American tradition."[44] Nonetheless, one comes away from reading King understanding why custodians of culture would be so invested in dismissing fantasy and those who write them as "high hackery."[45] Nor is it surprising that so much energy is invested in maintaining that the horror market is merely a "diversion," or that as "entertainment," it has no meaning. Read differently, these texts are horrific because they are too real, not because they are too unreal. This is the real reason why, from Nathaniel Hawthorne through Lovecraft and Stephen King, the fantasy text historically found itself shoved into literary basements. Nor does one wonder, as Leonard Wolf notes, why the dark implications behind Stoker's *Dracula*—a "fairly narrow Christian work" (p. 180)—were "carefully unacknowledged" for generations.[46] Frank McConnell writes that the "horror film is . . . a remarkable instance of submerged value" that only comes to full articulation through the development of "critical intelligence" (p. 110).[47] McConnell's insight is applicable here, since most people would rather *not* articulate. To acknowledge submerged values would indeed mean apocalypse and chaos. At the very least it would entail the discomfort of having to acknowledge a rhetoric that no longer lived, an ideal order that no longer could be real. It would mean having to change. King's readers therefore engage the text in much the same way that the townspeople of 'Salem's Lot engage each other—in vampiric, voyeuristic ways. Indeed, what else is reading but a sort of vampiric voyeurism in the model of Mabel Werts, the spiderlike telephone operator in The Lot?[48] Stephen King creates his characters to be ideal readers, and his real readers then are likely to be as boundary-defensive and as xenophobic as the townspeople. The horror—the "real" *meaning*—must stay *in* the text; its possible contamination of "real" life will not be allowed. The problem, of course, soon becomes apparent; what is adjudged the "real" seems more and more illusory, the illusions more and more real. To prevent this interpretive confusion, the reader casts about for a likely scapegoat on whom to blame the troubling implications of the horror text. Like the townsfolk, the reader finds it readily enough in Barlow. So long as Barlow could be identified as the vampire, the townspeople—and King's reader—can consider themselves free of taint. The monster, again, has served its purpose. It is a remonstrance and reminder, a spectacle, an expiation and judgment.

NOTES

1. John Demos, *Remarkable Providences: Readings on Early American History*, rev. ed. (Boston: Northeastern University Press, 1991), p. 414.
2. Cited in George Beahm, *The Stephen King Companion* (Kansas City: Andrews and McMeel, 1989), p. 56.
3. In *Danse Macabre*, King calls H. P. Lovecraft the "twentieth-century horror story's dark and baroque prince" (p. 41). King recalls his introduction to Lovecraft—an result of his father's "sudden disappearance" (100), since the paperback edition of Lovecraft found among his father's abandoned books was, King says, fortuitous—it was his "first encounter with serious fantasy-horror fiction" (p. 102).
4. The universe of Jonathan Edwards, or rather, its derivative, horrific copy, is a cosmology polarized between gestures of power and the rhetoric (usually ineffectual) of love; caught between the valorization of the individual and the

ruthless demands of communal awareness. And, as we have seen, Lovecraft's alignment of the discourse of the holy with the obsession of the conventional (the contested ground where the Other intruded) marks the return of the dark underside of American spiritual rhetoric, the sharply moralistic mode of its self-perception, evidenced in a need for transgression, as well as for *expiation*. The narrator in "The Dunwich Horror" comments on the "unnameable violence and perversity" of the citizenry (p. 101), suggesting, even implicitly, religious, aesthetic, and conventional canons of respectability. So while Lovecraft may be dismissed as one of the Pulps, writing on culture's margin, as it were, he certainly still speaks to its center.

5. Susan Sontag, "Piety Without Content," in *Against Interpretation, op. cit.*, p. 250.

6. Even as I write, *Time* magazine has for its cover story, "In the Name of God: What Happens When Believers Embrace the Dark Side of Faith," about the sectarian apocalyptic set in Waco, Texas; and the (putatively) religious-inspired bombing of the New York World Trade Center. *Time* magazine, vol. 141, no. 11, March 15, 1993.

7. *Selected Poems and Two Plays of William Butler Yeats*, M. L. Rosenthal, ed. (New York: Macmillan, 1962).

8. *The Complete Poems and Plays of T. S. Eliot* (New York: Harcourt, Brace and World, 1952), p. 69.

9. See, for instance, *Devouring Whirlwind: Terror and Transcendence in the Cinema of Cruelty*, Will H. Rockett (New York: Greenwood Press, 1988). Rocket argues that "in feeling a strong attraction toward certain films usually identified as horror, audiences are seeking transcendence, or at least confirmatory contact with the sublime or transcendent" (p. 6).

10. King made the remark with reference to the 1950s horror film, *The Creature from the Black Lagoon*; see *Danse Macabre*, p. 103.

11. Michael Levenson, "The Nayman of Noland." *New Republic,* July 6, 1987.

12. George T. Wetzel, "The Cthulhu Mythos: A Study," in *H. P. Lovecraft: Four Decades of Criticism*, S. T. Joshi, ed., *op. cit.*, p. 79.

13. As Michel Foucault demonstrates in *A History of Sexuality*, a dread of the body—its issues and fervors, its unspeakable and uncontrollable desires—profoundly influences western culture.

14. In what Mary Douglas defines as a "witch-finding cosmology" separation (or its failure) and transgression establish a central axis, or *ritual* of identity, by which the normative center is identified in terms of its repudiated "outside." In such a social taxonomic system, Douglas argues, dirt is function rather than material—it is matter in the *wrong* place, needing to be removed, re-*placed*. Analogously, the witch is the person who breaches the line, who crosses the categories, and makes dirt possible. He or she lets the Outside In—and conversely, permits the Inside Out. Perversely enough, in such a social order witch-making is a sign of social self-cleansing and health. In its preoccupation with dirt and uncleanness variously symbolized, Lovecraft's tale reflects how, in anthropological terms, the human body writes out a map of the universe, becoming *the* symbolized site of metaphysical tensions.

15. In the post-*Exorcist* cosmo-drama, *The Amityville Horror*, Jay Anson makes the

point, repeatedly, about the wife's cleanliness, as if to confirm her in her domestic role: "she keeps the children so clean." The demon, of course, tracks dirt in everywhere. (Englewood Cliffs, NJ: Prentice-Hall, Inc., 1977).

16. See her *Epistemology of the Closet* (Berkeley: University of California Press, 1990).

17. When Armitage learns that the invisible brother has escaped from the Whately farm, cutting a swath of destruction through the town, he and two others prepare to confront it. In a final effort to thwart the horrible invasion of Dunwich by extramortal agents, Armitage and the others "ascended the mountain alone," chasing the invisible creature. The scene recalls the story of Jesus's transfiguration, and insofar as Lovecraft echoes that narrative, the allusion directs a reader's attention to the systematic efforts, geographically as well as narratively, to underscore the distance between the Divine and the mortal. As the trio of *cognoscenti* perform rites and incantations on the hill, far below in the distance the townsfolk gawk through binoculars and gesticulate, their ineffectuality underscored by their remoteness from the scene.

18. The violent history of post-Reformation theology, from Luther through Calvin and their respective interpreters, can be read then as an act of containment, an attempt to deny what Updike (himself an accomplished theologian) calls the "scandalous Incarnation." In "Hawthorne's Creed," Updike writes, "Orthodox doctrine bridges matter and spirit with a scandalous Incarnation, Jesus Christ." *Hugging the Shore: Essays and Criticism* (New York: Knopf, 1983), pp. 76–77.

19. As we have seen Lovecraft knew it well enough to use it repeatedly to his own advantage, as he does in "The Dunwich Horror" (also in "The Shadow over Innsmouth" and "The Whisperer in Darkness"). In "The Call of Cthulhu," Lovecraft, for example, uses the expression "spectral intercourse" (p. 88), aware, I think, of its conflicting implications.

20. Even Garry Wills admits the "idea of the Incarnation may be monstrous." See "The Tragic Pope," *The New York Review of Books*, vol. XLI, no. 21: 6. Wills continues, "[the Incarnation] is hardly dull, or irrelevant to the way people think of themselves and their world." Which of course, as I am suggesting, is true—although perhaps not in the way Wills originally meant.

21. Leszek Kolakowski, *Metaphysical Horror* (New York: B. Blackwell, 1988).

22. Don Herron, "Stephen King: The Good, the Bad, and the Academic," in *Kingdom of Fear, op. cit.*, p. 148.

23. In *"The Exorcist: A Devilish Attack on Women,"* *Social Policy*, May/June 1974, Herbert J. Gans notes that Blatty's text had gone through twenty-nine printings before the film's release. He cites *Variety* to note that 5.5 million copies of the book were in print before the film's release, and that four million more were subsequently printed (p. 72).

24. Marsha Kinder and Beverley Houston, "Seeing is Believing: *The Exorcist* and *Don't Look Now,"* in Gregory A. Waller, *American Horrors: Essays on the Modern American Horror Film* (Urbana: University of Illinois Press, 1987), p. 46.

25. In *Possessed: The True Story of an Exorcism* (New York: Doubleday, 1993), Thomas B. Allen traces the historical events behind Blatty's novel.

26. In general, certain characteristics repeat in these narratives, as we have seen: the Self is overtaken by an Other, usually portrayed as the Divine, though increasingly violation comes through the agency of a demonized Other (Dickinson's "Because I could not Stop for Death," for example). This Other, though conventionally of supernatural origin, could, however, be mortal, to whom supernatural powers are *attributed* through rhetoric or other agency of language.

27. As Noel Carroll notes in *The Philosophy of Horror: or Paradoxes of the Heart, op. cit.*, "it is an affirmation of the existence of inexplicable evil in the world . . . and it has a theory about the real purpose of demonic possession" (p. 103). This supports Herbert Gans, who writes that the film "in the end advocates the necessity of religious concepts and insights." (p. 72) Gans also argues that "the social underpinnings of *The Exorcist* suggest . . . that it is about manly— and Christlike—priests of lowly origin in the service of a rational and modern Catholic church . . ." (p. 73).

28. "Crypto-religious" is the only adequate way to describe Friedkin's adaptation of Blatty's text; its cinematic chills and religious "thrills" connive with the comfortable disbelief of a viewer who, probably, has no practical use for God *or* a demon. The *Grand Guignol* effects and the Beauty-into-Beast transformation of the possessed girl marked a signal departure—and beginning—in the limits to which American cinema would go.

29. Of course one could almost formalize a genre—Public Woman as Spectacle, or perhaps, Woman Publicized as Spectacle—and extend the list to include most recently Anita Hill and Hillary Rodham Clinton (but not, of course, the safely domestic Barbara Bush).

30. Punter, *The Hidden Script: Writing and the Unconscious* (New York: Routledge and Kegan Paul, 1985), p. 114.

31. For an important discussion of the way that "horror spectatorship" is "registered as a 'feminine' experience," see Carol J. Clover, "Her Body, Himself: Gender in the Slasher Film" in *Fantasy Cinema*, James Donald, ed., *op. cit.*, pp. 91–135. Clover's general remarks provide good background for my discussion of *The Exorcist*. See also Vera Dika, *Games of Terror: Halloween, Friday the 13th, and the Films of the Stalker Cycle* (Rutherford, NJ: Fairleigh Dickinson University Press, 1990).

32. But recall Friedkin's *The Exorcist*. Despite all that is suggested about Pazzuzu's power, he seems essentially quite limited, able only to make off-color sexual references, rattle furniture, and bully a priest or two and threaten a small girl.

33. George Gerbner and Larry Gross, "Living with Television: The Violence Profile," *Journal of Communication*, Spring 1976, pp. 172–97.

34. Hicks, "Stephen King's Creation of Horror in *'Salem's Lot*: A Prolegomenon Towards a New Hermeneutic of the Gothic Novel," in Gary Hoppenstand and Ray B. Browne, *The Gothic World of Stephen King: Landscape of Nightmares* (Bowling Green, OH: Bowling Green State University Popular Press, 1987, p. 75).

35. Phyllis A. Roth, in *Bram Stoker* (Boston: Twayne Publishers), argues that part of Stoker's research for *Dracula* is "a clipping of an article from the *New York World*, dated 2 February 1896, headed 'Vampires in New England—Dead

Bodies Dug Up and Their Hearts Burned to Prevent Disease' " (p. 148). Roth suggests, then, a possible irony; that King returns the vampire to where Stoker may have originally found him in the first place—in New England. Stoker's papers, and this clipping, are in the Rosenbach Library, Philadelphia.

36. That "*Our Town* can be rendered into Jerusalem's Lot is a jackhammer blow at the psychological firmament of the pastoral myth, tearing away the small town facade to expose dark truths . . . " (Winter, *Stephen King*, p. 38). The xenophobia of the sentimental Christian tradition, however, was satirized long before King, by Twain in *Huckleberry Finn*, and alternately, and more canonically, by Flannery O'Connor. O'Connor and the rhetoric of victimization encoded in sentimental Christianity: "Good Country People," "Revelation," *Wise Blood*.

37. Edith Wharton, "The Great American Novel," *Yale Review 16* (July 1927): 646–56. See also Frank Peretti, whose first novel, a horror-apocalypse in the vein of King's '*Salem's Lot*, has sold 1.9 million copies. In *This Present Darkness*, angels and demons fight over the fate of a town.

38. After all, Twain's Pap Finn may have less finely developed sensibilities and delicacy of speech than Barlow, but his instincts for killing are as well-honed as the vampire's. As much as Barlow, Pap lives on the vitality and energy he steals from others. (Consider Pap's peculiar understanding of family values; consider, for example, the dark, emotional incest that characterizes his relationship with his son.) So it is easy to see why Twain's novel would be repeatedly banned over the years—it doesn't make a very good case for some cherished sentimental beliefs about the American Way.

39. Leslie Fiedler, *Love and Death in the American Novel*, rev. ed. (New York: Stein and Day, 1966).

40. Tony Magistrale, ed., *The Dark Descent: Essays Defining Stephen King's Hororscape* (New York: Greenwood Press, 1992), p. 2.

41. Fiedler again: "Nor has horror ceased to function for us as pornography even now . . . . Yet without quite ceasing to be experienced as porn (in part, indeed, for that very reason) Weird Fiction has in the last decades of the twentieth century turned into a best-selling commodity in the supermarket of popular culture" (*Kingdom of Fear*, p. 54).

42. *Speaking the Unspeakable: A Poetics of Obscenity* (Albany, NY: State University of New York Press, 1993). Michelson argues that other writers, Henry Miller, William Faulkner, and Philip Roth, for example, are representative of the American tradition of pornographic discourse. This tradition is "liberal," as opposed to "conservative." A conservative tradition, including writers like D. H. Lawrence and Anaïs Nin, "resist the idea of pornography in order to subdue it to their other purposes." The liberal tradition, on the other hand, is one in which pornography is "organically fused" into practice (p. 15).

43. Andrea Dworkin, of course, would argue that sexism *is* the most violent of tolerated violences, as her own pornogothic novel, *Mercy*, supposes. See "So Long as It's Not Sex and Violence: Andrea Dworkin's *Mercy*," *Sex Exposed: Sexuality and the Pornography Debate*, Lynne Segal and Mary McIntosh, eds. (New Brunswick, NJ: Rutgers University Press, 1993), pp. 216–29. In this

context, Dworkin's novel shares some suggestive similarities with King's telling of the battered author, *Misery*.

44. Paul Buhle, "Dystopia as Utopia: Howard Phillips Lovecraft and the Unknown Content of American Horror Literature," in *H. P. Lovecraft: Four Decades of Criticism*, p. 197.

45. In "Fantasy as Commodity and Myth," Leslie Fiedler comments, "By the end of the nineteenth century . . . not just Dark Fantasy but all hardcore fantasy had been ghettoized: demoted to the Nursery, on the one hand; and on the other, remanded to circulating libraries and railroad bookstalls. . . . Horror was left to modest hacks . . . content to be loved by the yahoos but despised or condescended to by the official guardians of literary standards" (See *Kingdom of Fear: The World of Stephen King*, pp. 52–53).

46. *A Dream of Dracula: In Search of the Living Dead* (New York: Popular Library, 1972), p. 181.

47. Frank McConnell, "Rough Beast Slouching: A Note on Horror Movies," *The Kenyon Review*, vol. 1, 1970: 109–20. McConnell has this interesting comment to make about Dracula: "for what Dracula comes to destroy is an insularity not primarily of space but of history" (p. 111).

48. Elizabeth Bird argues that the relationship between text and reader "should be seen as circular rather than linear, in that producers incorporate readers in their production of texts, and texts in turn may have an impact on readers, whose response then feeds back into the text." *For Enquiring Minds*, p. 162. See also *The Delights of Horror, op. cit.*, for a reader-response view of the machinery of horror (pp. 1–18).

End Runs: Toward the American Gothic

The world of memory breaks up more quickly, the mythic in it surfaces more quickly and crudely, a completely different world of memory must be set up even faster to oppose it.
—WALTER BENJAMIN, *STORM FROM PARADISE*, P. 49

We were fertile ground for the seeds of terror. . . . we had been raised in a strange circus atmosphere of paranoia, patriotism, and national hubris.
—STEPHEN KING, *DANSE MACABRE*, P. 23

———— ■■ ————

"This Horrid Nonsense"
—JONATHAN EDWARDS

Necessity may be the mother of invention, but memory—awe-ful memory—is what the founders of New England, by civic necessity, invented.[1] At some remove behind this study of cultic memory have been two primary assumptions: first, religious discourse, although legally "unspeakable" in public, never ceases to speak; its rhythms and cadences establish a critical civic hermeneutic. This apparent paradox directs attention to a second assumption, that terror and nostalgia—rather than love, as conventional rhetoric insists—drives the popular or mass-culture imagination.[2] As evidence for these assertions, I have considered in this study the genres of the unspeakable, the theologically shadowed tradition of American fantasy. In the formulaic tales of episodic attack and providential release that typify this discredited genre, a culture speaks, however indirectly, the nightmares to which it is most habituated. Gary Green writes that a "sense of negativity lies at the core of the American self, a void out of which the language of nightmare arises" (*Language of Nightmare*, p. 12). Green argues that this negativity reflects "a fear that perhaps ultimately there is no true concept of the American self" (p. 4). If Green is correct, and if the term "American" is worthwhile as any kind of critical generalization, its dark fantasy texts, riddled with anxieties, horrors, terrors, ideological fissures, and silences, arguably reflects what the rhetoric of being "American" means in practice.

What is popularly called "entertainment" is rarely value-free, and in the main, texts that declare themselves as fantasy have never fared well critically; when they are not shown the door immediately they are ignored or vilified. An early reviewer, for example, dismissed Gothic texts as "completely expurgated of all the higher qualities of mind" (cited in DeLamotte, *Perils of the Night*, p. 8), and opinions haven't changed much since.[3] In *The Development of American Romance*, Michael Davitt Bell writes about the place of imagination in American culture; "Imagination," he writes, "if not strictly controlled," was thought to pose "a threat both to individual happiness and social cohesion."[4] So when texts are dismissed as "fantasy" or "entertainment," the dismissal is at least as important as the text itself, because the "real world" of politics, theological prescriptions, and civic directives is present even if—especially when—these seem absent. William Patrick Day makes the point that the Gothic

> illuminates the unbroken connections between our imaginative life and our economic, social and political life. The genre grows out of the conventional ideas about families, about the definitions of male and female identity that dominated the nineteenth century and continue to affect our ideas today.[5]

So, far from being dismissible and of no importance, the genre of American Gothic *acts out*, in a manner of speaking, the conditions and collusions of the imaginative life, its possibilities and impossibilities. Indeed, a culture's politics enacts its spiritualities, and what a social order chooses to forget shows what it needs to remember.[6]

Paul Tillich argues that culture is the shape of religion. This study began with that premise applied to American imaginative life. Although not about religious experience directly, nonetheless I presume a cultic dimension to the *civitas* that in sometimes literal ways depends upon a prior theological metaphysical formulation. I have argued that those moments of self-reflection celebrated (and, importantly, memorialized) in national cultic life are, often enough, *tactics* of civil organization rather than *facts*. State and church, finally, do come together—if ever they were separate in the first place. The evidence for that entanglement can be found most readily in a history of fear and trembling, first in the pulpits, then at the movies. The chief secret of Gothic literature, as Porte and others have argued, is that it is theology at one remove. The chief secret of American popular identity is, then, the idealizing, negating theology that is kept well-hidden, out of view, wrapped up.[7] The "designs of darkness"—in Frost's phrase—points toward the idealizations of light that give them theoretical context and emotional conviction. Both show just how close the Holy and the Horrible are; how easily one's foot can slide, as Edwards warned, from ecstasy to terror.

From the literary low-basement view I have taken, cultural theologies—its nationalistic fantasies as well as its civic politics—are rarely distinguishable. For example, the post-Christian fervor of Blatty's moralistic *The Exorcist* echoes the political apocalyptics of Cotton Mather. Nor are the overlaps between polity and theology new. From 1630 till the present, American religious sentiment has been compounded partly of personal anxieties, civic sensibilities, and by pragmatic social needs. Glance through any Puritan text, religious or civil; early colonial broadsides echo recent election speeches. They share a common language and cadence, while evoking similar negations and repudiations. Yet historically one can detect a recent change—a growing awareness that whether or not Jesus saves, Jesus sells and gains votes. In short, the pomps of religion find themselves pressed into the service of the political market, as divine economies lubricate less holy ones. The reverse, of course, is equally true, and I argue that American religion is as much *produced* by culture as it has produced its own inimitable form. Nor is *this* a new story.[8] For instance, in *The Feminization of American Culture*, Ann Douglas demonstrates that Calvinism's once-rigorous philosophical/religious epistemologies were subsumed into a program of sentimentality, a conventionality that registered interiority on the surface, as it were. Citing Stowe's *Uncle Tom's Cabin* as an example, Douglas observes about Little Eva that her "sainthood is there to precipitate our nostalgia and our narcissism" (p. 4). The cultural historian Warren Susman describes the phenomenon similarly as a movement from a culture of character to a culture of personality.[9]

Reading Douglas and Susman prompted my initial observation about the semiotics of terror. In a society where religious discourse is both fundamental to self-identity *and* routinely converted, in Douglas's phrase, to "consumer pleasures," what will be the effects? Further, where shall we look to find traces of this silenced master narrative? I hope this study has been a tentative answer. Where a metaphysics of Christian love is discredited in practice yet idealized in cultural mythologies, the accompanying dissociation produces the oppositions of terror and nostalgia—memory forward and its backward look.[10] How do we think the Holy? We sentimentalize and thus deny it, a point Stephen Carter makes in *The Culture of Disbelief*.[11] Or else we rewrite the Holy as the terrible; the dream as the nightmare, the awe-ful as the awful. Then, by force of the tensions at work in the dialectics of denial, both the Holy and the Horrible are cast outward beyond the safe limits of an ideologically defined "real," where mutual gravity keeps each in neighborly though not always congenial tension. Finally, both the Holy *and* the Horrible suffer the favorite American put-down for what cannot, or will not, be taken seriously—they are dismissed as variant forms of fantasy, and they remain, in effect, unspoken and unspeakable.[12]

American Horrors, American Theologies

It is with fiction as with religion: it should present another world, and yet one to which we feel the tie.
—MELVILLE, *THE CONFIDENCE MAN*

I have suggested that Gothic epistemologies and theological structures serve parallel functions in demarcating cultural boundaries. It is time to consider this point more at length. While this study of the links between conventionalized terror and religious memory in American culture is not about the Gothic genre *per se*, I argue that formal resemblances between the discourses of theology (the "ineffable") and Gothic fantasy (the "unadmitted") (Punter, *The Literature of Terror*, p. 20) have permitted, even encouraged, the deflection of once-dominant theological rhetorics into different forms. As Louis Gross argues, the tradition of Gothic is "uniquely American in its sense of personal sin and national retribution" (*Redefining the American Gothic*, p. 89). In *The Supernatural in Gothic Fiction*, Geary argues that a close link exists between horror and belief, citing, as have other critics before him, the "religious impulse of the [Gothic] form" (p. 7).[13] Geary writes the "Gothic novel . . . becomes a lonely religious revival, of a primitive sort, against an age of desiccated rationalism and materialism" (p. 7). I would perhaps reverse the equation, suggesting that a religious impulse or habit shows itself as a pattern of self-annihilative terror, better understood as a debased form of the Sublime.[14]

It should be clear by now that the tropes of conversion appropriate to religious discourse, and the recurring anxiety of metamorphosis characteristic of much horror/fantasy describes a fear of self-loss common to both genres.[15] Each discourse, however, comes at the issue from a different perspective, fixing in its own terms the limits of permitted experience, charting the boundary beyond which it is death or annihilation to wander. Gothic discourses, then, both literary and theological, operate in similar ways, and both genres easily assimilate elements of political discourse as well. Gothic and theological discourses each foregrounds mystery, establishing an epistemology of entrapment or uncertainty by which little can be known, or known with certainty. Thus both move toward paradoxical closure, since in neither can anything be disclosed with certainty. Finally, each promises a revelation that comes, if it ever does, as a gesture of ultimate change, fulfilled in terror. Thematically, too, both genres operate in similar fashion. As it has been historically constructed, Protestant interiority is governed by three concerns: separation (from which derive anxieties about purity and its opposite, defilement); second, the presumption of scrutiny (and its corollary, a fascination with the ambiguities of transgression); lastly, a yearning for expiation (often experienced as a mix of fear, shame, and desire couched in the language of conversion or annihilation). In a bit of rhetorical legerdemain these concerns become silenced as theological motifs; instead they are allegorized, rewritten in moralistic ways. For example, fears of separation make possible a public speech saturated with communitarian metaphor and a heightened anxiety about familial bonding, as we have seen in John Winthrop. Anxieties of scrutiny give rise to a rhetoric of freedom, utopic and untrammeled—in itself, therefore, ultimately horrific. Finally, expiation becomes confessional: emptying of the self is, ironically, the new interiority. Thus, from two perspectives, old theologies become new social rhetorics; these, in turn, conservatively reaffirm a civic status quo.

In addition, theological and Gothic rubrics share similar apocalyptic teleologies. To borrow a phrase from G. R. Thompson, both are "fear-driven narrative" in which a hermeneutics of the unknown and the to-be-revealed assumes transcendent authority. Of course, in neither discourse is destiny manifest or stable; in each fate is hidden, oblique, secret, and subject to sudden change or loss of definition. Theology and Gothic structures are alike in that each establishes a domain of secrets and [dis]closures employing similar metaphors of intimacy and distance. Often the one (the secret) is the other (the intimacy), especially if the intimacy or secret is an unapproved variety. Terror, especially of exposure, is a crucial motivation. Terror is an emotion, and like any, it is habit-forming. But terror is not only habit, it is habitation, as well—a place to possess, as well as one by which to be possessed. Traditionally the Gothic reflects an interest in space and architectural form. Theology, too, organizes itself around boundaries and limits, establishing domains, sites, and areas of unknowability and mystery—of which Hell, of course, is the *locus classicus*. Unlike the Gothic's emphasis on space, however, in general the theological *eschaton* offers a temporal rather than spatial metamorphosis and fusion.[16] In a similar manner, democratic political forms and myths ostensibly create areas of "private" space, where an individual can exist supposedly free of, or beyond, the solicitations of culture ("A man's home is his castle," for instance). Nonetheless, terror, especially as it is invoked under various public covers, deconstructs that space, exposing the private "I" as still under the control of *res publica*.[17] As a consequence, dis-closure of the secret becomes a powerful social tactic and focus for communal energy.

To this end exist a variety of public and private forms of scrutiny which provide ritualistic methods for the discovery of the hidden and concealed.[18] In the collusion of metaphysics and politics, then, the secret defines the transgression whose disclosure and damnation first rectifies, then sanctifies, the body politic.

Theology and Gothic discourses are deflective, decentering: their subject, once disclosed, is *not*, in the end, the subject. Instead, the systematic arousal and manipulation of terror *is* the subject, while the possession and display of power is unspoken pretext and motivation of the discourse. Elizabeth Napier writes that the Gothic is "finally much less about evil . . . than it is a standardized, absolutely formulaic system of creating a certain kind of atmosphere in which a reader's sensibility toward fear and horror is exercised in predictable ways" (*The Failure of the Gothic*, p. 29). While theological (apocalyptic) narratives of the Divine move to apparent confirmation—comfort and reassurance—in the *eschaton*, in actuality they provide ongoing examples of disconfirmation and imbalance. As Frank Kermode argues in *The Sense of an Ending*, the end is always deferred; Jesus is always coming but never here. Likewise, while Gothic texts move to (apparent) knowledge and exposure of various mysteries, they usually do not, at least in the way originally promised. Mysteries are effaced or denied rather than resolved. Finally, and this is key: both discourses presume a grammar in which the unknown implicitly judges the known and in which terror is object as well as motivation. Finally, Gothic and theologic epistemologies ritualize mystery as the great secret, whose gradual revelation, in however complex ways, functions as the sacrament of Judgment and Revelation. Yet insofar as theology and the Gothic mode offer epistemologies of the mysterious and unknown (even the unknowable), they are, paradoxically, "genres of imbalance."[19] Their subject is logically odd; they deal in nonsense, as even Edwards found his theologies to sometimes sound. And while theology traffics in unfinished, or at least constantly deferred, business, it doesn't like to leave it that way, since it holds up as final the awe-ful dis-closure (unclosing) of Judgment.

Joel Porte observes that in the Gothic tradition of Ann Radcliffe, the "proper business of the orthodox novel of Terror was to expand the soul religiously" ("Sinners," p. 43). That is, in a kind of implicit spiritual metonymy, terror—characteristically associated with the sublime—easily substitutes for the sublime itself.[20] And so, mindful of the various ways in which critics interpret Gothic texts, the genre's formal structures replicate, echo, reaffirm some basic formulas of theological discourse—especially the motif of hidden power central to it, and knowing how to "read" its mysteries "rightly." Thus a metaphor of reading and literacy is central to theology and Gothic alike. In an earlier chapter I argued that "right reading" of selected, canonical (yet, perversely, "low" or vernacular) texts gave the proto-society its authority, and this mythicizing habit continues. In the foundational theological readings of American myth, the presumptive master text is the Bible, which can be read backwards (Genesis) or forwards (Revelation), a movement from nostalgia to terror along a range of sentimental expressiveness. Such a range also characterizes Gothic epistemologies of the secret, in which the issue is, formulaically, the origin (or hidden origins) and the end; authority to begin (and perversely enough) permission to end. Thus, the apparently serendipitous, incidental patterns of similarity between different apocalyptic narratives (Edwards's sermons and Lovecraft's minatory tales, for instance) demonstrate a metonymic substitution at work as Calvinism, in Porte's words, "pressed naturally into the service of a common Gothic fable of total decay" (Porte, "Sinners," p. 54). In either the semiotics of grace *or* the grotesque, not everyone is saved; not everyone can read rightly the signs.

While it is neither possible nor desirable to specify one single hermeneutic that adequately governs both discourses of secrecy, the language of love—metaphorized as sex, the biological imperative—comes closest (as I briefly considered in my previous discussion of "The Dunwich Horror"). Indeed, love and power are often mistaken for one another. Frank Gonzalez-Crussi, M.D., writes that one of the "oldest, but also least comforting, theories on the nature of the erotic. . . . views love as the imperialism of the soul, a tendency to impose our arbitrary rule on others."[21] It is understandable, then, and very often the case that hidden love (or at least its *public* threat) is *the* issue in Gothic texts; and the discourse of theology, of course, abstracts and idealizes an otherwise essentially erotic gesture—the covering and uncovering of the Divine. The Apocalypse, then—the final judgment—is, in effect, a mutual act of exposure: we shall see God as we are seen. However, remaining this side of that ultimate point, even the Western tradition of mystical texts—ranging from the Song of Songs through Dante and even through more recent poets—is, if nothing else, a chronicle of God's dalliances, recalled and eroticized by the one so favored.[22]

So to return to a point raised earlier, Gothic narrative strategies as well as theological ones move in varying ways to a similar form of Eros: mystical, annihilating experiences of self-loss, being captive and victimized, if not by love, then by its loss. To recapitulate: Todorov describes "the social function of horror" as a "pretext to describe things [authors] would never have dared mention in realistic terms" (cited in Blonsky, *American Mythologies*, p. 341). Much the same thing could be said of the varieties of religious discourse, especially in a society where *regulation* comes increasingly to be regarded as essential to interior, spiritual health. In other words, these twin grammars of the unspeakable—Gothic literatures and theologies—create spaces in which words, gestures, and symbolic presences can simultaneously be spoken *and* silenced as well. In this way, the unspoken is rendered compliant to systems of law and grammar in which the beyond-the-bounds is given permission (under strict conditions) to speak itself.[23]

It is not accidental, of course, that the languages of the erotic, the confessional, and the politic here again conjoin. Foucault reminds us that the regulation of love's hidden moments is the primary way the Christianizing *polis* extends its control over the body—and thus, over the *body politic*. In *The History of Sexuality*, he argues that the discourse of sexuality was constructed, paradoxically, to be most silenced especially where it was most present (the Divine, too, shares this trait). On "the subject of sex, silence became the rule" (*The History of Sexuality*, p. 3), and a "nearly infinite task of telling" accompanied the "transformation of sex into discourse" (p. 20).[24] In turn this produced a vast proliferation of subsidiary secrets of varying degrees of openness. The Word become flesh, after all, is a central religious metaphor; here it is raised to a principle of political organization. Similarly, confession becomes the modern sacramental moment or at least public *mode*.[25] The new transcendent moment, then—the soul's manifest destiny—is an ironic, self-effacing transubstantiation: the public rending and consumption, if not specifically of bodies, then of persons.

The essential ambiguity, then, of Puritan discourse and its

estrangement in the techniques of horror is nicely encapsulated by the word "apocalyptic," whose complex concealings and revealings governed the Puritan soul. Its terms shaped public discourse and private converse alike, couching the Divine in a language of moral declension and decline. Indeed, the public recitation of apocalypse seems to have made possible more private narratives of dark fate as over time sermon became minatory pulp. There was always something literal, even fundamental, about Puritan hopes (somewhat confusedly) for possession, inheritance, and for sanctity; and nowhere is this literalism of the imagination so evident as in their desire, found everywhere in their exhortations and fulminations, to bring history to its proper conclusion—in short, to call forth "a new Heaven and new Earth." Edwards thought it axiomatic that New England was to be the divinely chosen site. His sermons and treatises published posthumously, for instance, show Edwards concerned, in effect, to finish what the Divine had left unfinished—to *read* history to this culminating moment.[26] This anxiety about closure remains still as a sort of cultural unfinished business; it is evidenced in public discussions of meaning and purpose—identity, on the one hand; and, on the other, it is reflected in a public rhetoric of fate and destiny. Yet fate and destiny require prior authorities, beginnings, genesis; last things imply first things: so here we are again, forwards and backwards. Nostalgia and its twin, terror. Between Winthrop and contemporary practitioners of dread, then, one reads an ongoing argument, centuries later, trying to bring to closure the late lamented "errand into the wilderness." Previously I argued that Manifest Destiny represents a universalization of the American eschatological myth, an ultimately narcissistic way to read personal anxieties onto the universe. Yet this self-referencing is, of course, doctrinally correct, and one can reverse the equation, since shifted slightly, the metaphoric lens turns inward as well as outward. Narcissism is the other face of Judgment. Manifest Destiny could be read onto new-world geographies partly because its terms had already been established as a moral geography by which to map the wild terrain of the soul. In effect one mapping becomes two, or maybe three or four, which accounts for the anxiety that reading the map provokes. Is the proper epistemology here eschatological, or political, or Gothic: the Rapture, democracy, or the horrific last things?

It must be argued, however, that Manifest Destiny presents itself as technology as well as metaphor; it is a well-articulated cosmological map *as well as* a strategy for reading that map. At its most basic, this cosmological strategy implied an ability to read the map of Heaven right—even if, as was historically the case, the colonists in question could not always read terrestrial maps (as in the mislanding at Jamestown, for instance). And from the cosmological to the incidental: the terms implicit in the metaphor of Manifest Destiny established the will of God as the source and origin of a entire culture, whose terms authorized its widest transpersonal, and largely invisible, structures as well as the most detailed and intimate moments of personal interiority. Nor can these aspects be separated, for to do so, as Fredric Jameson argues, is only to fall prey to the illusion that a sphere actually exists that can be demarcated as "private."

Thus it is that without obvious force or coercive violence, a mythologized religious framework (a metaphysics) controls without seeming to control; shapes a political order while seemingly indifferent to shape; relentlessly publicizes the smallest of personal details while valorizing the private in its rhetoric. In summary, as a result of the blending of theological and political discourse in American civil life, the most intimate moments of the imagined life operate publicly under the most constraint, blending speech and silence; imperative and restraint; idealization and negation. In the increasing commodification of the American soul, a once-religious metaphysics of prescription and dissent wrote itself anew in a destiny that was not manifest, and in a fate that was inscrutable and interior. Everywhere claimed as unique, nonetheless the rhetoric of the American self remains conventional and formulaic.[27] The resulting confusions of discourse and debasement of ideas are most apparent in the forms of what is called "pop" culture.

Pop Goes the Culture: "Slip-Sliding Away"

"Horror films are rituals of pagan worship. There western man obsessively confronts what Christianity has never been able to bury or explain away. . . . The horror film uses rot as a primary material, part of the Christian west's secret craving for Dionysian truths."
—CAMILLE PAGLIA, *SEXUAL PERSONAE*[28]

In *The Thrill of Fear*, Walter Kendrick argues cogently that although the titillation of horror is an ancient practice, "full-fledged horror stories" (p. xx) are a relative newcomer to the literary arts, a product of an era in which "feelings for sale" (p. 35) merged with the technology to market, at will and repeatedly, specific emotions—particularly those associated with the aesthetizing of death, rot, and decay.[29] Kendrick argues, that is, for a "long, slow, immensely complex process of deliberate forgetting" (p. xiv), in which death slips from being a biologically important datum to an imaginative one. Horrid fiction, Kendrick might say, keeps death aesthetically alive in a society where death itself has been put to death. While this is true so far as it goes, I read the emphasis slightly differently. The process of "deliberate forgetting" involves "remembering as art." Kendrick notes that the "chills solicited [by the Gothic] were genteel, self-induced, and untroubled by either commitment or belief" (p. 83). However, I think it probable that a metaphysics of distress, clarified and perhaps unwittingly focused by Calvin and his interpreters, was easily appropriated to other uses. Gothic tales of claustrophobic mystery "distilled the pure essence of a tradition of religious terror" (Porte, "Sinners," p. 50) which then was placed in the service of marketing just the emotions Kendrick identifies.

It was perhaps fortuitous that the confluence of old-world Gothic and a habit of religious allegorizing occurred just when technology and audience made possible the conditions of "mass memory" (King, *Danse Macabre*, p. 23)—or "masscult," as King later terms it (p. 61). Nonetheless, marketing alone cannot explain the obsession with death, its confusing mix of terror and comforts, nor explain death's endless return, as it were, to haunt the living. There must be more here—or maybe less?—than meets the eye. As is often the case with the thrifty human imagination, in important matters nothing is wasted; and since death is the most important matter *of* matter, as an event it is symbolically dense, radiating meanings within meanings. Like other aspects of life— of which in fact death is a prime function—the act of dying also invites an allegorical reading. But death offers a uniquely multivalent perspective. As a moment weighed down by cumulative experience, the moment of dying offers a backward look from the end. Thus, death is metaphor as well as allegory, perhaps even the final metaphor. A bridge between worlds, it connects the like and the unlike, the known and the unknowable. Expressed in the religious language familiar to the tradition we have been examining, death is the ultimate conversion; in the language of horror, it is the ultimate metamorphosis—or, as Lovecraft would say, the final liquescent fusion. From a more doctrinal perspective, theologian Karl Rahner proposes that death is the shape human freedom takes when the spirit finally comes to ground. The last moment of biological life, then, in theological terms death is the beginning of the unveiling—the moment when God is to be revealed (and, of course, when *we* are revealed, or maybe exposed, as well). At this horrific juncture, mortality casts off its corporeal veil in dread anticipation of whatever comes next. So damned or saved, whether one of the many or one of Calvin's few, in the end the Self stands revealed as utterly transparent, facing a most horrific of final revelations in which the Self becomes its secret Other.

But conversion, even to death, was not always so fearfully anticipated. Early in the tradition, Edwards, for instance, thought that movements of terror and spiritual fear in the soul were "reasonable" signs of God's converting action in the soul. In other words, terror and fear were confirmatory signs of divine revelation in which the soul found itself possessed by God. A hundred years later, Emerson still conceived of fear in these transcendental terms—as something to be, in his words, "glad to the brink of." No more. While death is still a favorite subject for ritual narrative, tones of these narratives have changed. Stephen King, for example, is remarkable for his meditations upon the last thing. He has boundless energy for ritualizing death in exotic new ways, always in seemingly superfluous detail. Thinking on death always, King recalls the colonial Mr. Green's 1696 *Commonplace Book*: "Remember death; think much of death; think how it will be on a death bed—." Yet King's fetishization of death differs from Green's. In King's endless cataloguing of the ways to die, fear is just fear, and not spiritual movement—fear for the sake of fear, remembered again and again, the body's pain being metaphorized, even *memorialized*, as the *condition* of exteriority rather than spirituality. Thus, in the metaphysical resymbolization I have been tracing, the encounter with terror tells us not so much the state of the soul, saved or damned, but the condition of the body, the soul's last haunt and its final matter. Indeed, at this point *pain* comes to define interiority, if not spirituality, itself.

Stephen King can be taken as representative of contemporary horror fiction; some critics argue that the "cottage industry" of Stephen King is responsible for shaping the current horror market. If this is the case, then it is all the more interesting to observe that King's tales reflect how the religious sublime persists in the marketed horrible; how gut-clenching fear moralizes even the gross and banal. An interviewer asked King what he thought about being "America's Best-loved Bogeyman" and King dismissively responded, "Why America should *need* a Best-Loved Bogeyman is a question I'm not sure I want to think about too deeply, but it certainly seems to be true."[30] King's comment reminds me of James Twitchell's deprecatory analysis of horror writers: "I don't know why the teller of the horror tale should be so deferential unless he knows that he is doing something in public that really is rather private and it's also making him rich" (*Dreadful Pleasures*, p. 74). And Twitchell is right; surely King is rich enough on the leavings of terror to realize his own duplicity. His early work, in particular, shows that he has thought deeply about the intersection of the terrible and the commercial, the sublime and the slimy. He even wrote a book (*Danse Macabre*) in which he explains at length his opinions on the subject, while at the same time justifying why *he* writes. Even the master, it seems, needs authorization. Nonetheless, King's deflection marks him as a member of his commodity culture, visibly in denial of anything beyond the superficial. Remember the brutalizing narrator of Bret Easton Ellis's *American Psycho?* Patrick Bateman *does* American rhetoric very well. Constantly exhorting, ever preaching the delights of being an American, Patrick encourages, as he says, "a return to traditional moral values." We must, he says "promote social concern and less materialism in young people" (p. 16). And yet Patrick is obsessed with the surface of things that don't much count; he fills up page after page of narrative with a numbing litany of *name brands*, "a [world] of consumer horror," as Skal terms it (p. 375): "Both Bret Easton Ellis and Stephen King depict, from radically polar perspectives, the monstrous spectacle of the consumer consumed" (Skal, *The Monster Show*, p. 376).

But Bateman's endless litany of products seems offered as a propaeduitic of sorts, a necessary ritual of specificity to balance his aphasic, self-effacing life (Patrick Bateman kills woman after woman in hideous, monstrous ways as a form of recreation or therapy, or maybe both). I'm not saying King is like his characters, or that his characters are like Patrick Bateman. He is not and they are not (although *Misery*, by King, has similar moments). Even at his subversive best, King conforms to the moralistic and didactic "high church" American tradition (museums of the irreal) in which, historically, it has been the case that for religious, political, and social reasons, romance and fantasy are considered not worth thinking deeply about. King's purposeful forgetting is somehow like Bateman's convenient periods of forgetting (and Bateman, of course, recalls *his* famous ancestor, Norman Bates of *Psycho*). Both are functional; both explain behaviors not otherwise dealt with. I would like to suggest some reasons why America *needs* its haunts, and yet why, at the same time, it must continue to forget them. I base my answer partly on Durkheim's formulation of culture and partly on Freud's.

As one critic put it, Emile Durkheim argued that religion is "society's way of worshipping itself."[31] In other words, a society's religious investment reflects its pattern of self-awareness; culture, if you will, takes its identity from the gods it worships. Religion is social identity mystified (deified), ritualized in particular moments and gestures. Its rhetorics universalize and sustain certain values prized in theory—individuality, community, love—while disguising the fact that those values do not always, in practice, apply. The rhetoric of transcendence privileged by a culture thus embodies the society's contraries and oppositions, while hiding from immediate view powerful social hierarchies and motivations. Religious systems, then, *are* often a society's most congruent and compelling, if not always logically coherent, forms of civic management. And, while it might seem a leap at first, the horror market exists in a similar relationship to its culture: it is reflection, occasion, shadow, rite—sometimes all at once. Like religion, the discourse of horror embodies the meanings culture cannot or will not tell about itself, but which, nonetheless, it compellingly must live.[32] For example, the poetics of the transcendent terrible considered in this study—from Edwards to Frost, Mather to Lovecraft and King—derive their power from the metaphysics of revelation in which a validating, experiential encounter with God both grounds identity and annihilates it at the same time. Experience of the Divine, as we have seen, was longed for and anticipated to the extent that it was dangerous, even illegal—a moment *without* limits or boundaries, a moment of Burkean terror composed equally of radical self-possession and radical dispossession.

In *Devouring Whirlwind*, Will Rockett argues that the horror cinema provides audiences with "confirmatory contact with the sublime or transcendent" (p. 6). Rockett writes that this energy toward transcendence has been redirected into a "cinema of cruelty" (p. 3). This study would be remiss without glancing for a moment or two at the contemporary horror market, the commercialized mayhem by which we indulge our quotient of "daily dread" (Skal, *The Monster Show*, p. 82).[33] Consider, for example, what American society looks like from the breathlessly lurid perspective of B. Dalton's horror shelves or (more accessibly, perhaps, to the so-called common reader) from the horror shelves at Blockbuster Video.[34] Gregory Waller writes that 1968 "inaugurate[s] the modern era of horror," not so much because of the films produced that year (*Rosemary's Baby* and *Night of the Living Dead*), but because in 1968, the Motion Picture Association of America (MPAA) instituted its "Industry Code of Self-Regulation." The MPAA's action, says Waller, was "a response to (and an attempt to sidestep) public concern over the role of censorship in the media" (p. 5).[35] Since then—or really, since Lovecraft—it is customary to find a moralistic alignment of the blasphemous and the litigious, or a blending of the religious and the erotic.[36] But it was after the 1968 screening of *Rosemary's Baby* that the association of slightly perverse sexuality with divinity was no longer even subliminal or even optional.[37] In *The Exorcist* that linkage is, as they say, "in your face." Notice, too, the iconography of religious terror throughout these films and many others—as evident, for banal example, in the fire-of-hell imagery of *Terminator II: Judgment Day*. Even its title makes forcibly apparent the religious context of Arnold Schwarzenegger's pyrotechnics, though I doubt anyone could miss it. So how are we to read the candification of the demonic? How to read the Gothic theologies that cast dark shadows over the politicized sets of *Batman*?[38] Or, at another extreme, how to read *ET*, in which the transcendent becomes bubblegum and Ann Douglas's argument takes cinematic flesh? Perhaps the key is to accept the film's oleaginous spirituality and simply *pray* the film.[39]

As a whole, these fairly typical products of American cinematic horror have prompted me to this unspeakable act of my own—that is, to question the unquestioned content of cultic memory, and indeed, to speak at some length about the unspeakable. Yet to poke and prod this sort of cultural ephemera looking for signs of life may seem as macabre, even unnatural, an activity as Victor Frankenstein's midnight wanderings through "vaults and charnel houses" (p. 50) seeking material to equip his "workshop of filthy creation" (Shelley, p. 53).[40] The inevitable question ritually arises: what? Why does *everything* have to have a meaning? Regan in *The Exorcist* is *just* a helpless little girl, and the killer in *Nightmare on Elm Street* is *just* a boy, and his axe is *just* an axe.[41] It's just "entertainment," after all (to say nothing of the lethal charge associated to the word in the Salem witch-hunts). However, it is likely that since Freud, nothing can be dismissed for what it "just is." Nor, likewise, in a poststructuralist dispensation, can any text be thought merely to speak its piece and then quietly shut up. Nothing is just *just*. Because as human beings we either symbolize or die, and in the end (thank you Messrs. Edwards, Green, and King), that's *all* we do—symbolize the ways we imagine, or that society permits us to imagine, we will die. "Think on death; think how it will be." Indeed, we do so full-time. One could argue that the *practical* purpose served by religious discourse is, after all, to provide an adequate conceptualization of "the end," death's always hidden, always (as yet) undiscovered country that waits to be revealed. Consequently death's frame narrative—life—is not unlike the structure of Gothic. It gives a kind of spurious closure to mysteries that, in the end, are not resolvable in the terms in which they are posed.

The Story and Byword

> *God-in-his-heaven, moral certitude, and cultural unity cannot be restored by nostalgia.*
>
> —SUSAN SONTAG, *AGAINST INTERPRETATION*, P. 253

Any enduring community myth tells the story that a society most wishes to hear about itself, justifying the tensions it finds tolerable while denying those it cannot face. Yet with cultures as with individuals, self-descriptive narratives are rarely factual. As Roland Barthes argues, myth is a speech act whose importance is not limited by its putative truth or universality.[42] The articulation of social mythologies, then, is a complex process. Community mythologies must be resilient enough to survive time and change, and broad enough to include many disparate groups. Woven of words as well as of deeds, community myth is forged in war as well as in peace; it forgets as well as remembers, all in the public interest. Like any identity, the myth a community honors about itself must seem to be second nature, a matter of habit, perhaps even of necessity. Above all, it must be *normalized*, its contrived origins forgotten to such an extent that they appear universal common sense. In times past, the responsibility for maintaining these common places was largely the province of the preachers and ministers, those who decried public woe in order to enforce public weal. The very words themselves confess the connection between the *cleric*, the *author*, and *authority*: the cleric who could read and write—and thus who implicitly authorized social texts—and the author, who today still functions however basely as a kind of psychopomp or mage.

Nor is it an overstatement to suggest that the vigilance once handled by Jonathan Edwards and his peers is now increasingly left, perhaps by default, to the designs of the horror market. This fetishizing economy blends, on the one hand, a traditional rhetoric of the religious sublime (the awe-ful) with the economics of the awful, marketed to sell. But why this particular combination? Religious sentiment reforms men's hearts while conveniently conforming their lives. The invocation of the religious sublime in a parodic form is comforting because it re-enacts a habit of self-scrutiny that has a long association with a debased religious past. In essence this re-enactment is a gesture of transcendence without the actual intent (as one can observe in the pseudo-religious posturing of *The Exorcist*, for instance). Further, as indicated by Salem and other sites of ideological contention (Wounded Knee; Manzanar; Stonewall), the well-worn edges of Christian altruism only barely cover the violence accepted as necessary for enforcing civic righteousness, too often understood as public conformity. And, since the emotional life cannot distinguish between its theologies and its politics, the downward conversion of the sublime becomes only one part of the willfully unexamined life called commodity culture.

Perhaps King is right when he comments that "violence is something that unites us" (Blonsky, *American Mythologies*, p. 348). And what a marvelous clarification of the obvious to suggest, as he does, that "most of our culture is now symbolic violent entertainment, horror pictures, chase movies, suspense novels, that sort of thing" (p. 348).[43]

Culture, then, is a symbolic text, a reading activity as much about dismembering as remembering. Ritual, habit: Freud suggests that "whatever reminds us of this inner 'compulsion to repeat' is perceived as uncanny" ("The Uncanny," p. 238).[44] So the old haunts keep returning in new, ever-diminishing returns, in "ghostlier demarcations, keener sounds" (Wallace Stevens's expression). Apparently this is true for theologies as well as for genre fiction, since both are constrained, in odd ways, *not* to be either themselves or new, but to be something else, and old. In ritual theology or ritual fiction, repetition is the thing: Jesus returns; the witches return; so do ghosts; so does the sequel. Genre fiction recapitulates the familiar—which, as I hope I have shown, is in part a habit of fearful, formulaic theology: good, old-fashioned *pietas* become *tremens*. Thus it is that the horror market and its endless revenants can be read, at least in part, as the debasement of a religious discourse that set out, really, to do too much—as metaphysics, attempting to draw, map, and justify a religious cosmos; as politics, to authorize a social state. Practically speaking, its forms offered worship of the Divine while its rhetoric and *praxis* insured the policing of the soul. Nor should it be forgotten, of course, as the witch-hunts at Salem showed, these remembered forms of policement and uncertainty—the pursuit of disclosures and promised exposures— added color, drama, and spectacle to otherwise dreary lives.

Let's turn our focus just a bit. If formulaic horror and fantasy fiction, like their earlier theological counterparts, construct the "normative" American by mapping appropriate emotional terrain, horror fiction in addition does something else. Since John Winthrop, and probably long before, the pious fearsomes have also been implicitly charged with constructing the acceptable God— one created in our image, one who makes a virtue of what we *value*, not what we preach: a deity, that is, who values conformity, obedience, duty, and right thinking; expiation and victims. The genre serves up a deity who is not too close, not *too* loving; one who, like us, snoops, intrudes, and who loves by possessing or abandoning. It is an indication of the depth of spiritual schizophrenia that religious rhetoric and religious emotions go in opposing directions, and that what is said (often at length), about God and what the average believer *feels* about God are two very different matters. Pain, still, is the payoff; in the new Christology of victimization, self-effacement is most godlike. Thus Stephen King preaches the mainline tradition, confirming all the while Updike's insight that the haunted is a "degenerate form of the Sacred" (p. 78).[45]

So no matter how much we dismiss them as a culture's trash heap, contemporary markets for mayhem reflect what a social order, in rhetorical captivity to things ideal and spiritual, has conventionally defined as the good life—and this constitutes a formidable network of moralized negations, denials, and deflections. First, in the name of God, the good life means anticipated and continual conversion, an uncertainty secularized as an ideology of growth and self-development. Second, to the spiritualizing imagination, life means a denial of the body as *meaningful,* and this paradox has its own horrible consequence—repressed and denied, the body returns inescapably, vampirically seductive on billboard, totemistically splattered on screen. Finally, a society constructed around Judgment and Revelation—in Punter's terms, "sovereignty and surveillance" (*The Hidden Script,* p. 110)— institutionalizes violation and external judgment as a metaphor of self-knowledge as well as paradigm of religious experience.[46]

Gothic texts, says Punter, are about terror, its mystery and uncertainty—and perversely, I add, about terror's delights. I have been arguing that the Gothic genre represents a growing spiritual self-reflexiveness about the relationship between gods and societies, as well as describing the ways in which these limited encounters are encoded in language and commodified as products. One could argue that the Gothic tradition represents the final fate of interiority, the last resting place of spiritual energy driven by the Enlightenment underground—or into the new world of fantasy and geopolitics. Indeed, a Gothic sensibility has marked American literature from before the founding of the Republic, providing a focus for the theological zeal of a culture that is Protestant by historical choice and confessional by civic strategy.[47] In *Redefining the American Gothic,* Louis S. Gross argues that the Gothic vision of a world of darkness, terror, oppression, and perversity, seemingly so alien from the rational bias of the Founding Fathers, is as pervasive in our national consciousness as its daylight opposite. The texts Americans have traditionally viewed as the reflection of national identity—the Declaration of Independence and the Constitution—have their counter images, images in the long line of Gothic texts that show the land, people, and institutions of this country as participants in the nightmare of history (p. 89).

America's dark fantasies, then, can be read as the story a culture does not wish to tell about itself, but which, nonetheless, it necessarily speaks.

Chesterton remarked that the United States was a country with the soul of a church. And, he might have added, with the psyche of an abandoned church. Its tales are *religious* with a vengeance: not a binding back, but a binding up—even, in some cases, a throttling. It is a truism of narrative that we are heroes of our own stories. Or, less flatteringly, that the stories we tell tell us. The continuing evocation of religious terror affirms a profoundly central dimension of American public experience. It is a gesture toward the transcendent in a culture where the transcendent is secularized as nationalistic myth or sentimentalized as a moralized—and moralistic—political tradition.[48] American self-descriptive narratives, religious and political, have, through the years, echoed and shaped each other. Both are centered upon the Word and confirmed by a reference to texts. An enduring socio-political reliance upon biblical typology, sometimes dismissed as fundamentalism, gives rise to a secular variant, foundationalism. Both promote habits of allegory, and in each a rhetoric of transcendental imperative (the "Sacred") is invoked, sanctifying equally biblical texts *and* primary political documents: the Constitution, the Bill of Rights, the Declaration of Independence. Thus, a primary tension of American culture is one essential to its foundation, just as slavery is written into cultural fabric. At issue are certain basic anxieties, political in nature, theological in implication: questions of authority, boundaries, justice, and judgment; the theologies of fear and the annihilating ends of ecstasy. You might say that in our foundational texts spiritual tyrannies contest earthly democracies for power over the imagination.

Let me sum up my argument. Simply put, the imagining of the

terrible is religious cultic memory at its most binding. The appeal to terror is self-denial idealized and habituated, a rethinking of an old cliché: Jesus is coming again—with a twist of apocalypse—and boy is He—. If there is such a thing as American spirituality, it is interleaved here, in the ways transgression and expiation are licensed as civic violences, employed for shaping—scarifying, exacting—the public soul. These commemorative rhythms still engage neo-Christian rhetoricians who, for largely conservative economic ends, have organized a veritable taxonomy of the monstrous with which to apply formidable leverage against inconvenient political programs or social groups. As Clive Barker observes, "the old hypocrisies are gaining acolytes by the hour."[49] For it is still the case that the righteous invincibility of being chosen is used to buttress a political program in which (no surprises here, at any rate) violence is authorized against those unspeakables who are either theologically or politically incorrect—weird sisters (or brothers) of various kinds. Looking then to our dark literatures, we see why Carrie, Regan, and their possessed, captivated, and bewitched sisters retell a political narrative of expiation and exclusion. In the fictional bindings of these women we can read other bindings, and therein discern the beginnings of cultic myth. For their public—and publicized—transgressions play out the rite of denial, an inevitable chord accompanying the rhetoric of being chosen. Our fictions are only a different theater for our spiritual melodramas; the arousal of terror, with all its erotic possibilities, supports an ideology of comfort and containment at all costs, idealized as sacrosanct and untouchable tradition. So it is that Whitman's single, separate self, commodified as common-sense national myth, is quite literally constructed on the bodies of various discounted, dismembered selves.

Conclusion

> *[The] abject and abjection are my safeguards. The primers of my culture.*
>
> —JULIA KRISTEVA, *POWERS OF HORROR*, P. 2

The study of culture is a curious business. Like any organizing system, its strategies and forms of popular management recede from view, while much energy is invested in keeping them either unreflected upon or unreflecting. It is like a text, rewritten and overwritten, dense with meanings which are invisible to conventional (that is to say, to authorized) technologies of reading. To study the text properly, for insights and clues one must go, like Alice in Wonderland, the reverse of where one initially supposes. One must listen where one is told there is nothing to hear and look where culture forbids looking. One must make the connections that a society has carefully hidden. Of course, to return to my original point, the links I make here (between *polis* and police; *civitas* and civility; holy and horrible; the awe-ful and the awful) are precisely the connections that a culture of negative spirituality keeps purposefully unconnected—and thus, powerful. Finally, it may be observed that the economies of worship and horror are not dissimilar from the economics of consumption.[50] An unending thirst for goods substitutes for the unendurable love of God. Consumption is the new religious imperative, another variation on a theme of effacement in which the malls, reconfigured, become the new sacred space (or, alternately, the new site of captivity). And so, inverted and sentimentalized, love becomes sentimentality, the sublime becomes merely terror. The transformation offers an emotional habitation and economic fix by which citizen consumer rehearses the pleasures of remembered pain, even when—especially when—the originating impulse has been forgotten. Like the vampire, citizen consumer never casts a reflection, or proposes reflection as a possible "diversion." Meaning is confined to texts and reading is dismissed as private activity. In such a culture, original thought must be disowned and silenced so that patriotic mindfill can do its work. Citizens are kept from the dread-full encounter with the conditions of their often literal enthrallment by the unceasing, relentless and dis-centering swirl of background: sights, lights, and sound, words used in the service of lies. Movement is the thing; the slippage of a life of surfaces: style, bewitchment, a-musement; a-mazement.

So the habit of terror is, ultimately, not private at all, though it seems thoroughly to be so. It is ritualized in a variety of ways, and it is where the individual expression of terrible intimacies joins the wider public discourse of permission (and thus suppression) that warrant exists for calling patterns of terrorizing *religious*—in the widest sense of that word, a binding work of remembering. For we are bound again by what we believe, and bound mostly where we have forgotten the binds. That is to say, in the image of my title, that the theological mapping of the heavens not only made possible a map of Hell but made one necessary. God becomes flesh in social bones, and is born again in every age. Finally, theology resembles fantasy in that both are, in Ogden's expression, "logically odd"; both express the conditions of improbability. As I have attempted to show, theology texts and fantasy texts alike come to sharp focus at the edge of the abyss, whether at the limits of the state or the Self—indeed, wherever one experiences best the plasticity of the human, its unaccountable tendency to flux, change, even entropy. Following the example of Saint Augustine, the early church called this condition Original Sin, a primal terror whose telling is the daily doing of everyman and everywoman. Finally, politics may in fact demonstrate the art of the possible, or at least, what *is*. But fantasy, on the other hand, even the most artless, embodies the forbidden and out-of-bounds. Somewhere in this unholy trinity—theology, politics, fantasy—is where we make the connections that will set us free of enchantment; free, that is, of the chains we willingly assume, as Freud argues, in the interests of culture. In the film, *Forbidden Planet* (1956), one of the earliest efforts of science fiction to exploit the *pax Americana* later popularized by *Star Trek*, Commander Adams, chief officer of a planetary exploration team, assumes the role of guardian of the planet. Like Armitage, though in a different place and in another country, Adams moralizes about the reasons why the planet and all its dangers must be destroyed: "We are all part monsters in our subconscious. That's why we have laws and religion." Do you think he has the equation backwards? The laws and religion came first, as even the early Puritans realized. The law made the monster/transgressor, not the other way around; in turn, the monster must die for the good of the people. And where have we heard *this* before?

NOTES

1. See "Introduction: Inventing Traditions," in *The Invention of Tradition*, Eric Hobsbawm and Terence Ranger, eds. (Cambridge: Cambridge University Press, 1984). Hobsbawm writes, " 'Invented tradition' is . . . a set of practices,

normally governed by overtly or tacitly accepted rules and of a ritual or symbolic nature, which seek to inculcate certain values and norms of behavior by repetition, which automatically implies continuity with the past. . . . However, insofar as there is such reference to a historic past, the peculiarity of 'invented' traditions is that the continuity with it is largely factitious" (pp. 1–2). Regarding horror discourse, then, see Bruce Kawin's "The Mummy's Pool," where he implies that participants in horror films may be "indulging a nostalgia for ritual" (*Planks of Reason*, p. 4).

2. Definitions of mass culture are various and often contradictory. Mass culture has been read, as Yanarella and Sigelman observe, as a "cultural narcotic" or a "means of binding a society of atomized citizens together . . . generated by a huge culture industry . . . an enormous lens through which the mass public interprets social reality and a gigantic mirror by which members of the fragmented citizenry perceive their individual selves" (p. 1), "Introduction: Political Myth, Popular Fiction, and American Culture," in *Political Mythology and Popular Fiction* (Westport, CT: Greenwood Press, 1988). For an exploration of these and various other meanings of the term "mass culture" see "Introduction: Six Artistic Cultures," in *Modernity and Mass Culture* (Bloomington: Indiana University Press, 1991), James Naremore and Patrick Brantlinger, eds., pp. 1–24; also *The Study of Popular Fiction: A Source Book*, Bob Ashley, ed. (Philadelphia: University of Pennsylvania Press, 1989), esp. pp. 40–81; and Slavoj Zizek, *An Introduction to Jacques Lacan through Popular Culture* (Cambridge: The MIT Press, 1992).

See, in particular, "Consumer Society" and "The Mass: The Implosion of the Social in the Media," in *Jean Baudrillard: Selected Writings*, Mark Poster, ed. (Stanford: Stanford University Press, 1988).

3. For extensive bibliographies of the American Gothic, see Frederick S. Frank, *Through the Pale Door: A Guide to and through the American Gothic* (New York: Greenwood Press, 1990); see also his *Guide to the Gothic: An Annotated Bibliography of Criticism* (Metuchen, NJ: The Scarecrow Press, Inc., 1984), esp. 204–92; also *Gothic Fiction: A Master List of Twentieth Century Criticism and Research* (np: Meckler, 1988); and lastly, Marshall B. Tymn, ed., *Horror Literature: A Core Collection and Reference Guide* (New York: R. R. Bowker Co., 1981).

See also *The Fantasy Tradition in American Literature From Irving to LeGuin* by Brian Attebery (Bloomington: Indiana University Press, 1980).

4. *The Development of American Romance: The Sacrifice of Relation* (Chicago: University of Chicago Press, 1980), p. 12.

5. *In the Circles of Fear and Desire: A Study of Gothic Fantasy* (Chicago: University of Chicago Press, 1985), p. 191.

6. See Dana Polan, *Power and Paranoia* (New York: Columbia University Press, 1986), especially her chapter "Knowledge and Human Interests: Science, Cinema, and the Secularization of Horror." Also of interest, and cited earlier, is Will Rockett's *Devouring Whirlwind: Terror and Transcendence in the Cinema of Cruelty*. Rockett argues a point similar to mine: "people create these works and people pay to read or to see them, and they repeat the process over and over again because human beings continue unconsciously to crave contact

and even interfusion with a transcendent world beyond their own . . ."
(pp. xiii-xiv).

Noel Carroll argues that "one structure for the composition of horrific
beings is *fusion*. On the simplest physical level, this often entails the construction of creatures that transgress categorical distinctions such as inside/
outside, living/dead, insect/human . . ." (See *The Philosophy of Horror*,
pp. 43–46).

7. See "The Origins of The Paranoid Style in American Politics: Public Jealousy
from the Age of Walpole to the Age of Jackson," James H. Hudson, in *Saints
and Revolutionaries: Essays on Early American History*, David D. Hall, John M.
Murrin, and Thad W. Tate, eds. (New York: W. W. Norton & Co., 1984),
pp. 332–72; and Emory Elliott, "The Puritan Roots of American Whig Rhetoric," in *Puritan Influences in American Literature*, pp. 107–27.

8. Important to my argument throughout is Fredric Jameson, *The Political Unconscious: Narrative as a Socially Symbolic Act* (Ithaca: Cornell University Press,
1981), especially his chapter entitled "On Interpretation: Literature as a
Socially Symbolic Act," pp. 17–103. Also useful is William C. Dowling's *Jameson, Althusser, Marx: An Introduction to The Political Unconscious* (Ithaca: Cornell University Press, 1984).

An example of this sideways movement of culture might begin with Stephen King's '*Salem's Lot*. Slotkin argues that the English Puritans who settled
in the New World "repudiated . . . blood myths and blood rituals" (p. 37) and
that "Puritanism was founded on opposition to blood myth and blood ritual"
(p. 58). King, then, precisely enacts the counter ritual the society denies.
Quite emphatically the blood will out.

9. Warren Susman, " 'Personality' and the Making of Twentieth-Century Culture," in his *Culture as History: the Transformation of American Society in the
Twentieth Century* (New York: Pantheon Books, 1984), pp. 271–87. Also, Santayana anticipates Douglas's argument. In "The Genteel Tradition in American Philosophy," Santayana argues "an indigenous evolution from Calvinism
to Transcendentalism to Pragmatism," *The Genteel Tradition; Nine Essays*,
Douglas A. Wilson, ed. (Cambridge: Harvard University Press, 1967). See also
Martha Banta, *Failure and Success in American Culture: A Literary Debate* (Princeton: Princeton University Press, 1978).

10. Nostalgia, says Jonathan Boyarin, is "a formalized longing for a parodically
constituted past." See *Storm from Paradise: The Politics of Jewish Memory* (Minneapolis: University of Minnesota Press, 1992), p. 35. See also Susan Sontag's
"Piety Without Content" in which she addresses contemporary "religious
fellow-travelling": "a piety without content, a religiosity without either faith
or observance . . . [which] includes in differing measures both nostalgia and
relief . . ." ("The Imagination of Disaster," p. 250).

11. In *The Culture of Disbelief: How American Law and Politics Trivialize Religious
Devotion*, Carter writes, "Having lots of public religion is not the same as
taking religion seriously. . . . The seeming ubiquity of religious language in
our public debates can itself be a form of trivialization—both because our
politicians are expected to repeat largely meaningless religious incantations

and because of the modern tendency among committed advocates across the political spectrum to treat Holy Scripture like a dictionary of familiar quotations. . ." (New York: Harper Collins, 1993).

12. "The Death of God" is of course by now a cultural cliché, useful, as early as the late sixties, for selling *Time* magazine and the film *Rosemary's Baby*. In "The Fascination Begins in the Mouth," Mary Gordon obliquely addresses this point, as well as the larger cultural issues of this study: "If the word sin has any useful meaning at all in a time when there is no possibility of redemption, it must speak about a distortion so severe that the recognizable self is blotted out or lost . . . Sin makes the sinner unrecognizable" (*The New York Times Book Review*, June 13, 1993, section 7, p. 31).

13. In *The Supernatural in Gothic Fiction*, Geary cites Devendra Varma, who in *The Gothic Flame* (1957) writes that "Primarily the Gothic novels arose out of a quest for the numinous. They are characterized by an awestruck apprehension of divine immanence penetrating diurnal reality" (*Supernatural*, p. 7).

14. However, by suggesting that theological patterns have been deflected into other forms, I do *not* mean to imply the existence of what is called *civil religion*—that is, religious emotions in civilian dress. Such a concept, in fact, seems to support precisely the point I am making, since in practice the notion of a civil religion distracts attention away from just how emphatically *religious* American civic and imaginative structures are in the first place.

15. See Noel Carroll, *The Philosophy of Horror, op. cit.*, p. 43, for his discussion of metamorphosis and "fusion" as source of horror. Also, Irving Massey's *The Gaping Pig: Literature and Metamorphosis* (Berkeley: University of California Press, 1976) offers an extensive discussion of the varieties of metamorphosis in the Gothic tradition.

16. See Leslie Fiedler's *Love and Death in the American Novel* for his analysis of the transformation of "space" as metaphor in Gothic American texts, particularly how "wilderness" and "frontier" substituted for the haunted spaces of Continental Gothic. See esp. "James Fenimore Cooper and the Historical Romance," pp. 162–216.

17. G. R. Thompson, "Washington Irving and the American Ghost Story," in *The Haunted Dusk: American Supernatural Fiction, 1820–1920*, Howard Kerr, John W. Crowley, and Charles L. Crow, eds., *op. cit.*, p. 16.

18. See Michel Foucault, *Discipline and Punish: The Birth of the Prison*, trans. Alan Sheridan (New York: Pantheon Books, 1977); also D. A. Miller, *The Novel and the Police* (Berkeley: University of California Press, 1986), esp. pp. 1–32.

19. Elizabeth R. Napier, *The Failure of the Gothic: Problems of Disjunction in an Eighteenth-Century Literary Form* (New York: Oxford University Press, 1986), p. 5.

20. Theoreticians since have elaborated and focused this point, usually beginning with Rudolph Otto's *The Idea of the Holy* in which he discusses the "numinous" quality of certain liminal experiences. See, in particular, S. L. Varnado, *Haunted Presence: The Numinous in Gothic Fiction* (Tuscaloosa: University of Alabama Press, 1987); a slightly different take is offered by Kirk J. Schneider in *Horror and the Holy* (Chicago-Open Court, 1993). Angela Carter, an unlikely contemporary theorist, perhaps, also argues that t

"moral function" of Gothic discourses is "to provoke unease." *Fireworks: Nine Profane Pieces* (London: Chatto & Winds, 1974), p. 122.

21. Frank Gonzalez-Crussi, M.D., *On the Nature of Things Erotic* (New York: Random House, 1988), p. 13.

22. See, for instance, David Daiches, *God and the Poets, op. cit.*

23. For example, in *Speaking the Unspeakable: a Poetics of Obscenity, op. cit.*, Peter Michelson writes that "dirty words [verbal pornography] are at once an aphrodisiac and a repudiation of social restrictions. . . . Pornography is not merely a subcultural sign of depravity but is in fact a relatively common way for individual personalities to relate to their environment and exorcise some of its power over them." (p. 48)

24. Michel Foucault, *The History of Sexuality: An Introduction*, trans. Robert Hurley (New York: Random House, 1978); also Foucault's *The Care of the Self*, trans. Robert Hurley (New York: Pantheon Books, 1978).

25. Foucault's discussion, similarly, echoes Georges Bataille's consideration of taboo and transgression. Bataille argues that in Christianity, transgression necessarily intersects with transcendence: "By introducing transcendence into an organized world, transgression becomes a principle of an organized disorder" (p. 118). Georges Bataille, *Death and Sensuality: A Study of Eroticism and the Taboo* (New York: Arno Press, 1977).

26. Edwards's *Concerning the End for Which God Created the World* (1765), and especially *The History of the Work of Redemption* (1774).

27. Space and Manifest Destiny: the Moral Majority transforms the quasi-religious discourse into, first, a geographic imperative and then a moral one. Similarly, they appropriate the religious exclusivity of "chosen people" into a different kind of xenophobia. Essentially racial categories underlie these religious formations, not only with biblical warrant, but with historical; as a result we have a geo-religious drawing of the U.S. map.

28. Camille Paglia, *Sexual Personae: Art and Decadence from Nefertiti to Emily Dickinson* (New York: Vintage Books, 1991), p. 268.

29. Walter Kendrick, *The Thrill of Fear: 250 Years of Scary Entertainment* (New York: Grove Press, 1991).

30. *Entertainment Weekly*, no. 77, August 2, 1991, p. 29.

31. Michael Harrington, *The Politics at God's Funeral: The Spiritual Crisis of Western Civilization* (New York: Holt, Rinehart and Winston, 1983), p. 132.

32. For an insightful psychoanalytic reading of the American horror film, a model "developed out of Freud by Marcuse" (p. 165), see Robin Wood, "An Introduction to the American Horror Film," in *Planks of Reason, op. cit.*: "Repression [is] fully internalized oppression" (p. 166). Wood's "basic formula" for the horror film: "Normality is threatened by the Monster. I use 'normality' here in a strictly non-evaluative sense, to mean simply 'conformity to the dominant social norms'; one must firmly resist the common tendency to treat the word as if it were more or less synonymous with 'health.' " (p. 175) Frank McConnell, in "Rough Beast Slouching," *op. cit.*, argues that "the horror movie as a genre is . . . distinctively American" (p. 111).

33. See also "Tired Blood Claims the Horror Film as a Fresh Victim," Janet

Maslin, *The New York Times*, Sunday, November 1, 1981, pp. 15–16; "Have Horror Films Gone Too Far?" Elliott Stein, *The New York Times Art And Leisure*, Sunday, June 20, 1982, pp. 20–21; "Riding the Crest of the Horror Craze," William Wilson, *The New York Times Magazine*, May 11, 1980, pp. 42–50, 54, 63; Marshall Blonsky, "Hooked on Horror," *Washington Post*, Sunday, August 13, 1989; pp. B1, B5. Blonsky writes, "American media and our personal behavior are an immense enterprise to simulate happiness, welfare, communication. Why horror? Horror portrays the danger of losing this material world that Americans so highly cherish. Horror films and fiction are the dark side, the other face of America: not apple pie but the oozing monster; not the American dream but the American nightmare. . . . But hell is still with us. In fact, modern-day materialism has spawned a new sort of damnation and created its own sub-genre of horror." Blonsky is the author of *American Mythologies*, cited elsewhere in this study.

34. In "An Introduction to the American Horror Film," Robin Wood argues that the contemporary horror film is "dominated by five recurrent motifs" (p. 180), including "The Monster as human psychotic or schizophrenic"; "The revenge of Nature"; "Satanism, diabolic possession, the Antichrist"; "The Terrible Child"; and "Cannibalism." (p. 181) He comments that these "apparently heterogeneous motifs are drawn deeper together by a single unifying master-figure: the Family" (p. 181).

   Will Rockett, in *Devouring Whirlwind*, presents "various views" of the attraction of horror. (pp. 3–5) He cites the *Encyclopedia of Horror Movies* (1986) which compiles a listing of over 1,300 horror films produced between 1896 and 1985.

35. Gregory A. Waller, ed., *American Horrors: Essays on the Modern American Horror Film* (Urbana: University of Illinois Press, 1987). Concerning the implication of the cinema in "the country's first national mass culture" (p. 1), and especially its place as bearer of social value, see Brian Neve, *Film and Politics in America: A Social Tradition* (London: Routledge, 1992). Neve argues, "It is generally suggested that in the second half of the thirties few important films had much social or political relevance. The campaign by the Catholic Legion of Decency in 1934, and the establishment in the same year of the Production Code Administration, had led to the strict enforcement of a code which was designed both to restrict the portrayal of sex and violence and, as Black argues, to 'use popular entertainment films to reinforce conservative moral and political values' " (p. 2). See esp. his chapter "*Film Noir* and Society," pp. 145–70. Also of interest is "'Fairy Tales for the Apocalypse': Wes Craven on the Horror Film," in *Literature and Film Quarterly*, 13 (1985), pp. 139–47.

36. It is also clear, as Waller notes, that "without *Night of the Living Dead* and *The Exorcist*, we would have had to wait much longer for made-for-television movies to bring child pornography and nuclear holocaust into our homes during primetime viewing hours" (*American Horrors*, p. 6).

37. While this is not the place to consider the problematics of sex and gender in the horror film, Robin Wood argues that the "general sexual content of the horror film has long been recognized, and the list of monsters representing a

generalized sexual threat would be interminable . . ." ("An Introduction to the American Horror Film," p. 171). See Linda Williams, "Film Bodies: Gender, Genre, and Excess," *Film Quarterly*, Summer 1991, pp. 2–13. See also James Twitchell, *Dreadful Pleasures, op. cit.*, whose general thesis about the "attraction of horror" argues that "horror has little to do with fright; it has more to do with laying down the rules of socialization and extrapolating a hidden code of sexual behavior. Once we learn these rules, as we do in adolescence, horror dissipates" (p. 66).

38. See, for instance, Tim Blackmore's "The Dark Knight of Democracy: Tocqueville and Miller Cast Some Light on the Subject," *The Journal of American Culture*, vol. 14, no. 1, Spring 1991: 37–56.

39. A similar treaclification of the Divine occurs in the "beatific" fantasies (Carroll, p. 17) of *Close Encounters of the Third Kind, Starman*, and *Resurrection*. Using terms slightly different from mine, Noel Carroll calls these films examples of the "beautific/beatific" fantasy genre, in which the "discovery" is "an object of reverence rather than revulsion" (*The Philosophy of Horror*, p. 233).

40. Mary Shelley, *Frankenstein* (New York: Signet, 1983).

41. Not, of course, to Jonathan Rosenbaum to whom the film is, as Wood writes, an "instrument of Puritan vengeance and repression . . ." ("An Introduction to the American Horror Film," p. 196). See Rosenbaum, "*Halloween,*" in *Take One*, vol. 7, no. 2, January 1979: 8–9. For a discussion of the social function of the fantastic cinema, see *Fantasy and the Cinema*, James Donald, ed. (London: British Film Institute Publishing, 1989). Two of its essays in particular deserve note: Carol J. Clover, "Her Body, Himself: Gender in the Slasher Film" (pp. 91–136) and James Donald, "The Fantastic, the Sublime and the Popular: Or What's at Stake in Vampire Films?" (pp. 233–53). Clover indirectly confirms my general point about the reconstitution of the captivity narrative as social text. She argues that "Abject terror . . . is gendered feminine, and the more concerned a given film with that condition—and it is the essence of modern horror—the more likely the femaleness of the victim" (p. 117). Of course, if we wish to read the religious-metaphysical strategies as examples of patriarchy, and God the Powerful Father, then one can more clearly see the entrapment motif of the early Puritans as, indeed, a gendered role. Finally, see Philip Brophy, "Horrality—The Textuality of Contemporary Horror Films," *Screen*, vol. 27, 1986: 8–10.

42. Roland Barthes, *Mythologies*, trans. Annette Lavers (New York: Noonday Press, 1988).

43. *American Mythologies* (New York: Oxford University Press, 1992). In "Living With Television: The Violence Profile," *op. cit.*, George Gerbner and Larry Gross argue that television is an "agency of the established order and as such serves primarily to extend and maintain rather than to alter, threaten, or weaken conventional conceptions, beliefs, and behaviors." (p. 175) Thus, violence becomes "dramatic stories of . . . symbolic violations" (p. 177).

44. Sigmund Freud, "The Uncanny," *The Standard Edition of the Complete Psychological Works of Sigmund Freud*, ed. and translated James Strachey, et al., 24 vols. (London: Hogarth Press, 1953–74), vol. 17: 217–56.

45. So, too, is the treacle, as Peter Gay observes about the religious opposition to Jonathan Edwards's theology: "the old God wore new, almost unrecognizable, guises; his yoke was easy, and his burden light" ("An American Tragedy," in Levin, *Jonathan Edwards*, p. 250).

46. Slotkin concludes *Regeneration through Violence:* "Set the statuesque figures [cultural heroes] and their piled trophies in motion . . . and a more familiar landscape emerges—the whale, buffalo, and bear hunted. . .; the buffalo meat left to rot; the Indian debased, impoverished, and killed in return for his gifts; the land and its people, its "dark" people especially, economically exploited and wasted . . . the piles of wrecked and rusted cars, heaped like Tartar pyramids of death-cracked, weather-browned, rain-rotted skulls, to signify our passage through the land" (p. 569).

47. As for the possibly antecedent quality of American Gothic to its continental variants, G. R. Thompson writes, "It is . . . apparently accurate to claim that the ambiguous mode of the Gothic, with its intricate manipulations of frames, its metafictional implications of point of view, its intrusions of humor, and its general polyphony of tone, was not much in evidence in Britain until after the publication of Le Fanu's later tales. . . . In America, however, the ambiguous mode is dominant. The early American ghost story is one manifestation of the Gothic impulse of American dark Romanticism. After Irving, the ambiguous Gothic tale reaches an apex with Hawthorne and Poe, who tend to work within the larger Gothic tradition rather than focusing on the ghost story." See Thompson, *The Haunted Dusk*, pp. 32–33.

48. For example, Bellah (and later Wills) isolate the genre of the Election Day speech (post-colonial) and demonstrate how the Election Day speech formally presents a distinct civil religion—aspects of which I call foundationalism. Wells argues, and I follow him, that Lincoln was crucial in this formulation. See Garry Wills, *Inventing America: Jefferson's Declaration of Independence* (Garden City, NY: Doubleday, 1978); *Under God, op. cit.*; and Peter Conrad, *Imagining America* (New York: Oxford University Press, 1980).

49. Clive Barker, "Surviving the Ride," in *Kingdom of Fear*, p. 68.

50. J. Baudrillard, in "The Consumer Society," demonstrates the appropriateness of a market economic mythology to the American fetishization of horror. Conspicuousness of consumption and affluence, established by the "multiplication of objects, services, and material goods . . . now constitutes a fundamental mutation in the ecology of the human species." (p. 29) We have reached, he says, "the point where 'consumption' has grasped the whole of life; where all activities are sequenced in the same combinatorial mode . . . ." (p. 33) See *Jean Baudrillard: Selected Writings, op. cit.*

Selected Bibliography

———— ■ ————

General and Cultural Studies

Aldiss, Brian. *Trillion Year Spree: The History of Science Fiction.* New York: Avon, 1973.

Altman, Dennis. *AIDS in the Mind of America.* Garden City, NY: Anchor Press, Doubleday, 1986.

Ashley, Bob, ed. *The Study of Popular Fiction: A Source Book.* Philadelphia: University of Pennsylvania Press, 1989.

Bataille, Georges. *Death and Sensuality: A Study of Eroticism and the Taboo.* New York: Arno Press, 1977.

Battilana, Marilla. *The Colonial Roots of American Fiction: Notes Toward a New Theory.* Firenze: Leo S. Olschki Editiore, 1988.

Banta, Martha. *Failure and Success in American Culture: A Literary Debate.* Princeton: Princeton University Press, 1978.

Barthes, Roland. *Mythologies.* Trans. by Annette Lavers. New York: Noonday Press, 1988.

Bell, Michael Davitt. *The Development of American Romance: The Sacrifice of Relation.* Chicago: University of Chicago Press, 1980.

Blonsky, Marshall. *American Mythologies.* New York: Oxford University Press, 1992.

Burke, Edmund. *A Philosophical Enquiry into the Origin of Our Ideas of the Sublime and Beautiful.* Notre Dame: University of Notre Dame Press, 1968.

Carter, Stephen. *The Culture of Disbelief: How American Law and Politics Trivialize Religious Devotion.* New York: Harper Collins, 1993.

Chiappelli, Fredi, ed. *First Images of America: The Impact of the New World on the Old.* Berkeley: University of California Press, 1976.

Douglas, Mary. *Natural Symbols: Explorations in Cosmology.* New York: Pantheon Books, 1973.

Elliott, Emory, general ed. *Columbia Literary History of the United States.* New York: Columbia University Press, 1988.

Foucault, Michel. *The Care of the Self.* Trans. by Robert Hurley. New York: Pantheon Books, 1978.

———. *Discipline and Punish: The Birth of the Prison.* Trans. by Alan Sheridan. New York: Pantheon Books, 1977.

———. *The History of Sexuality: An Introduction.* Trans. by Robert Hurley. New York: Random House, 1978.

Freese, Peter. *America, Dream or Nightmare?: Reflections on a Composite Image.* Essen: Ver Die Blaue Eule, 1990.

Gerard, René. *Violence and the Sacred.* Trans. by Patrick Gregory. Baltimore: Johns Hopkins University Press, 1977.

Gonzalez-Crussi, Frank, M.D. *On the Nature of Things Erotic.* New York: Random House, 1988.

Grixti, Joseph. *Terrors of Uncertainty: The Cultural Contexts of Horror Fiction.* London: Routledge, 1989.

Hobsbawm, Eric, and Terence Ranger, eds. *The Invention of Tradition.* Cambridge: Cambridge University Press, 1984.

Hunter, Diane, ed. *Seduction and Theory: Readings of Gender, Representation, and Rhetoric.* Urbana: University of Illinois Press, 1989.

Jameson, Fredric. *The Ideologies of Theory: Essays 1971–1986.* Minneapolis: University of Minnesota Press, 1988.

————. *The Political Unconscious: Narrative as a Socially Symbolic Act.* Ithaca: Cornell University Press, 1981.

Kristeva, Julia. *Powers of Horror: An Essay on Abjection.* Trans. by Leon S. Roudiez. New York: Columbia University Press, 1982.

Lawrence, D. H. *Studies in Classic American Literature.* New York: The Viking Press, 1964.

Luce, A. A., ed. "On the Prospect of Planting Arts and Learning in America." In *The Works of George Berkeley, Bishop of Cloyne.* London: Nelson (1948–57), vol. 7: 373.

Martin, Richard C. "The Study of Religion and Violence." In *The Morality of Terrorism,* ed. by David C. Rapoport and Yonah Alexander, second edition. New York: Columbia University Press, 1989.

Michelson, Peter. *Speaking the Unspeakable: A Poetics of Obscenity.* New York: State University of New York Press, 1993.

Miller, D. A. *The Novel and the Police.* Berkeley: University of California Press, 1988.

Moore, Thomas. *Dark Eros: The Imagination of Sadism.* Dallas: Spring Publications, 1990.

Morey-Gaines, Ann-Janine. *Apples and Ashes: Culture, Metaphor and Morality in the American Dream.* Chico, CA: Scholars Press, 1982.

Naremore, James, and Patrick Brantlinger, eds. *Modernity and Mass Culture.* Bloomington: Indiana University Press, 1991.

Neve, Brian. *Film and Politics in America: A Social Tradition.* London: Routledge, 1992.

Paglia, Camille. *Sexual Personae: Art and Decadence from Nefertiti to Emily Dickinson.* New York: Vintage Books, 1991.

Polan, Dana. *Power and Paranoia.* New York: Columbia University Press, 1986.

Poster, Mark, ed. *Jean Baudrillard: Selected Writings.* Stanford: Stanford University Press, 1988.

Shelley, Mary. *Frankenstein.* New York: Signet, 1983.

Slotkin, Richard. *Regeneration through Violence: The Mythology of the American Frontier, 1600–1860.* Middletown, CT: Wesleyan University Press, 1973.

Sontag, Susan. *Against Interpretation.* New York: Anchor Books, 1990.

Spacks, Patricia. *Gossip.* New York: Knopf, 1985.

Spengemann, William C. *A Mirror for Americanists: Reflections on the Idea of American Literature.* Hanover: University Press of New England, 1989.

Stallybrass, Peter, and Allon White. *The Politics and Poetics of Transgression*. London: Methuen, 1986.

Stoller, Robert J. *Observing the Erotic Imagination*. New Haven: Yale University Press, 1985.

Susman, Warren. *Culture as History: The Transformation of American Society in the Twentieth Century*. New York: Pantheon Books, 1984.

Watney, Simon. *Policing Desire: Pornography, AIDS and the Media*. Minneapolis: University of Minnesota Press, 1987.

Wills, Garry. *Under God: Religion and American Politics*. New York: Simon and Schuster, 1990.

Yanarella, Ernest J., and Lee Sigelman. *Political Mythology and Popular Fiction*. Westport, CT: Greenwood Press, 1988.

Zizek, Slavoj. *An Introduction to Jacques Lacan through Popular Culture*. Cambridge: The MIT Press, 1992.

Gothic

Attebery, Brian. *The Fantasy Tradition in American Literature From Irving to LeGuin*. Bloomington: Indiana University Press, 1980.

Barron, Neil, ed. *Horror Literature: A Reader's Guide*. New York: Garland Publishing, 1990.

Blatty, William Peter. *The Exorcist*. New York: Harper & Row, 1971.

Brophy, Philip. "Horrality—The Textuality of Contemporary Horror Films." In *Screen*, vol. 27, 1986: 8–10.

Carroll, Noel. *The Philosophy of Horror: Or Paradoxes of the Heart*. New York: Routledge, 1990.

Carter, Angela. *Fireworks: Nine Profane Pieces*. London, Chatto & Windus: 1974.

Clover, Carol J. "Her Body, Himself: Gender in the Slasher Film." In *Fantasy Cinema*, ed. by James Donald. London: British Film Institute Publishing, 1989, pp. 91–136.

Coad, Oral Sumner. "The Gothic Element in American Literature Before 1835." In *Journal of English and Germanic Philology*, vol. 24, 1925: 72–93.

Craven, Wes. "Fairy Tales for the Apocalypse," In *Literature and Film Quarterly* 13 (1985): 139–147.

Dadoun, Roger. "Fetishism in the Horror Film." In *Fantasy Cinema*, ed. by James Donald. London: British Film Institute Publishing, 1989.

Day, William Patrick. *In the Circles of Fear and Desire: A Study of Gothic Fantasy*. Chicago: University of Chicago Press, 1985.

DeLamotte, Eugenia C. *Perils of the Night: A Feminist Study of Nineteenth-Century Gothic*. New York: Oxford University Press, 1990.

Dika, Vera. *Games of Terror: Halloween, Friday the 13th, and the Films of the Stalker Cycle*. Rutherford, NJ: Fairleigh Dickinson University Press, 1990.

Docherty, Brian, ed. *American Horror Fiction: From Brockden Brown to Stephen King*. London: Macmillan Press, 1990.

Ellis, Bret Easton. *American Psycho*. New York: Vintage Books, 1991.

Evans, Walter. "Monster Movies: A Sexual Theory." In *Planks of Reason: Essays on the Horror Film*, ed. by Barry Keith Grant. Metuchen, NJ: Scarecrow Press, 1984.

Fiedler, Leslie. *Love and Death in the American Novel.* Revised edition. New York: Dell Publishing Co., 1966.

Frank, Frederick S. *Guide to the Gothic: An Annotated Bibliography of Criticism.* Metuchen, NJ: Scarecrow Press, Inc., 1984.

———. *Through the Pale Door: A Guide to and Through the American Gothic.* New York: Greenwood Press, 1990.

Geary, Robert F. *The Supernatural in Gothic Fiction: Horror, Belief, and Literary Change.* Lewiston, NY: Edwin Mellen Press, 1992.

Green, Gary L. *The Language of Nightmare: A Theory of American Gothic Fiction.* Ann Arbor: University of Michigan Research Press, 1992.

Gross, Louis S. *Redefining the American Gothic: From Wieland to Day of the Dead.* Ann Arbor: University of Michigan Research Press, 1989.

Heller, Terry. *The Delights of Horror: An Aesthetics of the Tale of Terror.* Urbana: University of Illinois Press, 1987.

Jackson, Rosemary. *Fantasy: The Literature of Subversion.* New York: Methuen, 1981.

James, Henry. Preface, *The Altar of the Dead and Other Tales.* New York: Scribner's, 1909, p. xxi.

Jones, Stephen, ed. *Clive Barker's Shadows in Eden.* Lancaster, PA: Underwood-Miller, 1991.

Kendrick, Walter. *The Thrill of Fear: 250 Years of Scary Entertainment.* New York: Grove Press, 1991.

Kerr, Howard, John W. Crowley, and Charles L. Crow, eds. *The Haunted Dusk: American Supernatural Fiction, 1820–1920.* Athens: University of Georgia Press, 1983.

Lovelace, Linda, with Mike McGrady. *Ordeal.* New York: Berkley Books, 1981.

Luce, John. "Literary Prototypes of Atheism: Prolegomena to a Hermeneutics of the Ecstasy of Horror." In *Dialog* 19 (1980): 256-62.

Masse, Michelle A. *In the Name of Love: Women, Masochism, and the Gothic.* Ithaca: Cornell University Press, 1992.

McConnell, Frank D. *The Spoken Seen: Film and the Romantic Imagination.* Baltimore: Johns Hopkins University Press, 1975.

Napier, Elizabeth. *The Failure of the Gothic: Problems of Disjunction in an Eighteenth-Century Literary Form.* New York: Oxford University Press, 1986.

Punter, David. *The Literature of Terror: A History of Gothic Fictions from 1765 to the Present Day.* New York: Longmans, 1980.

———. *The Hidden Script: Writing and the Unconscious.* New York: Routledge, 1985.

Ringe, Donald A. *American Gothic: Imagination and Reason in Nineteenth-Century Fiction.* Lexington: University Press of Kentucky, 1982.

Rockett, Will R. *Devouring Whirlwind: Terror and Transcendence in the Cinema of Cruelty.* Westport, CT: Greenwood Press, 1988.

Sage, Victor. *Horror Fiction in the Protestant Tradition.* New York: St. Martin's Press, 1988.

Schneider, Kirk J. *Horror and the Holy.* Chicago: Open Court, 1993.

Skal, David. *The Monster Show: A Cultural History of Horror.* New York: W. W. Norton & Co., 1993.

Thompson, G. R. *The Gothic Imagination: Essays in Dark Romanticism.* Pullman: Washington State University Press, 1974.

Tuska, Jon. *Dark Cinema: American Film Noir in Cultural Perspective.* Westport, CT: Greenwood Press, 1984.

Twitchell, James. *Dreadful Pleasures: An Anatomy of Modern Horror.* New York: Oxford University Press, 1985.

Tymn, Marshall B., ed. *Horror Literature: A Core Collection and Reference Guide.* New York: R. R. Bowker Co., 1981.

Varnado, S. L. *Haunted Presence: The Numinous in Gothic Fiction.* Tuscaloosa: University of Alabama Press, 1987.

Waller, Gregory A., ed. *American Horrors: Essays on the Modern American Horror Film.* Urbana: University of Illinois Press, 1987.

Wilson, William, "Riding the Crest of the Horror Craze." In *The New York Times Magazine,* May 11, 1980, p. 42.

Wolf, Leonard. "In Horror Movies, Some Things Are Sacred." In *The New York Times Arts and Leisure,* Sunday, April 4, 1976, pp. 1, 19.

Religious Culture

Bellah, Robert. *The Broken Covenant: American Civil Religion in a Time of Trial.* New York: Seabury Press, 1975.

Bercovitch, Sacvan. *The American Jeremiad.* Madison: University of Wisconsin Press, 1978.

————. *The Puritan Origins of the American Self.* New Haven: Yale University Press, 1975.

Boyarin, Jonathan. *Storm from Paradise: The Politics of Jewish Memory.* Minneapolis: University of Minnesota Press, 1992.

Caldwell, Patricia. *The Puritan Conversion Narrative: The Beginnings of American Expression.* Cambridge: Cambridge University Press, 1983.

Chidester, David. "Aesthetic Strategies in Western Religious Thought." In *Journal of the American Academy of Religion,* vol. 51, no. 1, 1983: 55–66.

Daiches, David. *God and the Poets.* Oxford: Clarendon Press, 1984.

Davies, Horton. "Calvinism and Literary Culture." In *John Donne Journal,* vol. 3, no. 1, 1984: 106–12.

Dawson, Lorne. "Otto and Freud on the Uncanny and Beyond." In *Journal of the American Academy of Religion,* vol. 57, no. 2, 1989: 284.

Demos, John. *Entertaining Satan: Witchcraft and the Culture of Early New England.* Oxford: Oxford University Press, 1982.

————. *Remarkable Providences: Readings on Early American History,* revised edition. Boston: Northeastern University Press, 1991.

Elliott, Emory, ed. *Puritan Influences in American Literature.* Urbana: University of Illinois Press, 1979.

Erikson, Kai T. *Wayward Puritans: A Study in the Sociology of Deviance.* New York: Wiley, 1966.

Gilkey, Langdon Brown. *Society and the Sacred: Toward a Theology of Culture in Decline.* New York: Crossroad, 1981.

Hall, David D., John M. Murrin, and Thad W. Tate, eds. *Saints and Revolutionaries: Essays on Early American History.* New York: W. W. Norton & Co, 1984.

Hall, David D. *Worlds of Wonder, Days of Judgment: Popular Religious Belief in Early New England.* New York: Knopf, 1989.

——., ed. *Witch-Hunting in Seventeenth-Century New England: A Documentary History, 1638–1692.* Boston: Northeastern University Press, 1991.

Hancock, Ralph Cornel. *Calvin and the Foundations of Modern Politics.* Ithaca: Cornell University Press, 1989.

Harrington, Michael. *The Politics at God's Funeral: The Spiritual Crisis of Western Civilization.* New York: Holt, Rinehart, and Winston, 1983.

Hatch, Nathan O. *The Democratization of American Christianity.* New Haven: Yale University Press, 1989.

Heimert, Alan, ed. *The Puritans in America: A Narrative Anthology.* Cambridge: Harvard University Press, 1985.

Karlsen, Carol F. *The Devil in the Shape of a Woman: Witchcraft in Colonial New England.* New York: Random House, 1987.

Lowance, Mason I. *The Language of Canaan: Metaphor and Symbol in New England from the Puritans to the Transcendentalists.* Cambridge: Harvard University Press, 1980.

Mather, Cotton. *Days of Humiliation, Times of Affliction and Disaster.* Gainesville, FL: Scholars' Facsimiles & Reprints, 1970.

——. *The Wonders of the Invisible World.* London: J. R. Smith, 1862.

McLoughlin, William Gerald. *Revivals, Awakenings, and Reform: An Essay on Religion and Social Change in America, 1607–1977.* Chicago: University of Chicago Press, 1978.

McLoughlin, William G., and Robert N. Bellah. *Religion in America.* New York: Houghton Mifflin, 1968.

Miller, Perry. *The American Puritans: Their Prose and Poetry.* Garden City, N.Y.: Doubleday, 1956.

——. *The New England Mind: From Colony to Province.* Boston: Belknap Press, 1961.

Moseley, James G. *A Cultural History of Religion in America.* Westport, CT: Greenwood Press, 1981.

Mullin, Robert Bruce. *Episcopal Vision/American Reality: High Church Theology and Social Thought in Evangelical America.* New Haven: Yale University Press, 1986.

Nicgorski, Walter, and Ronald Weber. *An Almost Chosen People: The Moral Aspirations of Americans.* Notre Dame: University of Notre Dame Press, 1976.

Otto, Rudolph. *The Idea of the Holy.* Trans. by J. W. Harvey. New York: Oxford Galaxy Books, 1958.

Reid, W. Stanford, ed. *John Calvin, His Influence in the Western World.* Grand Rapids, MI: Zondervan Publishing House, 1982.

Richey, Russell E., and Donald G. Jones, eds. *American Civil Religion* (Notre Dame Press, 1968). New York: Harper and Row, 1974.

Robinson, Douglas. *American Apocalypses: The Image of the End of the World in American Literature.* Baltimore: Johns Hopkins University Press, 1985.

Ruland, Richard, and Malcom Bradbury. *From Puritanism to Postmodernism: A History of American Literature.* New York: Penguin, 1991.

Shea, Daniel B. *Spiritual Autobiography in Early America.* Princeton: Princeton University Press, 1968.

Stout, Harry S. *The New England Soul: Preaching and Religious Culture in Colonial New England.* New York: Oxford University Press, 1986.

Thomas, Keith. *Religion and the Decline of Magic.* New York: Scribner's, 1976.

Walzer, Michael. "Puritanism as a Revolutionary Ideology." In *History and Theory* III (1963).

Weisman, Richard. *Witchcraft, Magic, and Religion in Seventeenth-Century Massachusetts.* Amherst: University of Massachusetts Press, 1984.

Jonathan Edwards

Bushman, Richard. "Jonathan Edwards as Great Man." In *Soundings* 52 (1969):15–46.

Cady, Edwin Harrison. "The Artistry of Jonathan Edwards." In *New England Quarterly* 22 (1949): 61–72.

Edwards, Jonathan. *Apocalyptic Writings*, ed. by Stephen J. Stein. New Haven: Yale University Press, 1977.

———. *Freedom of the Will*, ed., by Paul Ramsey. New Haven: Yale University Press, 1957.

———. *Religious Affections*. New Haven, Yale University Press, 1959.

———. *Representative Selections, with Introductions, Bibliography, and Notes*. New York: American Book Co., 1935.

———. *Scientific and Philosophical Writings*, ed. by Wallace E. Anderson. New Haven: Yale University Press, 1980.

Hatch, Nathan O., and Harry S. Stout. *Jonathan Edwards and the American Experience*. New York: Oxford University Press, 1988.

Kolodny, Annette. "Imagery in the Sermons of Jonathan Edwards." In *Early American Literature* 7 (1972): 172–82.

Lensing, George. "Robert Lowell and Jonathan Edwards." In *South Carolina Review* 6 (1974): 7–17.

Levin, David. *Jonathan Edwards: a Profile*. New York: Hill and Wang, 1969.

Miller, Perry. *Jonathan Edwards*. New York: Delta Books, 1949.

Scheick, William, J., ed. *Critical Essays on Jonathan Edwards*. Boston: G. K. Hall, 1980.

Shea, Daniel B. "The Art and Instruction of Jonathan Edwards." In *American Literature* 37 (1965): 17–32.

Simonson, Harold Peter. *Jonathan Edwards, Theologian of the Heart*. Macon, GA: Mercer University Press, 1982.

H. P. Lovecraft

Joshi, S. T. *H. P. Lovecraft*. Mercer Island, WA: Starmont House, 1982.

———. *H. P. Lovecraft and Lovecraft Criticism: An Annotated Bibliography*. Kent, OH: Kent State University Press, 1981.

Joshi, S. T., ed. *H.P. Lovecraft: Four Decades of Criticism.* Athens: Ohio University Press, 1980.

————. *The Weird Tale.* Austin: University of Texas, 1990.

Levy, Maurice. *Lovecraft: A Study in the Fantastic.* Trans. by S. T. Joshi. Detroit: Wayne State University Press, 1988.

Lovecraft, H[oward] P[hillips]. *At the Mountains of Madness, and Other Novels.* Sauk City, WI: Arkham House, 1964.

————. *The Best of H. P. Lovecraft: Bloodcurdling Tales of Horror and the Macabre.* Introduction by Robert Bloch. New York: Ballantine Books, 1982.

————. *Supernatural Horror in Literature.* Introduction by E. F. Bleiler. New York: Dover Publications, Inc., 1973.

Samuels, Charles T. "Usher's Fall: Poe's 'Rise'." In *Georgia Review* 18 (1964): 208–16.

Shreffler, Philip A. *The H. P. Lovecraft Companion.* Westport, CT: Greenwood Press, 1977.

St. Armand, Barton Levi. *The Roots of Horror in the Fiction of H. P. Lovecraft.* Elizabethtown, NY: Dragon Press, 1977.

Robert Frost

Bloom, Harold, ed. *Robert Frost.* New York: Chelsea House Publishers, 1986.

Frost, Robert. *The Poetry of Robert Frost,* Edward Connery Lathem, ed. New York: Henry Holt, 1969.

Kemp, John C. *Robert Frost and New England: The Poet as Regionalist.* Princeton: Princeton University Press, 1979.

Stephen King

Beahm, George. *The Stephen King Companion.* Kansas City: Andrews and McMeel, 1989.

Hanson, Clare. "Stephen King: Powers of Horror." In *American Horror Fiction: From Brockden Brown to Stephen King,* ed. by Brian Docherty. New York: St. Martin's Press, 1990. 135–54.

Hoppenstand, Gary, and Ray B. Brown. *The Gothic World of Stephen King: Landscape of Nightmares.* Bowling Green, OH: Bowling Green State University Popular Press, 1987.

King, Stephen. *Danse Macabre.* New York: Berkley Books, 1982.

————. *Carrie.* New York: Signet, 1974.

————. *'Salem's Lot.* New York: Doubleday, 1975.

Monteleone, Thomas F. "King's Characters: The Main(e) Heat." In *Kingdom of Fear: The World of Stephen King,* New York: New American Library, 1986, pp. 279–94.

Underwood, Tim, and Chuck Miller, eds. *Kingdom of Fear: The World of Stephen King.* New York: New American Library, 1986.

————. *Fear Itself: The Horror Fiction of Stephen King.* New York: New American Library, 1982.

Whissen, Thomas Reed. *Classic Cult Fiction: A Companion to Popular Cult Literature.* Westport, CT: Greenwood Press, 1992.

Winter, Douglas E. *Stephen King: The Art of Darkness.* New York: New American Library, 1986.

Mary Rowlandson

Derounian, Kathryn Zabelle. "The Publication, Promotion, and Distribution of Mary Rowlandson's Indian Captivity Narrative in the Seventeenth Century." In *Early American Literature,* vol. 23, 1988: 239–61.

Green, David L. "New Light on Mary Rowlandson." In *Early American Literature,* vol. 20, 1985: 24–38.

Rowlandson, Mary. *Narrative of the Captivity, Sufferings and Remarks of Mrs. Mary Rowlandson.* Boston: Printed & Sold by Thomas Fleet, 1682.

Sieminski, Captain Greg. "The Puritan Captivity Narrative and the Politics of the American Revolution." In *American Quarterly,* vol. 42, no. 1, March 1990: 35–56.

Thorne, Melvin J. "Fainters and Fighters: Images of Women in the Indian Captivity Narratives." In *Midwest Quarterly,* vol. 23, 1981–82: 426–36.

Index

transgression: as communal rite, xvi,
42–45; as civic display, 46–47
Trevor-Roper, Hugh, *The European
Witch-Craze of the Sixteenth and
Seventeenth Centuries*, 43
Trilling, Lionel, "A Cultural
Episode," 122–123, 127
Twain, Mark, xxxi, 80, 95, 100, 105,
136, 146; reading Edwards, 101–
102; *Huckleberry Finn*, 180; "The
Great Dark," 106–107, 118
Twitchell, James, *Dreadful Pleasures*, xi,
xv, 204

U

Utopia, xvii, 2 as discourse, xvi, xix

V

Voyeurism, as rite of communal
identity, xi, xv

W

Waller, Gregory A., *American Horrors*,
206
Weird Tales, xxx, 179
Weisman, Richard, *Witchcraft, Magic
and Religion in Seventeenth-Century
Massachusetts*, 70
Wharton, Edith, 180

White, Dennis L. "The Poetics of
Horror," 98–99
Whitman, Walt, 103, 212; "Chanting
the Square Deific," 84, 88, 95
Wigglesworth, Michael, xxxi; "The
Day of Doom," ix, 16, 17, 31, 78,
81, 83, 94, 105
Williams, Roger, xx
Wilson, Edmund, "Tales of the
Marvelous and Ridiculous," 147
Winslow, Ola, *Jonathan Edwards*, 78,
85
Winthrop, John, xiv, xvii, xxx, 53, 63,
78, 80, 100, 137, 143, 156, 163,
196, 200, 209; "A Model of
Christian Charity," xv, xxvii, 1, 8,
9–12, 31, 39, 83; Governor, 39
Wolf, Leonard, *A Dream of Dracula*,
184
Wyden, Peter and Barbara, *Growing
Up Straight: What Every Thoughtful
Parent Should Know About
Homosexuality*, xxii, xxiii

Y

Yeats, William Butler, "Leda and the
Swan," 171; "The Magi," 158;
"The Second Coming," 158

Z

Ziff, Larzer, *Puritanism in America*, 4

S
1201